PRAISE FOR *THE WRITER'S WORKOUT*

The Writer's Workout is like having a personal trainer for your brain—every day of the year. Christina Katz will turn you into a lean writing machine, preparing you to face the challenges of the Too Much Information Age.

—Marc Acito, author of *How I Paid for College* and *Attack of the Theater People*

For years, I searched for one book to offer my students—a book that would walk them with kindness and respect through the maze of learning to live as a working writer. Christina Katz's *The Writer's Workout* is that book.

—Melissa Hart, author of *Gringa: A Contradictory Girlhood*

Christina Katz is a writing coach in every sense of the word. This book is absolutely packed with tips, techniques, and pearls of wisdom. One can use this as a reference book, curriculum of study, or motivational guide—or all three.

—James Scott Bell, author of *The Art of War for Writers* and best-selling suspense novelist

Christina Katz is the warm, funny, inspiring, and enthusiastic mentor every writer dreams of having in her corner. Like any good workout, this book will make you feel strong, energized, and ready to take on whatever comes next!

—Dallas Woodburn, young writer activist

If you want great tips for writing and great tips for publishing all in one place, this is the book you need!

—Eric Maisel, author of over thirty-five books including *Coaching the Artist Within*

Christina Katz's *The Writer's Workout* is like a writer's devotional—366 entries, from inspirational to practical to cautionary tips, advice, and exercises—to get you through the seasons of your writing life. It's perfect for aspiring writers who want to get in the driver's seat rather than leave it to fate to jumpstart their careers.

—Hallie Ephron, author of *Never Tell a Lie* and *Writing and Selling Your Mystery Novel*

As in sports, success in writing is half psychology. Coach Christina Katz builds both your word skills and your confidence. Get ready to flex your muscles—and harness your mind!

—Donald Maass, literary agent and author of *Writing the Breakout Novel*

The grounding metaphor of the workout is beautifully developed throughout the book, and Katz's tone is warm and encouraging as she takes on the role of coach. Her comprehensive work is an inspiring pleasure to read.

—Caroline Grant, editor-in-chief of *Literary Mama* and co-editor of *Mama Ph.D.*

No more excuses! Writing is hard work, arguably harder than physical exercise, but Christina Katz's insightful regimen offers a holistic body/mind/soul workout that will rejuvenate even the flabbiest of authors. From the motivational to the practical, her coaching style is an appealing blend of warm encouragement and a no-nonsense kick in the pants that almost every writer needs at some point in their career.

— Guy LeCharles Gonzalez, digital publishing expert and poet

The Writer's Workout will take you from *wanting* to be a writer to thinking, acting, and working as a writer should. An indispensable daily read, with a leap year's worth of lively, thought-provoking, and invariably useful information.

— Randall Albers, Chair of the Fiction Writing Department, Columbia College Chicago

The Writer's Workout is a must-read for any writer on this path for the long haul. Christina Katz is the teacher we all want—supportive and understanding, but handy with a good kick-in-the-butt when we need to get down to work.

— Becky Levine, author of *The Writing & Critique Group Survival Guide*

What writers want to know is: What's the shortcut to success—the fast and easy way to get a book deal? Hint: There isn't one. That's why I am so glad that Christina Katz wrote *The Writer's Workout* because it clearly shows aspiring writers what to do, when to do it, and how to do it.

— Lee Silber, best-selling author of fifteen books including *Time Management for the Creative Person*

THE WRITER'S

366 TIPS, TASKS, & TECHNIQUES
FROM YOUR WRITING CAREER COACH

WORKOUT

WD
WRITER'S DIGEST
BOOKS
WritersDigest.*com*
Cincinnati, Ohio

Christina Katz

For more resources for writers, visit www.writersdigest.com/books.

To receive a free weekly e-mail newsletter delivering tips and updates about writing and about Writer's Digest products, register directly at www.writersdigest.com/enews.

15 14 13 12 11   5 4 3 2 1

Distributed in Canada by Fraser Direct
100 Armstrong Avenue
Georgetown, Ontario, Canada L7G 5S4
Tel: (905) 877-4411

Distributed in the U.K and Europe by F&W Media International
Brunel House, Newton Abbot, Devon, TQ12 4PU, England
Tel: (+44) 1626-323200, Fax: (+44) 1626-323319
E-mail: postmaster@davidandcharles.co.uk

Distributed in Australia by Capricorn Link
P.O. Box 704, Windsor, NSW 2756 Australia
Tel: (02) 4577-3555

Edited by Melissa Wuske
Interior Designed by Claudean Wheeler
Cover Design by Terri Woesner
Production coordinated by Debbie Thomas

DEDICATION

For Jane Friedman, former publisher of Writer's Digest, a champion of writers for more than a decade, and a dear friend.

ACKNOWLEDGEMENTS

Jane Friedman helped me brainstorm the original concept for this book and got the pub board approval process rolling. Kelly Messerly took over steering the project and got it green-lighted. Melissa Wuske shepherded the book through production and helped it find a new focus and the traction it needed. Terri Woesner created a terrific cover design and Claudean Wheeler designed the book's interior.

The watchful eyes and sage advice of my agent, Rita Rosenkranz, have been a boon to my career, and this book was no exception. Sharon Cindrich has been an unwavering source of support, cheer, and inspiration ever since we signed the contracts for our first books.

My students from the last ten years were the muses for this book. Deep gratitude to my former students, who have inspired me and schooled me, session after session, over the past decade. Special thanks to: Cindy Hudson, Judy M. Miller, Malia Jacobson, Jen Henderson, and Lela Davidson for your enthusiasm and example.

Pats on the back from me to all the folks who work so hard at *Writer's Digest* Magazine and Writer's Digest Books. I have appreciated your thoughtful dedication over the years, especially: Jessica, Robert, Chuck, Brian, Zac, Mark, Phil, and Scott. Thank you for actively supporting my work over the years: Bill Johnson, Leona Grieve, Diana Jordan, and Pat Duke.

Randy Albers has set a great example for me since 1992. I appreciate his dedication to writers and his gentle heart.

Thanks to Mom and Dad for everything, as well as for the rest and relaxation.

I am eternally grateful to Jason and Samantha. I feel blessed every day to know you and to share this life with you. Our pets provide a constant source of fuzzy companionship.

I am ever appreciative of the power that moves me to write, that gives me a sense of connection and serenity, and leads the way to whatever is coming next.

CONTENTS

SUMMER: FIND YOUR STRIDE

FALL: BECOME RECOGNIZABLE 188

WINTER: COACH YOURSELF

INTRODUCTION
WRITE YOUR WAY TO A SUCCESSFUL CAREER

Writing is not an enigma. It is a sport.

—NATALIE GOLDBERG

You don't have to have been a world-class or even a junior varsity athlete to know that a body feels powerful in motion. Writing is just the same. You won't feel powerful writing until you are making strides, moving forward, and inching your way up your own career trajectory.

Until you get to the point where writing becomes an everyday occurrence, this book can serve as a coach who puts you through the training paces until they become muscle memory. It will do all the same things any good coach does. It will challenge you, encourage you, push you, push you some more, remind you to be humble and respectful and hungry, and teach you how to become more instinctive about the choices you make on your way to success.

The Writer's Workout contains information and advice that can help any creative person hunker down and start writing. By the time you are done reading it, you will be the best writing career coach you could possibly have, because you will know what you need to do. And you will be ready to dive in and take the necessary steps. And the necessary steps you take will ultimately add up to increased success.

But nobody can just hand you success. You have to work for it. Happily, the encouragement in this book will help keep you going. *The Writer's Workout* is writer centric; that is, it focuses on the point of view of the writer, not the publisher, the editor, or the agent. What's best for the writer is what this book is all about.

With so much emphasis on the social and networking aspects of creative careers these days, you might expect this book to promote an extremely social approach. But *The Writer's Workout* is focused on the creative person as an expressive individual instead. Although the perspectives of others are touched on here and there, the primary objective of the book is to help you cultivate creative confidence and express literary ability through writing. This is what belongs at the center of your writing career. Period.

HOW THE WRITER'S WORKOUT IS ORGANIZED

This book takes a very grounded approach and honors the natural rhythms of everyday life, therefore it is divided into seasons. It is written to echo the seasons of the year—like a full circle, like the chapters of your writing career, like the cycle of the creative process.

You can start at the beginning or wherever you like. Read one chapter a day for a year or blaze through the whole book, if you want. Pick it up once in a while and open up to a particular page to read a message for you. There is no wrong way to read it.

The purpose of *The Writer's Workout* is to help you get jazzed about whatever you are working on or are planning to write next. And because folks will be coming to it with professional experience ranging all the way from none to decades, I use the Spring section to lay down basic premises, the Summer section to discuss challenges facing intermediate writers, the Fall section to discuss how to start becoming visible, and the Winter section to encourage you to make the most of your strengths so you can coach yourself to future success.

Here are three possible ways you can interpret the tip-a-day approach:

1. You can think of *seasons* as the seasons of the year. The message of *The Writer's Workout* is to stop pushing your writing career, to give rushing a break, and instead let your creative efforts grow your career in a more natural, authentic way.

2. Or you can think of the seasons as referring to the seasons of *your* writing career. Creativity cycles through phases, and your writing career will also likely have springs and falls, summers and winters. What season is the season that best describes the current cycle you are in? You might want to start there.

3. Whether you are growing and developing a single idea or many, it's always shrewd to put yourself through learning cycles that stretch your creative horizons. Consider each year a new learning cycle and get used to putting your skills through new paces if you want them to grow.

Writing career growth takes root and flourishes when you give it ample time and plenty of practice. When you rush it or push it beyond its capacity, you get diminished results. This is not a get-rich-quick or make-six-figures type of book; it's a slow-and-steady- wins-the-race kind of book because creativity should not be rushed and writing careers take time to mature. The series of simple tips, tasks, and techniques demonstrate how any writer who can focus on and complete one task after another can produce and eventually prosper as a writer.

HOW TO USE THE WRITER'S WORKOUT

I hope you enjoy your writer's workout. I know you are busy and you like to get the most out of every minute of time that you invest, so I'd like to make a few suggestions of ways you can get the most out of this book:

HAVE A METHOD FOR CAPTURING YOUR IDEAS AS YOU READ. Valuable epiphanies may occur to you. Don't let them get away. Snatch them up and put them to good use.

TAKE YOUR TIME. Many writers are in a huge rush to arrive at a destination that they believe is going to relieve them of the stress of where they are today. It doesn't exist. If you can accept and embrace exactly where you are in the process, you will enjoy the journey more.

RELAX AND HAVE FUN. You are exactly where you are supposed to be. What is going to happen tomorrow is up to you and depends on whatever choices you make next. This book is here to give you a gentle kick in the caboose, no matter where you are in your journey.

Ready to begin your writing workout? *The Writer's Workout* will help you make the most of every single writing day. Enjoy the burn.

SPRING:

GET GOING

Exerting yourself to the fullest within your individual limits: that's the essence of running, and a metaphor for life—and for me, for writing as well.

—HARUKI MURAKAMI

Getting started and finding a workable writing rhythm are big steps. Just like baseball players go to spring training every year, writers need to recommit year after year to getting into the game. This means getting off the couch and getting warmed up, loose, and strong again. The tips and exercises in this section are designed to help focus your energy and get your writing career off to a solid start so you can eventually write, sell, get published, specialize, and promote yourself. A lot of eager writers never get past the reading-about phase, but you will be different. You will not only be prepared, you will be encouraged. You will channel your wishes into actions. You will get on track and stay the course. You will realize your creative potential. You will be a winner, whatever winning means to you.

Creativity is a habit, and the best creativity is a result of good work habits. That's it in a nutshell.

—TWYLA THARP

Craft is the center of everything you do as a writer. However, craft is an aspect of writing that some writers treat altogether too preciously.

So instead of focusing overly on craft, think about writing as a habit. As something you practice until you can't not do it. Writing is a lifelong process where you start out green and write and write and write until the words just flow and you no longer think about what you are doing because you lose self-consciousness.

Write until writing becomes as natural as breathing. Write until *not* writing makes you anxious. The end of self-consciousness is what we are after. Without self-consciousness, rewriting and editing simply become a fluid, natural part of the process, not anything to fear or obsess about.

Banish your self-consciousness from the room and get back to scribbling. Write stuff down. Breathe in. Breathe out. Do it all over again. This is the writing habit. You'll get used to it.

Breathing is easy. You just did it and you didn't even notice. However, unlike breathing, which you usually get right on the first try, you may never produce your best work on the first try. Maybe once in a blue moon you will nail it the first time around. And hey, that's great. But that's so much less important than reaching the point at which writing becomes as natural as breathing. Because then you will consistently be writing, and writing better and better all the time. Once you make writing a habit, craft will come down from her pedestal and join you in the dance.

First become a habitual scribbler; then watch your writing craft evolve. Write at least a full page a day on one of your ideas. Anyone can manage a page a day. If you accomplish more on any given day, that's a good habit paying off.

2 SELL YOUR WORDS

If you wrote something for which someone sent you a check, if you cashed the check and it didn't bounce, and if you then paid the light bill with the money, I consider you talented.

—STEPHEN KING

To sell your words means simply to offer your words to others. No one is going to come knocking on your door, demanding to view the contents of your hard drive.

You will need to package your words so that someone besides you can read them. Selling your words helps you find readers as a writer. It bridges the gap between going unread and getting read. I don't know too many writers who are happy with the idea of never getting read.

If you don't pitch your work, your writing career will falter, then stall, and eventually possibly disappear. But once you learn how to sell your work, you won't be inclined to blame others for your lack of career success.

As a professional writer, you'll need to write and also to persuasively offer your work to folks who can pay you for it. You will need to learn how to encapsulate your work and summarize your offerings in the sexiest of terms so you can submit a steady stream of work to editors.

Don't wait to get in the mood to sell because it's never going to happen. If you don't care enough about your hard work to muster the courage to share it with anyone, why should anyone else care?

Selling is one of the most important parts of a writer's job. When you become willing to make your work available to the masses, you will earn money for your words.

So fire up your computer and print out all of your previous writing on hole-punched paper. Gather it up in a three-ring binder without hyperanalyzing its quality. Put the notebook on a shelf within reach. There are probably some decent ideas in there, but we are not selling them just yet. Let's honor what's already been written while moving ahead with the intention of creating a fresh stream of new writing to sell.

3 SERIAL FOCUS

I think there is a choice possible to us at any moment, as long as we live. But there is no sacrifice. There is a choice, and the rest falls away.

—MURIEL RUKEYSER

WHAT IS YOUR CURRENT CAREER THRUST?

If you don't know, your career might be drifting off course.

One thing that all successful writers know how to do is focus.

But until you can focus on one task at a time, you won't meet your short-term goals because you won't finish anything.

Once you can complete one task and then another and another and another in a focused manner, that's when you will start finishing projects.

And it won't matter if previously you had dozens of false starts with no projects ever completed. Once you can focus, you can pretty much finish anything.

We are going to talk about specializing in section two, but before you can specialize, you need to learn how to focus on one thing at a time and finish it.

Once you can finish projects, you can serial focus on one goal after another throughout the rest of your career until you are able to slam-dunk your goals like a pro.

But until you can serially focus, your career can't take root, and therefore it can't grow.

You can be the greatest writer in the world and pretty good at selling yourself, too, but if you don't establish consistent focus as a central skill, you won't ultimately succeed in this business.

So, if you want to be a one-shot-wonder or a sometime success, go for it. Most people can do that. What most people can't do is commit for the long haul, stay with the process when it's not going well, and keep their focus on the single next more important goal and task.

Can you? Think of a time in your life when the going got tough and you kept going. And then repeat after me: What do I need to do next? You'll be asking this an awful lot.

4 PROMOTE YOURSELF

Remember that our lives are connected with other people all over the world. By identifying a specific cause and recruiting a small army, you can achieve far greater success than you otherwise could on your own.

—CHRIS GUILLEBEAU

When a writer is ready, a compelling Web presence can make all the difference. Writers who promote themselves succeed beyond writers who merely work hard at writing, selling, and staying on track. Therefore, if you do everything else but remain unwilling to promote yourself, this omission is going to handicap your potential in the long run.

Self-promotion describes your willingness to make yourself visible, heard, buzzed, recommended, and respected and typically follows an upwards-slanting trajectory when you work at it steadily. Expanding your self-promotion skills can take you from completely unknown to internationally known over time.

Typically, self-promotion is the make-it-or-break-it point for getting a book deal. Even if you self-publish—especially if you self-publish—platform-building skills are crucial to selling your work and becoming more known.

There is an art to craft, an art to selling, an art to perseverance, and an art to self-promotion. All of these efforts can be done so artfully as to never appear shallow or crass. Folks who are artful at self-promotion are so natural you don't even notice they are doing it. The skill becomes a seamless part of their professional identity.

If you are unwilling to become visible and known, maybe a professional writing career is not for you, unless you would prefer ghostwriting or business writing, which are ways of becoming successful as a writer, yet remaining anonymous.

However, if you plan to become an author, or wish to become widely recognized in the field you write in, you'll need to learn as much as you can about self-promotion on an ongoing basis. Visibility opportunities are constantly evolving, shifting, and expanding. Once you become willing to promote yourself, you will be amazed at what this simple skill can do to advance your career.

For now, just say yes to self-promotion instead of steeling yourself against it. This is a good enough start for now.

Those long, unpaid hours at the computer or keyboard often feel "wasted" or "self-indulgent." Worse, many writers have family members who share this view.

—MOIRA ALLEN

One of my former students once snuck the payment for a writing class onto a credit card without telling her husband. When she asked me to be complicit, I was uncomfortable. But when a writer understands the importance of microinvesting in her writing career, even when a spouse doesn't, how can I argue?

A couple years later, this writer has an agent and a book deal on a topic she loves, so apparently the class she secretly took turned out to be a good investment in her writing future.

Often writers are resistant to the idea that they need to invest in their career. They expect a payoff before they invest or at least the guarantee of a payoff. But you won't typically get paid consistently until you pay for information and training first. Having an informed guide can make all the difference between failure and success.

Continuing education may be more complex and multifaceted than you anticipated. No matter what kind of writer you are, you'll need to get and stay informed about:

- Your topic (whatever your specialty is)
- Your audience (what makes it tick)
- Your field (the latest news)
- Your industry (the trends)
- Business skills (self-publishing and entrepreneurship)
- Technology tools (the latest and most helpful)
- Publications (the top three)
- Associations (for your specialty and your field)
- Conferences/conventions/events (for your specialty and your field)
- Blogs (for your specialty and your field)
- Online networks (for your specialty and your field)

Ongoing learning is key to growing as any kind of professional and is the best way to stretch your mind, stay current in the marketplace, and evolve with the times. Staying loosely abreast of the latest trends and tools will help you compete, expand your professional credibility, and increase your income over time. You need to keep up. It's not optional.

When you can accept this, turn the page.

6

TAP YOUR CHUTZPAH

You can't test courage cautiously ...

—ANNIE DILLARD

There is only one thing that separates an aspiring writer from an actual writer: actual writers actually write.

Aspiring writers do a lot of other things. They talk about writing, read about writing, and think about writing, but at the end of the day, they often accomplish little in the way of actual words on the page.

But you practically can't stop actual writers from writing. They will write on anything you put in front of them: a napkin, a menu, a hand. If they have a phone, they record wisps of ideas on it as they walk.

If they have a computer at home or in their shoulder bag it is likely bursting with written stuff. They collect words in dribs and drabs, ideas are scrawled on papers and stuffed into folders and tacked up on the wall. You get the picture.

If you ask them, "Hey, can you write (some obscure form)?"

They will say, "Hmmm, I don't know," and pull out a pen or a laptop and start writing their way to finding out.

Fantasizing about writing without actually doing it can feel self-defeating and become a self-destructive habit. Writers have to get comfortable taking up space with words, and this willingness to occupy airtime takes a certain amount of chutzpah.

Chutzpah is a Yiddish term, which means courage verging on arrogance. It also means to have nerve, to dare. At some point, most writers acknowledge that they have a desire to write. But putting your desire into action despite the pressures of daily life is the real challenge.

My advice: Prove you are a writer by writing often. Don't just put on airs of being a writer; actually write. Write anything. Anytime. Anywhere. On anything. Because you are a writer, that's why.

Quickly, before you have a chance to talk yourself out of it. Number a page from one to ten and write down every topic you could write about right now. Go with whatever ideas bubble up.

7 TAKE STOCK

Writing is a dog's life, but the only life worth living.

—GUSTAVE FLAUBERT

A coach's job is not to give strokes, gratify egos, and indulge players. A coach's job is to motivate, rally, and push players to new levels of accomplishment. A coach's role is to help players win, whatever winning means.

Therefore, don't try to get strokes for your writing accomplishments. Giving yourself credit for writing career strides is your job, not anyone else's. If you take responsibility for the task of taking pride in your own work, you won't be looking for others to do the job for you.

Taking ongoing pride focuses your sense of accomplishment on what matters most to you, rather than on what has been impressive to others. It also helps you bless your work as "good enough" so you can keep moving on to the next project without getting hung up on the last.

Make as thorough a list as you can muster of all your past writing-related accomplishments. Here are a few prompts to get you started:

1. All the forms you know how to write
2. All the topics you typically write about
3. All the publications you have written for
4. All the expert sources you have met and quoted
5. Every milestone you've accomplished in your writing career
6. All the people who have helped you in your writing career
7. All the people you have helped with their writing careers
8. All the writing career development books you've read
9. All the panels you've appeared on or appearances you've made
10. All the self-publishing you have done
11. All the curricula you have developed or the teaching you have done
12. All the types of training or consulting you have done
13. All the books you have written or edited

Seeking strokes puts others in an awkward position, so if you do it, stop. Pause regularly and take pride in all your hard work as you go along. Then move on.

You'll forge ahead content, rather than seeking praise. Then the road ahead is wide open.

FORGET FRETTING

> *Ability is what you're capable of doing. Motivation determines what you do. Attitude determines how well you do it.*
>
> —RAYMOND CHANDLER

You might be concerned about the publishing industry right now. You've probably heard the end is nigh. I've been watching the industry evolve for years and I've learned a bit by paying attention. Here's my take.

THINGS HAVE NOT CHANGED MUCH. Publishing, as an industry, has collectively cleaned house, scaled back, and made changes to evolve in tough economic times. Just like most of us, they have had to look closely at spending, profits, and ways they can protect their bottom line. The less profitable publications and imprints have gone out of business, leaving behind plenty of others that have stayed in business. Most publishing houses have reorganized the way they do business. Regardless, there are still plenty of places to get published.

COMPETITION WAS ALWAYS STIFF AMONG WRITERS. Folks who want to write today can't fake it. That means you have to practice the skills that publishers expect writers to have. Ironically, the folks who seem to have been most affected by the cutbacks are those writers who were making the big bucks (over 100K). They are struggling to maintain the lifestyle they'd become accustomed to. Many of them had to change their strategies to adjust to industry-wide changes. By now they have adjusted their strategies, diversified their approaches, or moved on.

ADVANTAGES EXIST FOR RISING WRITERS. When publishers are trying to save money, they look to up-and-coming writers because they can pay them less than they pay seasoned writers. Therefore, what is making life tough for experienced writers is creating an opportunity for less seasoned writers. If you are not new, at least act like you are new. Remember what it was like to be hungry and flexible. There are plenty of opportunities for writers who want them, perhaps more than there were before.

So don't worry too much about the industry. Worry will only immobilize your self-expression. Just learn, write, and earn. The industry will be fine. New opportunities to earn will continue to crop up as publishing evolves.

9 EMBRACE THE REASONS

We should write because writing yields us a body of work, a felt path through the world we live in.

—JULIA CAMERON

There are hundreds—maybe thousands—of reasons to write. Therefore this list only scratches the surface.

Whatever motivates you to write is important on good writing days and bad writing days.

I used to think I wrote for only one reason on this list. Come to find out, I write for almost every reason on this list and probably more I have yet to uncover.

So don't feel like you have to wax poetic about why you write, or make it sound really noble, or try to justify why you write. Some people like to write. This is just the way it is, like some people like to paint or sing or act.

But it's a good idea to know why you write, for your own benefit. Understanding your motivations can be powerful. If you know why you write, you can call on that power if you hit a snag or stall out.

Check off all the reasons that suit you. Expand on the list, if you like.

Why do you write? The truth. Mark the ways:

___ To express   ___ To individuate
___ To tell   ___ To leave a legacy
___ To heal   ___ To become known
___ To listen   ___ For love
___ To share   ___ Because you can't not write
___ To connect   ___ For pleasure
___ To respond   ___ For revenge
___ To participate   ___ To avoid housework
___ To inspire   ___ To make money
___ To explore   ___ To create tax write-offs
___ To grow   ___ To establish a career
___ To discover   ___ To remember
___ To transcend   ___ To meditate
___ To play   ___ To process
___ To report   ___ To stop the voices in your head
___ To inform   ___ To channel your ideas
___ To persuade   ___ More:
___ To rant   ___ More:
___ To ramble   ___ More:
___ To advocate

Every athlete knows this: Warm up before playing or you'll pull a muscle. If I am warm, I feel I can do anything.

—TWYLA THARP

Ready to brainstorm some writing ideas? On a fresh piece of paper, answer these questions and use the answers as starts for future writing.

1. Who are you? When I ask that question, what are three key values you'd like me (and the world) to know?
2. What jobs have you held? List them briefly. Any expertise in that line of work you would like to write about? Any lessons learned that might help others? If so, make notes.
3. What are your hobbies?
4. What would you love to learn more about? What topic could you immerse yourself in, sharing information with others as you go along?
5. What subject are you an expert on that is also a hot topic right now?
6. Finish this sentence ten times: "I know how to _____. (Number one through ten and come up with ten different answers to this one question.)
7. If you had to choose one topic, and only one topic, to write about for one year, what would that topic be?
8. If you were going to create your own publication, what would it be called and whom would it be for?
9. A collection of poetry you wrote about your life thus far has what as the theme?
10. After you have passed away, in the biography of your life, you will have made great strides for which group, how?

INCORPORATE NONFICTION

Writing is writing, and stories are stories. Perhaps the only true genres are fiction and nonfiction. And even there, who can be sure?

—TANITH LEE

As a professional writer, you are going to end up writing plenty of nonfiction throughout the course of your career, no matter what genre you specialize in. So be smart, learn nonfiction forms and plenty of them, and put them to good use in your career.

Last time I checked, the most widely respected writers these days are writing across genres without feeling a need to apologize. The writers who are most likely to survive the many changes in publishing, even while remaining true to their own mission and the people they serve, write across the genres, reaching a wider variety of readers, ultimately expanding their appeal and growing their readership as a result.

So look to nonfiction writing as a lifelong friend rather than a genre you are going to waste energy proving you are too superior to write in. Genre is a publication preference, not a hierarchy. And nonfiction is going to be your career-long friend, regardless of the genre you enjoy writing most.

Nonfiction requires just as much inspiration and conjures just as many creative juices as fiction writing or any other kind of writing. The more effortlessly you can move between genres, without complaint, the more appealing you are going to be to book publishers, who are looking for more content return for their investment buck.

Even if you write in another category, like screenwriting or comic books, you are going to write tons of nonfiction alongside your chosen genre. This is not something to dread; it's something to celebrate.

Every writing career ends up having an ultimate thrust whether you initially intend it or not, and this thrust carries through across the genres. So write across the genres, across as many as you like, but especially embrace nonfiction because nonfiction writing will support everything else you write. All of the nonfiction writing skills you acquire will serve you in the long haul as you go along.

Mighty oaks from little acorns grow.

—ENGLISH PROVERB

Aristotle viewed entelechy as "the condition in which a potentiality has become an actuality." Therefore, an acorn does not merely have the potential to become an oak; the proper and complete fulfillment of an acorn is a mighty oak.

Being at work in the particular way it takes to go from acorn to mighty oak is an acorn's daily tendency, until completeness is reached. Writers have an internal code similar to the acorn that unfolds day by day, whether we see the evidence or not.

And certainly, just as an acorn can avoid the fertile ground where it can hunker down and get to the business of growing, a writer can also avoid safe harbor and fritter away his creative energy.

But this is not what any aspiring writer is hoping for. To realize your potential, recognize that entelechy is about a realization, or actuality, of what is already inside of you. Given consistently secure circumstances, your creativity can flourish and grow into something bigger than you can likely imagine.

Your job as a writer is to recognize that your creative path is unfolding from this vital tendency. As soon as you feel a disconnection from natural growth, your path diverges from your potential.

When we are in a place where we can hunker down and grow, we can feel it. Not that the growth will go perfectly from that moment onward, but if you keep seeking safe harbor where daily growth is assured, your long-term career prospects can become mighty.

If you are not interested in finding safe harbor, you might squelch, squander, or sabotage your natural ability to grow and thrive. Writers are no strangers to self-destructiveness. Maybe it comes part and parcel with the creative tendency, I'm not certain. It does not matter. What matters is that a mighty oak grows better in a safe harbor than on shifting ground.

Do you cultivate a safe harbor for yourself? Or do you tend to squelch, squander, and sabotage your natural growth? Choose one path or the other.

TRUST YOUR INSTINCTS

The best article ideas are related to comfort, survival, fear, anxiety, hope, love, joy, security, curiosity, even death. And what do all of these have in common? They concern readers.

—GORDON BURGETT

You can write about whatever you want. And you should.

But if you want your words to be read, you might want to pay attention to the types of topics that typically compel readers.

Try topics:

- You are passionate about
- That might make the world a better place
- That might make you a better person by writing about them
- That will satisfy your curiosity
- That will change your life for the better
- That may include write-offs when you finish your taxes
- That will help you meet people you respect whom you'd like to meet
- That will expand your expertise
- That will exercise the expertise you already have
- That energize you
- That preoccupy you
- That inspire you
- That you keep tripping over
- That fall into your lap
- That might become a good specialty
- That will earn you money
- That have anything to do with sex, money, love, and time
- That are local but might have wider appeal
- That will help you solve your personal challenges as you also help others
- That move you
- That you think will move others

Trust yourself. If a topic concerns you, it's also likely to concern readers. Your ability to stay in touch with your instincts and follow them to topic after topic will determine how satisfied you feel at the end of each writing day.

If you allow what instinctively concerns you to become your subject matter, you will always serve readers.

Which topics concern you?

If there's any message I want you to take away, it's that true success—financial, personal, and professional—lies above all in loving your family, working hard, and living your passion.

—GARY VAYNERCHUK

Because writing careers take time to grow, you're going to need some money to make all of this work in the long haul. Ways writers typically stay afloat so they can continue to write include:

- Holding down a day job
- Having a patient/understanding partner or spouse with a steady paycheck
- Creating a business that earns so as to support your writing habit

And even if you have any or all of these things, there is still always the chance that your company could go out of business or that your position could be eliminated through no fault of your own. If you are married or partnered, you could become divorced or separated or your spouse could pass away. And even if you create a business and are successful in the short term, your business could fail or peter out.

Other sources of income for your writing career may include:

- Finding a patron who will pour money into your career with no strings attached
- Applying for grants
- Raising your own funds

There is nothing wrong with any of these strategies, except that none of them are likely to create permanent cash flow. Most of us perform at our peak creativity when we are less spoiled and more hungry, when we are more involved in the hum and thrum of life and less permanently sequestered.

Even if you have a consistent financial base today, no one can guarantee it will be there tomorrow. Basic needs come first and foremost. When you have those covered, you can grow your writing career from a solid foundation.

Create your solvency plan. What's yours realistically going to look like in the next year? If you are going to err, err on the conservative side so you can keep your attention on your writing.

Writing is the core of my wealth. Not wealth of money, wealth of knowledge—wealth of new ideas—wealth of creativity—wealth of material for seminars.

—JEFFREY GITOMER

Author and speaker Scott Ginsberg says that writing is the basis of wealth. He says he got the idea from best-selling author Jeff Gitomer, but I don't care where he got it. The statement rings true because the process of writing, from start to finish, can make you feel rich, and you are only as rich as you feel.

Any writer who can translate that feeling of wealth into results, and some writers do, can literally become rich in the long haul and profitable in the short run.

If nothing else, Gitomer's mantra is a good reminder to keep writing and the writing process at the center of your focus, even as you work on other important skills. It's easy to forget or to think other skills should take precedence.

There have been plenty of times I have forgotten and I see other writers catch this contagious amnesia all the time. Remember, at the end of the day, you are not in sales, you are not in marketing, and you are not a workshopaholic. You are a writer. Keep your eye on the prize.

At the point where working all five skills (writing, selling, focusing, learning, and self-promotion) become as familiar and natural as the things you do every day, like making coffee or brushing your teeth or driving your car, you will have internalized everything you need to create writing-career success.

For now, take a look at the image and imagine yourself moving effortlessly from writing to whichever skill you need next. Once you've got the hang of all of these skills, you can start tapping into your earning potential. You can translate the feeling of being rich into the result of money earned.

6
NURTURE YOUR IDEAS

If something inside of you is real, we will probably find it interesting, and it will probably be universal.

—ANNE LAMOTT

You can grow something huge out of something slight, if you plant it and nurture it appropriately. From a writer's point of view:

- Every moment is a seed because there is always a new idea to write about right now.
- Every idea is a seed with the potential to bear new fruit over and over and over again in the future.
- Every topic is a seed because you could build an entire line of products or services or columns or books from just one idea.
- Every writer is a seed because that writer's essence will permeate everything she writes.
- Every piece of research is a seed because any one discovery can turn your thoughts in a whole new direction.
- Every expert source is a seed with the potential to send you off and running in a new direction.
- Every publication is a seed with the potential to give you many ideas specifically suited to that editor. And if things don't work out, some of those ideas can carry over to similar publications.
- Everything you've already written is a seed because you can take it in a new direction or keep developing the material more widely and deeply.
- Every time two or more qualities intersect is a seed. For example, the intersection of the writer and a topic might lead to a personal story on the subject. The intersection of a topic and a publication might lead to an article assignment.
- Every article, class, speech, podcast, etc., is a seed because you might discover a new thought in the process and then take that thought and run with it in new directions and numerous forms.

Let your current writing feed your future writing by learning how to grow your ideas. Follow the threads of your ideas that make the most sense to you in the moment and seem to have the most future potential.

TARGET YOUR WORDS

Now is the operative word. Everything you put in your way is just a method of putting off the hour when you could actually be doing your dream.

—BARBARA SHER

Which audiences demand continual fresh content, and how can you position yourself to write regularly for the editors who put out publications that fulfill these readers' needs?

Writers get paid when a publisher has the intention to pay writers for completed work. Any updated market guide will help you narrow the seemingly infinite and constantly evolving possibilities for where you can get your writing published.

If you are new to writing for publication and you want to sell your work quickly, you are probably better off focusing on writing for an existing and wide market of potential buyers (like parents, hobbyists, or professionals) because you will get off to a more targeted start.

Here are some benefits for new writers who write for a wide audience hungry for a constant stream of timely content:

- You gain valuable writing experience.
- You learn how to compose basic publishable forms.
- You make some money.
- You learn that writers succeed by writing, re-slanting, and recycling ideas.

I teach unpublished mom writers how to delve into their ideas and come up with general parenting articles that they can sell and resell to regional parenting publications. Because there are hundreds of these publications out there seeking content, this approach consistently achieves positive results for my students.

You can put this strategy to work for you and your first or next audience, as well. But remember, if there were not hundreds of editors out there looking for fresh parenting articles, my students would not land as many sold articles.

When you want to write content in advance, without doing a ton of market research first, write for audiences you already know that demand a lot of fresh content on an ongoing basis. This kind of focus will get you off to a good start.

8
ADJUST YOUR ATTITUDE

Most authors are born to be failures, and the publisher knows it. He makes his living out of the few successes, and if he is indulgent with less successful writers, it is not only because there is always the possibility that today's failure may become tomorrow's bestseller.

—MICHAEL JOSEPH

Here's how to impress editors, agents, publishing industry insiders, and yourself:

- Take 100 percent responsibility for your writing career. Don't ever expect it to be as important to anyone else as it is to you.
- If you've been burned (or ignored) by publishing insiders in the past, acknowledge and own any grievances. You are not a victim. Choose to be continuously proactive instead of accumulating resentments.
- If you've been successful, celebrate and study your success strategies. If you haven't been successful, back off and reexamine your approach. What needs improvement?
- Be positive, flexible, service-oriented, and communicative. Don't whine, brood, suffer, or listen to groups of people who like to whine, brood, or suffer. Getting in the habit of whining, brooding, and suffering instead of developing professional habits will definitely slow your path to success.
- Don't get addicted to venting. "I'm just venting" can become a bad habit of creating drama and holding others hostage to listen to your whining. The only helpful reason to vent is to move through any negative feelings quickly and get back to work.
- Everyone's negative needle gets stuck sometimes. Go ahead and unstick yours now by giving a confidante permission to remind you that focusing on the negative gets you nowhere. Always proceed in as positive, constructive a manner as possible.
- Imperfection reigns. Know yourself, but don't let self-knowledge inhibit you or lead you to believe that you can't do something. You can succeed and you will succeed, when success really matters to you, regardless of your predispositions or quirks.
- Memorize this: "I succeed because of my willingness to go deeper in understanding myself, to stretch beyond my comfort zone, to take what I learn and turn it into action, and to ask for help when I have gone as far as I can on my own."

19
CULTIVATE A BODY OF WORK

Forget the concept of the "paperless office"—while you may find that you can store some records on your computer, you're still going to amass large quantities of files.

—MOIRA ALLEN

You won't get a big payoff as a writer until you accumulate a body of work. So instead of imagining some future greatness, imagine the kinds of results that are going to get you there: the books read, the piles of paper collected, the journals filled up, the boxes of notes poured over, the tax forms you submitted to report the money you made, the ephemera, the personal notes from people you met, the photographs of happy meetings, the conference lanyards dangling from a hook.

A writer's progress is measured in the completion of project after project. If you are experiencing serial rejection, are you sure you are not aiming for targets that are over your head?

Embarking on a short-term goal and taking care of the next steps is the best way to nurture your brightest future. Writers sometimes think if they are not entertaining some larger-than-life vision of their writing career they are not doing something right.

But you have no idea what you are going to be writing in twelve years, so how are you supposed to get started on it? Don't obsess so much about some huge future fantasy and miss the power of this moment. A writer's day-to-day existence is composed of a million right-now moments.

When we focus too much on an image of where we think we are going, we miss out on the opportunities right in front of us. We don't learn what we need to learn to get from where we are to the next level. We cut off the legs that are going to walk us to where we could be in twelve years when we try to leap there prematurely.

Embrace the idea that what writers do over the course of a lifetime is cultivate a body of work one project at a time. Writers write, one day at a time, toward a destination that will eventually become something that can be viewed retrospectively but typically cannot be perceived in advance.

Create the artifacts of a well-written life. Set one short-term goal you can accomplish this week, and start walking bravely toward it. Forget the future; leave behind evidence that you hit your short-term goal this week instead.

IDENTIFY YOUR AUDIENCES

You are never going to please everyone, so you shouldn't try. If you do, you'll fail at pleasing anyone. Instead, imagine who your very best audience is and go straight for the heart of that group. Ignore everyone else.

—SETH GODIN

Once you know whom you are writing for your ideas can come in a steady flow. But first you need to know: Whom are you writing for?

I can help you come up with some simple keywords to describe potential audiences that might relate to your work. For example, mine are *mother, wife, writer,* and *teacher.*

I have been sharing the concept of using keywords to discover possible writing topics for years. Used as a starting point, keywords can launch writers in powerful directions that might have been otherwise overlooked. Jot down a bunch of keywords that describe your roles in life so you can narrow the list to just the four most important to you right now.

At any given time you need to know whom you are writing for. For example, writing for children is not the same as writing for adults. Nor is writing for tweens the equivalent of writing for seniors.

To identify your audiences, list four keywords that describe your roles in life very simply (no compounds). Once you have them, mix them up. Put a couple keywords together and what do you get? You get some pretty interesting potential audiences. I got some pretty interesting results from writer + mama.

If you want to find more audiences for your writing, take each keyword and describe it in some detail. For example, what kind of mom am I? I am not a hip mom, nor a conservative mom, nor a moderate mom. I tend to stick to the middle, slightly to the left of center. These are also the folks I tend to write for. Take each of your words and describe them further so you can see which kinds of audiences might be a good match for your writing.

YOUR KEYWORDS: 1. _____ 2._____ 3. _____ 4. _____

ADD THEM TOGETHER:

_____ + _____ = _____
_____ + _____ = _____
_____ + _____ = _____
_____ + _____ = _____

THREE WORDS TO DESCRIBE EACH FURTHER:

1. _____ , _____ , _____
2. _____ , _____ , _____
3. _____ , _____ , _____
4. _____ , _____ , _____

So I went out and bought myself a copy of the Writer and Artist Yearbook, *bought lots of magazines and got on the phone and talked to editors about ideas for stories. Pretty soon I found myself hired to do interviews and articles and went off and did them.*

—NEIL GAIMAN

Pick the low-hanging fruit first because success builds success.

Match your level of writing experience to opportunities available. Rack up successes, then take a deep breath and stretch yourself a little more.

Build up your confidence over time and then aim higher.

Look at a lineup of possible writing markets from easiest to hardest to break into and lowest to highest pay (usually):

1. Association newsletters
2. Online markets/blogging
3. Nonglossy regional publications
4. Glossy regional publications
5. Local and regional newspapers
6. Custom and closed-circulation publications
7. Anthologies
8. Daily newspapers
9. National trade magazines
10. National glossies

Where should you break in? At the level, starting at the top and working your way down, where you have the most likelihood of breaking in. If you are unpublished, that's 1 through 5. And if you are already published or you have a good handle on the basic writing-for-publication skills, try tackling 6 through 10.

If you have a fresh and timely idea that is appropriate for readers, you'll have a good shot at getting your words in the door.

This can work in any genre, assuming you create a list like this appropriate to the types of markets for your genre and work your way down it. What would this list look like for fiction? For memoir? For children's books?

Create a target market list that works for you and use it as a workout ladder. Start with the easiest markets and work your way up.

22
DISCOVER YOUR RHYTHM

Stride forward with a firm, steady step knowing with a deep, certain inner knowing that you will reach every goal you set yourselves, that you will achieve every aim.

—EILLEN CADDY

I've got rhythm. You've got rhythm. And every person's rhythm is unique to them.

Creative progress has a thrum, a beat, and movement. So if you want to establish a writing rhythm, what matters the most is writing regularly, getting in a productive routine that works for you, hitting your marks, and pausing once in a while to take an objective look at your progress.

Long-term writing success comes from finding your rhythm and staying with it, not following someone else's formula. Just as you really can't find your writing rhythm if you are not writing regularly, you can't imitate someone else's groove, no matter how much you like or admire. You have to get your own groove, get down into it, and stay in it.

You can tell a writer has found her rhythm because she has momentum. A writer who hasn't found her pattern of success may still be trying to get going. Needless to say, once you have gotten moving, it's easier to maintain your momentum.

A writer who can't stay in his own rhythm may have found it but may not trust it. A writer who has embraced his own creative momentum feels strange if he does not experience its rhythm regularly.

Certainly, when you have a major life interruption like a move or an illness or a death in the family, you are going to lose your writing rhythm. Life is bound to interfere once in a while. Successful writers spend most of their days in their writing rhythms letting the small stuff that might distract a less focused writer roll off their backs so they can keep on keeping on.

Once you have experienced your own groove for any length of time, it's easier to get it back when you lose it. If you lose your momentum, you can quickly rebound and move forward again because you know what your groove feels like. Find your groove by writing regularly in a schedule that works for you.

23 BRAINSTORM TOPICS

If you are truly a creative writer you'll find it almost impossible to separate yourself from your material, whether you're writing fact or fiction. Your memories, emotions, convictions, experiences, and unique personality will permeate whatever you write.

—MARJORIE HOLMES

Once you know whom you are writing for and what your audience reads, you can begin to brainstorm topics and write on them. By identifying a topic with a clear, specific audience from the outset, you increase your chances of being published exponentially in both the short and long runs. Consider topics you know about and topics you are interested in learning more about. Try to view each potential article idea as an opportunity to dive into a topic and learn as you earn.

If I use my keyword "wife," possible topics might include:

- How to communicate better with your spouse
- How to spend more quality time with your spouse
- How to find the perfect holiday gifts for your spouse

Now your turn. Come up with three possible topics for each keyword.

If you have been writing for a while and you are looking to deepen your niche, you may want to use compound words for your audience.

AUDIENCE	POSSIBLE TOPIC	POSSIBLE TOPIC	POSSIBLE TOPIC
KEYWORD 1:			
KEYWORD 2:			
KEYWORD 3:			
KEYWORD 4:			

Just get it down on paper, and then we'll see what to do with it.

—MAXWELL PERKINS

Editors prefer informed ideas, not off-the-top-of-the-head or from-the-hip kinds of ideas, even if that's where your idea originated. You can always pitch faster and looser once you get to know an editor and she is comfortable working with (and perhaps even brainstorming with) you. But it's always a bad idea to approach a new-to-you editor with this expectation rather than with fully formed ideas.

So, if you want to make a professional impression, do your homework and offer substance. When I say homework, here's what I mean:

- Statistics
- Facts
- Quotes by well-known people
- Definitions
- Anecdotes (short illustrative stories about yourself or someone else)
- Quotes from people like the reader
- Quotes from experts
- Quotes from popular books on the subject
- References to other media (film, television, radio, the Internet)
- Helpful tools, resources, or products

Go ahead and choose one of the ideas you brainstormed in the previous chapter and consider which kinds of research would enrich any writing you will do for your intended audience.

Then, spending no longer than one hour on research, compile every piece of research you can in one folder, virtual as well as actual.

Once you have immersed yourself in the latest research on your idea, you are ready to locate a target publication for your idea (if you haven't already thought of one along the way) and start drafting content to suit.

Make the compilation of research a habit before you write and you will automatically start writing content that is more likely to sell than content that was written casually. When you are engaged in the process of writing and learning as you go, your reader will be engaged and learning as well.

You have your laptop computer: The whole world is your office, if you will let it be.

—ERIC MAISEL

It seems to me the "place" where writers write is more of an internal construct than an external construct. This idea was validated for me when I read psychologist and creativity coach Eric Maisel's book, *A Writer's Space*.

In the book, Maisel uncovers deep implications of the idea of place: We are not merely seeking "a quiet room" but also "mental health." Writers are seeking a sane inner space as well as a calm external space so we can start to write and maintain a steady output.

Say you are a working dad, already juggling the demands of family and work, writing on your way to or from work on the commuter train. You will need to become a master of your mental heath to be able to focus on your writing while you are in motion and surrounded by others.

We all need to cultivate a calm, quiet interior space that goes everywhere we go and does everything we do. From this place we can create because wherever we go, our creative "space" is always right inside of us.

What props will you need to take you to this space? How about a decent laptop? It needn't be expensive. New or used doesn't matter as long as you back up your work often.

Maybe you need a pair of headphones with an audio player to block the distraction of the chatter around you. These are inexpensive enough to purchase. Would you like to have a spiral pad and a handful of gel pens handy? Anyone can afford them.

Heck, you can start building a writing career with a couple of found pens, a few scraps of recycled paper, a library card, and access to computers at your local library. Just start with whatever tools you can afford.

Once you have the knack for maintaining your inner space, regardless of your tools, you can write here, there, and anywhere, filling up notebooks and hard drives and file cabinets as you go along your merry writing way.

Cultivate the "room" you write in. Take it with you everywhere you go. Watch your productivity increase.

26
CRAVE THE PAGE

I want to say, wake up, open your eyes, there's a snow-covered road ahead, a field of blankness, a sheet of paper, an empty screen.

—BARBARA CROOKER

Harvesting your epiphanies is key when you are a writer.

Take out an empty piece of paper. Put it somewhere where you can easily sit down and write on it. But then walk away. Do some chores or whatever you need to accomplish. Just get in the habit of leaving an empty, ready page sitting with a writing instrument within reach until you swoop in as the urge strikes and scrawl something on it.

Exercise your awareness that the paper is there, waiting for you, ready for your next best idea. So when one flies through your mind, you will know where to put it.

Every time you use up a page, put it in a folder or bin and set out another page. Don't reread what you wrote or judge it or critique it. Just enjoy the feeling of putting words—or whatever—on the page. Fill page after page.

Get in the habit of leaving a piece of paper there, waiting, and walk away from it. You'll be back when you are ready to write. And when you come back, it will be there.

Perhaps filling an empty page is not as dramatically dangerous as some have made it out to be. You can get used to the idea of filling an empty page and then another and another and another, if you just make it part of your everyday life.

I start off every New Year with a new sketchbook full of empty pages and a fresh set of markers. Get yourself a sketchbook, if this idea appeals to you. Or just keep leaving one piece of paper out where your ideas can come swooping in for a landing. Printer paper works well. A legal pad could also work. Just about anything could work.

Epiphanies run the gamut from tiny to huge. If you are a person who is intimidated by the empty page, practice this exercise until the sight of a space to write fills you with enthusiasm. Practice it until your life starts to feel like a series of empty pages you are excited to fill.

27
DON'T RAMBLE

If you are serious about writing, burn the journal and get to work.
—ROBERT MASELLO

One of the best ways I have found to teach writers to write well over a short period of time is by asking them to compose short forms. This advice squarely conflicts with a lot of advice that suggests writers scamper off and fill journal after journal after journal with every thought, hope, and fear. Or just blaze through their first novel without a care in the world.

I think there can be a benefit from writing for therapeutic reasons and for practice writing. I also believe that when you are ready to write for others, it's time to start mastering short, not long, forms. It's time to stop rambling and start writing tight.

If you have a trust fund that keeps a steady and generous flow of money coming into your checking account and a decade worth of health care coverage prepaid, why not go ahead and get to work on a novel, since most published novels take anywhere from two to ten years to complete? Just keep in mind that most first-time novelists write on the side while also writing to earn money or by holding down a day job.

What I love about short forms is that any writer can learn valuable lessons from writing them (which may also strengthen your writing in other genres), like:

- How to write tightly
- How to make every word count
- How to select powerful verbs
- The value of the active voice
- How to avoid repetition
- How to make and support a point
- How to say a lot in a few words

One of my favorite books on grammar and usage is Strunk and White's *The Elements of Style*. It's also my favorite book on writing concisely.

I ask all of my students to read it because it's mercifully short, and the lessons never go out of date. Every piece of advice in the book will improve your writing. Get a copy, if you don't have one already.

28
OBTAIN STICKY BRAIN

A writer is someone who begins by trying to catch insights as fire-flies in a jar, but in the end needs to see them pinned to the page.

—JANE YOLEN

I'm going to guesstimate that you probably have one writing idea per minute on a slow day. We could increase that number tenfold with just a few exercises. The sad part is you will probably only execute a fraction of your ideas. The rest will bounce off your brain and spill out like rainwater running down the roof gutters.

So the first order of business, if you plan to be a prolific writer, is securing your best ideas. Since you don't know the difference between a good idea and a bad idea until you actually try to use it, you want to capture as many of your ideas as possible and keep them handy, just in case.

Over the years, I have recommended many ways to do this—carrying around note cards or notepads with you, recording the ideas into your cell phone, placing white boards, bulletin boards, and clipboards strategically around the house—but there is only one place you have a giant idea web that can catch a fleeting idea, and that is in your mind.

You can train your mind to become "sticky" like a spider's web so your best ideas will get stuck long enough for you to write them down. You don't need fancy techniques to accomplish this. You just need to care about what you think. You have to believe there is value in your thoughts. You have to trust your observations.

Here are three simple steps to capture more of your ideas:

1. Notice what you are thinking.
2. Respond to what you notice when you next write.
3. Accumulate writings until you want or need them.

Collect words in formats you use regularly, like your blog, journal, or sketchbook. You'll be amazed how quickly you can compile writing of value by pinning down the tiny little fireflies in your mind before they flicker out. Catch your best ideas while you can. Don't let them fade away. Find out what you think by writing down your thoughts as they occur. Let what you think pile up.

29
ALWAYS BE RESPONDING

We are a species that needs and wants to understand who we are. Sheep lice do not seem to share this longing, which is one reason they write so very little. But we do. We have so much we want to say and figure out.

—ANNE LAMOTT

The favor of your response is always requested when you are a writer. Everything in your life is trying to communicate with you. I say *trying* because everything that is trying to communicate with you will only succeed if you respond.

What do you think, not just about this theory but about everything? What do you want to chime in on? Turn up the volume on the sound of your voice responding. The world is waiting to hear what you uniquely think.

I am talking about your response to your dog's diagnosis at the vet, your response to your daughter's intense interest in all things equine, your response to your husband's stress at work and the way it impacts your family at dinnertime. Start with the daily things and work your way up to the big things, whatever the big things are for you.

The diseased trees in your yard are talking to you. Your steadily increasing electric bill is talking to you. And don't forget the subtle, less easy to perceive things, like the whisperings of your soul, which is also speaking to you. What is your response?

Naturally, people are talking to you. Your sister who calls from Florida to say that your nephew has been diagnosed with Type 1 diabetes might be talking to you. Your parents' concerns about their dwindling retirement account might be talking to you. The way your friend's husband used social networking to find a new job might be talking to you.

Get in the habit of jotting these responses down as they come up and then respond fully to one or two ideas each week. You can do this publicly, as in a blog, or privately, in a notebook or sketch pad, as practice for developing your creative confidence.

Everything in your life right now is talking to you. Your job is to listen, filter out the most significant parts of what you hear, and decide if and when to respond. Responding is a choice, of course. And when a writer responds, the alchemy of the writing process begins.

*The faster I write, the better my output. If I'm going slow, I'm in trou-
ble. It means I'm pushing the words instead of being pulled by them.*

—RAYMOND CHANDLER

Don't abuse your muse. When you get an inner prompting, listen. In the process of dis-
missing your best ideas, you deprive others of ever knowing about them.

Writers usually have the most enthusiasm for an idea when it is new. By the third
time we've had an idea (especially if we have failed to write it down once again), the
idea may already feel like old news—even though we never bothered to capture it or
share it with anyone.

Here's a trick that can help you get the hang of using your best ideas when they first
dawn on you, since so often an idea will come fully feathered the first time it lands. At
Columbia College Chicago, when I was in graduate school, we used pretend letter writing to quickly scoop a lively idea out of thin air.

Today, pretending to write an e-mail would work just as well. At the top of the page,
write "Dear [name of a person who will be receptive to your inspiration]:" Then start
writing or typing as fast as you can until you either fill the page or exhaust the idea.

If you don't know anyone receptive to the idea, make someone up. It's okay to go
on for a few pages with an idea, but 500 words is usually enough to get the nut of an idea
down—the part of the idea you are most jazzed about sharing.

Don't try to write perfectly. You can edit or re-slant the idea later, if needed. In the
meantime, use this exercise to sketch out the idea before it gets away. Once you have it
down, it's yours.

Going forward, when an idea alights, take five minutes to run a 500-word dash.
There's no need to send the letter. You were writing to yourself, all along.

31 MAKE MULTIPLE OFFERS

You create your opportunities by asking for them.

—PATTY HANSEN

One of my students made five hundred dollars last month from submitting her work part-time. Another has sold 150 articles in the past 18 months. Others, who are just getting started, are making their first sales with glee.

How about you? Does the idea of selling your words stop you in your ink-tracks?

Fear of selling might come from a fear of rejection, the dread of not knowing whether or not what seems like a good match to you really is a good match, or good old-fashioned editor phobia. Good faith is required to sell your words because most of the work that writers do in exchange for money is done in advance. The money comes later.

Look at selling as offering your words in exchange for money and perhaps you can leap over the hesitation many writers have. Like most things that have to do with writing, selling takes practice. Successful selling means finding the most appropriate markets for your work and choosing wisely among them.

If your mission as a writer is to serve parents, parenting publications would be good markets for you. If your mission as a writer is to serve literary readers, literary magazines would be good markets for you.

Sometimes the market match is not so obvious, as with humor writing. When this is the case, don't be too quick to give up. The Internet is full of experts you can track down, who offer advice to writers just like you. Go find that advice, read it, and apply it to your sales strategy.

Selling is simply making an offer you can fulfill. What kinds of editors do you wish to write for? List up your leads, study the publication, and prepare work for those markets one at a time. Start with the easiest target to hit and work your way up.

Selling is simple, so keep it simple. Step one: Find folks you'd be happy to write for. Step two: Make them an offer. Step three: Move on to the next market. Repeat.

Whatever you say, say it with conviction.

—MARK TWAIN

An element of poetry results when you thrust what you want to say onto the page, like banging your fist on the table.

It's okay if your first draft comes out like a fist, like something furious and impatient though you had intended something pretty and poetic. If you are in the habit of spilling out your opinions as quickly as you bang your fist on the table, great. Don't apologize. You can pretty up that prose later.

However, many writers have to overcome a sense of inner oppression and feelings that what we think and feel does not matter and could not possibly be worth writing about. Therefore, it may take time before we can even pick up our fist, never mind banging it back down on the table.

Perhaps this explains why sometimes that energy, if it's been building up long enough, wants to come out all at once. So go ahead and bang your fist on the table.

If you bang your fist on the table enough times, and capture the words that go with it, that fist will eventually open up, blossom, and express something important.

A rosebud is tight, like a fist. But an open rose extends up and out like an out-stretched hand.

If writers see their first drafts as buds instead of fully open flowers, they can get those drafts written faster and with a lot less fretting.

Give us the bud and don't expect it to become a rose too soon. It will blossom when it's good and ready.

So go ahead and pound your fist on the table. Your fist won't break. The table won't break. And no one else has to see what you've written until it is good and ready.

You want the rose. We want the rose. If you are going to get the rose, you are going to have to give us the bud first.

33
TARGET SPECIFIC MARKETS

The point is that as writers, we are individuals, and our tastes and values are as important as those of the markets we are trying to penetrate.

—MOIRA ALLEN

If you want to write for publication, you'll need to compile a list of potential markets and topics to suit the specific type of audience you are targeting. Here are some tips or reminders.

- Identify what kind of person you are, for example, twenty-something, single, urban, etc.

- Identify what kind of publication targets a person like you. Gather these publications or go to the library or bookstore so you can study them. If you are a parent, try breaking in to parenting publications. If you just got married, try wedding magazines. If you were involved in the art field in a former job, you may enjoy writing in an art-related market.

- Think incrementally. If you have no clips, it makes sense to start with local and regional publications and work your way up to larger publications. Make a list of the publications you will submit to.

- Start gathering all of the writer's guidelines on your target publications. File them for easy access.

- Make a list of the best publications to approach. Start at number one on your list. Read the guidelines. Study the publication and come up with an appropriate idea far enough in the future to merit consideration. Write and submit one article at a time to those that allow unsolicited manuscripts.

- Work your way down your list without waiting to hear back on each piece submitted. Your goal is to get your twelve articles written and submitted, one publication at a time. Twelve isn't a magic number; it's simply a good first goal. Most of my students have mastered the basics of article writing after writing about twelve fresh articles in a row.

- The more you write for publication, the more you will become familiar with the types of topics featured in the kinds of publications you write for. Why not keep an ongoing list as you notice topics? The more evergreen (fresh and vital year after year) your ideas and the more compelling they are to you, the more successful you will be in writing and placing them.

34
FLEX YOUR VOICE

Voice is the articulation of all perceptions in verbal expression, written and oral, including the so-called nonverbal which we want to get into writing too. Voice is the expression of the whole person, an extension of speech, an extension of the body.

—JOHN SCHULTZ

You are the writer. You are the responder. You are the lens. You are the filter. You are the point of view. Your voice is in everything you write. Therefore the more you write, the more distinct your voice will become.

You could be tentative about this. You could consign your writing to journals while you wait for your elusive "voice" to make itself known. Or you could start small, writing with the understanding that sometimes you will use more of your voice and sometimes you will use less, depending on what is called for in each particular piece.

For example, you might hold back your voice in favor of letting the material lead. This is a more journalistic approach. Other times, like when giving your opinion or advice, you might go heavy on voice to get your points across.

If you are blogging, you will most likely use your most natural voice. You may pump it up for effect because blog readers read quickly and might not take the time to absorb your words otherwise.

When you write for a publication, you want to be sure you adjust your voice to fit the tone and style of the publication. Fortunately, your most natural and relaxed tone is usually the voice folks want to hear most.

So have a voice. Use your voice. But don't bow down and pray at the church of the almighty "Voice" as though you are waiting for your one and only "Voice" to make its debut and then everything in your career will fall into place.

Your voice will not work this way. It is not forged in steel; it's more pliable than that. So play around with your voice and see how many variations you have that you can put to use in a multitude of ways. And then let your many voices rip.

NOTICE PATTERNS

One huge advantage of magazines is that the publisher prints and distributes your work to thousands of readers, giving you exposure to a wider audience than you might garner on your own.

—ROBERT W. BLY

Writers who are just getting started often write and publish best when they choose a specific kind of target publication and serve that type of editor over and over and over.

The reasons are obvious: If you are constantly serving regional parenting publication editors, for example, after a short time, you can become familiar with the types of topics, forms, and styles of writing those types of editors prefer. This helps you stay focused on the writing and not on having to re-create the marketing wheel every time you want to get published.

You can do the same with trade magazines, alumnae magazines, or newspapers. I know writers who continue working the same lower paying gigs over long periods of time because those gigs are so wired into their writing habit that the process of doing so helps them focus so they can ramp up to higher paying, more sophisticated topics.

Based on the audience keywords that you've come up with and the types of markets you've looked over, which types of publications do you think might make the best market grooves for you to serially approach with your ideas?

Don't approach them yet. But start gathering the writer's guidelines for several of the publications you feel you have the best shot of breaking into.

Read the publications and guidelines as a collection and see what kinds of patterns you notice. How could you cultivate a body of ideas that would allow you to serially publish in this target market groove?

You will want to keep their contact info on file or, if they are online, use electronic bookmarking to keep track of the contact info all in one place.

36

EXPECT TEN DRAFTS

Because of my writing practice, I understood when I joined the running club that I just had to shut up and do it even though I thought I was incapable of running.

—NATALIE GOLDBERG

Any time you expect to write anything, expect to write ten drafts.

Thinking in terms of ten drafts takes the pressure off early drafts. Once this pressure is gone, you realize that even if the first draft is a wreck, you still have nine more tries to get it in shape.

Drafts one through nine don't have to be that great, as long as the tenth draft really works. Things usually start to come together somewhere around the middle of the drafting process for most writers, but there is no set rule. How slowly or quickly a final draft comes together will depend on the writer and what the writer is attempting to accomplish.

You will likely need to write less drafts as you progress in your career. Reasons for this vary. The writer may become more confident, relaxed, and experienced. But inevitably a project will still come along every once in a while that will send you right back into the double drafting digits.

The volume of drafts is not a reflection on the quality of the writer. Writers simply have good writing days and less good writing days. Some writers write quickly, some write slowly, most write both ways on different days.

The more writing days you have under your pen, the less drafts you will likely need for each project. By the time you get to the point where you are writing as naturally as you breathe, you will be writing a lot less drafts. In the meantime, I'm going to ask you to plan to write ten, just to keep your quality up and so you will always allow enough time for each and every draft you undertake.

START A BIZ

> *Modern poets talk against business, poor things, but all of us write for money.*
>
> —ROBERT FROST

Go to your local bank or credit union and open a checking account in your name. Use this account as the depository for all of your writing income going forward. You may be tempted to deposit checks in other accounts, but don't. You need a strict record of your business income for tax purposes today and ten years down the road.

By keeping one account purely for business and depositing only writing-related income in it, you will be able to keep an accurate accounting of exactly how much you have earned from your writing and writing-related work. If the account is empty, get something in there, check by check, deposit by deposit.

Decide realistically how much you would like to earn monthly in the next year. What kinds of writing will you do to reach your goal? Do you need to take continuing education to accomplish your goal? Inexpensive classes are always available, if you look for them.

In her website bio, Janet Evanovich says, "I motivate myself to write by spending my money before I make it." Don't imitate this example. In fact, do the opposite. Motivate yourself by investing half the money you earn writing back into your business. This is what you must do if you want your business to grow.

Start saving your expense receipts for tax purposes and plan to file your taxes next year as a business. Get help with this if you need it, or use one of the many tax-prep software tools available. It's easier than you think. Once you start making serious money, I suggest you hire an accountant, whose advice you can likely afford with the money you will save on your taxes.

In the meantime, congratulations! Open your checking account. You are in business.

Life is either a daring adventure or nothing.

—HELEN KELLER

Negativity is a pervasive problem among creative people. Negative thinking crops up most often in response to things we either don't want to do or are afraid to do. When we are unconscious about our negativity, it tends to come out sideways and can become debilitating.

Negativity may sound like this inside your head:

> I'm not trying that.
> This (or that) is stupid.
> Why would anyone care about my work?
> Editors never even get back to writers, so what's the point?
> This is taking too long.
> This is too hard.
> Other people are having an easier time than me. What's wrong with me?

So what can a writer who is struggling with negativity do?

First, recognize negativity for what it is: poisonous thoughts that serve no one, including you. Find a way to notice negative thoughts. After you've isolated each thought, talk back to your negativity.

For example, if the thought is, "Editors never get back to writers," challenge the thought. Really? Is this true or not true? I'm thinking editors do get back to writers, but perhaps more often when they want to make a purchase than when they don't.

Take the power away from negative thinking by seeing it for what it truly is: a bunch of lies, based on assumptions, hearsay, or an all-or-nothing perspective. Let willingness and courage drive your choices instead of negativity. Reframe your negative thinking as the truth like so:

> The truth about _____ is _____.

Example: *The truth about editors is they are just as busy as everyone else. They might be interested in what I submit, but only if I give them a chance to consider my best work by sending it in. Just for today, I will stop demonizing editors and do my work.*

Once you recognize the threat negativity can wield over your best intentions, you'll realize that even one little lie can derail an entire day. Expose your negative thinking for what it really is: a bunch of stinking lies that will keep you scared and stuck, if you let them.

39
DIVERSIFY AS YOU GO

Reach high, for stars lie hidden in your soul. Dream deep, for every dream precedes the goal.

—PAMELA VAULL STARR

Are you in for the long haul? I sure hope so because there is no reason to limit your dreams unless you intend to write for a short time. The longer you write regularly, the more you can accomplish. You can achieve quite a bit over the course of a lifetime. After all, you never have to retire from writing unless you want to. So plan to write for as long as you want.

Quite likely, your quickest path to success is to pursue one genre at a time. But in the long run, you can publish mysteries, nonfiction, poems, essays, and write a screenplay and songs, if you want to. It may not make sense to pursue three genres all at once in the short run, but there is no reason to limit your genres in the long run.

Get out a piece of paper or pull up a fresh document and write down every goal you intend to accomplish in your literary lifetime. Write down all your ultimate dreams and then try to write your way to them.

Pull all the hopes you hope to realize within the next year together in one list. Write them down in a letter from your present self to your future self. Be specific about what you want. Don't go for size and celebrity; go for the truth of what you want as a result of what you think it looks like. How do you want to feel?

Fold the piece of paper up and put it away somewhere safe. Mark your calendar to look at the list at the same time next year. Then, next year, write a new letter and add it to your old letter. Let them stack up over the years. Keep reading them. Keep writing them.

If you work slowly and steadily, and practice letting go of the outcome in between letters, you will start to see your hopes and dreams manifest in real time. But don't forget the steady effort part of the equation. You won't get an outcome if you don't invest the effort.

If you are like most writers, you have dreams. So write your way toward them.

40
CHOOSE REACHABLE GOALS

Like a surgeon, your goal is to focus. You want to muster your resources and canalize your energy.

—ERIC MAISEL

All creative success is a result of good energy management. Sure, there are other factors like permission and spontaneity and trusting your instincts and so on. But when it comes right down to it, folks who succeed in any creative endeavor know how to manage their energy.

Writing is a predominantly mental exercise that also involves our physical, emotional, and spiritual energies. But the act of putting thoughts into words, or if you prefer, capturing thoughts on paper, is done via mental effort.

You can't write if your mind is a mess—if you are distracted, undisciplined, lacking in follow through, and unmotivated. If this describes you, you won't likely be able to channel your ideas into words. It's as simple as that.

If you want to succeed as a writer, one of the first things you need to do is build up a reserve of time you can use to channel your energy toward your creative goals.

Eric Maisel has a great word for this: *canalize*. What writers do is create time and space in their lives where they can canalize their mental energy into written work.

Making space is not enough; you also need to make the best use of your time. You need to direct your energy toward reachable writing goals.

Having short-term goals will help canalize your mental energy into words. NaNoWriMo (National Novel Writing Month) is a great example of this. It's a steep, short-term, timed, thirty-day goal that forces participating writers to find the time to draft a novel. Notice it's not just about finding the time, nor just about fantasizing about writing the novel; it's actually about writing the novel.

Build a canal for your creative energy. Direct your creative energy toward your objective. Let it flow through that channel. Put words on the page or on the Internet or wherever you think is best until the result is whatever you intended to write.

4

If you don't have the time to read, you don't have the time or the tools to write.

—STEPHEN KING

To inspire yourself on an ongoing basis, you are going to need two kinds of idea files: writing forms you wish to emulate someday, and topics or content you think would be fun to write about in the future.

Think of the writing samples you keep in these files as energy to fuel your mind and get your creative juices flowing, like rocket juice for your writing brain. When you refresh yourself by exposure to a power pack of your favorite forms or ideas, watch what happens.

If you alternate reading the two types of inspiration—forms and content—I think you will be amazed at how you can come up with ideas seemingly unrelated to the forms and topics you are using for inspiration. These brain ticklers creatively converge in mysterious ways.

You can use electronic bookmarking to create a tickler file, archiving both digital and paper formats over time. The key factor is to organize your documents and bookmarks in ways that are accessible for you so they can feed your creative process when you need them.

I keep a plastic tub handy and toss in writing I fancy. I don't even bother to organize the docs as they flow in. I just print and toss, rip and toss, or copy and toss. I let papers pile up over time without a second thought. Then, when I need inspiration, I simply flip through them by hand, and that works for me.

Tickler files collect what has inspired you in the past so you can call upon your particular muse whenever you need a surge of inspiration. When you review piles of material that are compelling to you, your brain will reach new stratospheres.

So clip, clip, clip. Pile, pile, pile. File, file, file. (Or the virtual equivalent.) And take your writing to new levels of creativity.

42
PROGRESS INCREMENTALLY

O snail
Climb Mount Fuji,
But slowly, slowly!

—KOBAYASHI ISSA

Professional writers have a range of skills at their disposal. They don't balk or get intimidated when they need to take the next step toward completion of a project, like an inexperienced writer might.

They don't say, "I need a quote from a certain kind of expert right here," and then freeze up because they don't know how to proceed in a professional fashion or because the prospect of interviewing an expert is too daunting.

Professional writers juggle multiple steps of the creative process, getting them done in an organized fashion, whether that means cranking out the first full draft of the novel, deepening the scenes that aren't rich enough, increasing the tension to keep the pages turning, or reworking chapter twenty for the twentieth time.

Professional writers get more done because they have the muscle memory that it takes to get project after project "in the can." And this is a great feeling once you become familiar with it.

Of course, if you are ramping up bigger and bigger goals, there will always be new steps to master, new muscles to exercise.

A writer who writes a personal essay column for the local paper won't have the same skills as a journalist who writes feature stories for the same paper.

A writer who writes how-to articles does not necessarily have a nonfiction book under her belt.

And a short-story writer is not (yet) a novelist.

Once you can collapse a creative process that used to take you a hundred discrete steps into one that only takes you ten fluid strides, you know you are becoming a professional.

You are like the piano student who once practiced scales but can eventually play a whole concerto. Once you get to this point, you won't likely be thinking much about how challenging each step once was. But we can all use the reminder that every published, prolific, celebrity author had to start somewhere. And this "somewhere" very likely looked a lot like the same place a beginning writer starts today.

MINE YOUR RELATIONSHIPS

My mother wanted us to understand that the tragedies of your life one day have the potential to be comic stories the next.

—NORA EPHRON

Can't come up with enough good ideas to write about?

Here's a one-million-dollar idea that will never let you down: relationships.

If you look to your own relationships, I bet you will realize that you could never run out of ideas.

Examine your relationships with:

- Your parents
- Your child or children
- Your partner or spouse
- Your friends
- Your enemies
- Your pets
- Your grandparents
- Your siblings

See how you could write forever just by taking a closer look at your relationships?

And if writing about the people close to you makes you feel uncomfortable, why not choose more abstract relationships? Try writing about your relationships with:

- Your alma mater
- Your neighbors
- Technology
- Your hometown
- The world

Go for the human element in your writing no matter what the genre, and your readers will be interested and engaged.

And if you can't come up with a way to get started, try using a compare-and-contrast technique. Make two columns on a blank page. Then put two contrasting topics at the top of each column. For example, everything that was right vs. everything that was wrong. Or everything that was glorious vs. everything that was tragic. Or best moments vs. worse moments.

You get the idea. Once you start a list of comparisons and contrasts, I have a feeling you won't be able to resist jumping into a story.

44
DISREGARD GOOD GRAMMAR

Here is a lesson in creative writing. First rule: Do not use semi-colons. They are transvestite hermaphrodites representing absolutely nothing. All they do is show you've been to college.

—KURT VONNEGUT

Are you comma crazy?

Dash happy?

Colon confused?

These three forms of punctuation—commas, dashes, and colons—befuddle writers more than any others.

I have three simple suggestions that will set your submissions apart from the crowd:

1. Use commas, dashes, and colons lightly.
2. Use them only when needed.
3. Don't use them if you can say what you need to say without them.

That's it. Don't overindulge in slick, hip grammar guides. There are currently as many grammar guides out there as there are colors, with new ones coming out every season. The time you have to write is way too short to get bogged down in grammar obsession.

Perusing grammar guides is not going to make you a better writer, although it might make you a better editor. Then again, it also might make you a person who goes around correcting other people's grammar, which is annoying, unless a person has engaged you or partnered with you to edit her work.

Editors can afford to oooh and aaah over the grammar guides because editing is what they do. Their job is to know all about grammar and usage, and make writing the best it can be. Writers can use their time better by staying inspired and keeping focused on stringing words together.

I already suggested that you pick up the latest copy of Strunk & White's *The Elements of Style* when you need to conduct a quick edit of what you just wrote. Stunk & White (what many call it for short) can help protect you from the temptation of grammar guide addiction.

A modicum of proper usage can take you a very long way in this biz. So put your grammar guides aside for now and get back to writing.

SECURE EXPERT QUOTES

Experts are merely people, just like you and me.

—ELAINE FANTLE SHIMBERG

You are writing a piece that would benefit from the addition of expert quotes or input. But contacting experts often brings up fears. We don't want to trouble them or take up too much of their time. Yet plenty of experts would love to benefit from increased exposure, especially when that exposure comes via an interaction with a seasoned writer.

If you are cordial, respectful, and professional with experts, you will typically garner the quickest responses. You can save time by querying several experts serially via e-mail. Here's how to get quotes from experts quickly yet respectfully.

LOCAL/REGIONAL EXPERTS
- Contact your local chamber of commerce and see who they can refer.
- Grab a copy of a community college class offerings and contact instructors.
- Go to the websites of local universities and search by department.
- Conduct a Google search with topic, city, and state.
- Use your local yellow pages or business guides.

THE MAN OR WOMAN FROM YOUR STREET
- Flex your Rolodex (mark people's interests in the notes section).
- Ask your friends, friends of friends, and neighbors for input.
- Call local people with lots of contacts (hairstylists, vets, and mom-and-pop shops) and ask for referrals.

THE MAN/WOMAN FROM SOMEONE ELSE'S STREET
- Use your social networks (be explicit about what you are looking for).
- Check with moderators of online groups (tell them exactly what you need).
- Put a request out on Help a Reporter Out (HARO).

A NATIONALLY KNOWN EXPERT
- Try HARO (be specific about level of expertise, verify all sources).
- Try Profnet (this service prefers if you have an assignment in hand).
- Google the topic + association or group to look up an association administrator.

AN INTERNATIONALLY KNOWN EXPERT
- HARO is a good choice for the widest selection of experts (don't take the expert's word for his reputation; do some background research and verify credentials).
- Google the topic + words like *international authority*.

PRESTIGIOUS SOURCES
- Go through Profnet, universities, or contact traditionally published authors.
- Investigate sources listed at the bottom of academic journals.

46

CONTAIN CREATIVE CHAOS

Perfectionism is a mean, frozen form of idealism, while messes are the artist's true friend.

—ANNE LAMOTT

If you think you are going to grow and cultivate a writing career and keep your writing efforts the picture of neat and tidy perfection all the time, not only will you be disappointed, you will surely miss out on opportunities that might have been enjoyed by embracing a little more of what is natural along the way.

Writers are often habitually messy. Brainstorming is inherently messy. Piling up ideas creates clutter. So much of writing nonfiction well has to do with how well you can compress information. Before the compression, there is often a tower or flurry of papers. New ideas often emerge out of a sheer density of information.

At some point you may need more space to contain your projects, especially if you have several going on at once. Even more space may be needed if your piles start to become unsightly. But why not let your projects become what they want to become while they are in process? Put them somewhere out of sight, rather than trying to tame them too much, so you won't inadvertently tame the life right out of them.

Screenwriting teacher and playwright Cynthia Whitcomb suggests that writers think of writing projects as pots of soup. Human potential leader Jean Houston speaks of "cooking with all of your burners on" instead of just one or two.

So go ahead and start multiple projects. The idea of alternating between multiple projects of loosely controlled chaos can be used to your creative advantage. You can focus on one project while still preparing to work on others either simultaneously or later.

But first you have to give yourself permission to create contained chaos while working on one project. If you are a control freak, don't worry. The process of managing controlled chaos is like making soup. You can make a pot of soup without letting that same soup take over your whole life, right?

Your writing career will benefit when you work on a series of projects over the years. Go ahead: Make a mess or two. Make however many contained messes are necessary for your creative success.

The most common money-related mistake artists make is a reluctance to invest in their own careers.

—CAROLL MICHELS

Here are six reasons to microinvest in local or online classes rather than plunking down the dough (or taking out a huge loan) for an expensive master of fine arts right out of the gate:

1. CUSTOMIZATION
Taking short class after short class is an easy way to create a learning plan based on your own interests and needs. When you steer your own continuing online education plan, learning becomes like a buffet table. You can take a little basic journalism over here, a little short story writing over there, and go deeper into science fiction if it makes your heart sing.

2. SKILLS = OWNERSHIP
Learn skills rather than shortcuts or formulas to accomplish your goals. Once you learn a skill, practice that skill, and master it, it becomes yours. If you are following someone else's shortcuts or formulas, you may be stuck if their tricks stop working for you or if the marketplace shifts enough to throw those methods off.

3. RACK UP SHORT-TERM SUCCESSES
Once you have enough skills under your belt, you can parlay them into publication and earnings. You shift from being a hobby writer to professional writer. You stop saying you're going to be a writer someday and start being a writer today.

4. APPLYING SKILLS CREATES MOMENTUM
My teaching colleague Abigail Green says she takes classes because she always makes a sale or two as a result, eventually earning enough to counterbalance the class cost. Stalled writers can take classes for a kick in the pants as needed.

5. LOW INVESTMENT YIELDS A HIGH RETURN
Let's say a student invests five hundred dollars in two classes. After the classes, she begins averaging over two thousand dollars a year using the skills she learned, with no end in site to her earnings. A modest investment in the short run can provide not only immediate cash flow but also lasting returns.

6. VARIETY IS UP TO YOU
Let's say you are the type of student who likes to learn a little from many instructors. Or maybe you like to learn a lot from one instructor. No one way is going to work for everyone. You design your continuing education, so you get to choose who you enjoy working with most.

48
FOSTER YOUR IDEAS

Home wasn't built in a day.

—JANE ACE

In one of my classes over the past five years, I have been teaching writers how to jot down tips from their everyday life and then choose one of those tips to use as the basis for a list of tips (aka a list article).

A tip is a simply a solution to a problem addressed to an audience that will appreciate the information. I bet you give and receive tips all the time without even noticing. I might read tips for saving money on taxes or raising healthy kids or having a more enjoyable vacation. Sometimes we seek out tips only once. But on certain topics we probably read all the tips that come down the pipe.

Everyone has tips. And anyone can give tips. So go ahead and give us a few from your everyday experience. What do you know how to do? Make a killer chocolate cake? Use a GPS without getting lost? Start a business? It doesn't matter what the topic is because you can offer a tip about anything, so long as it's specific.

First imagine your ideal reader. Then draft your tip about five sentences long. Lay out the problem first and then offer your clever solution. That's a tip. Pretty easy, right?

Tips need to be short, tight, and descriptive. The best tips tell a little story. For our purposes, just get the gist of your tip down in draft form.

You could eventually build a communications empire on the germ of one little tip, if you wanted to. I've had students turn everyday life tips into articles and even, eventually, books. And books beget more ideas for more writing projects.

Continually having something helpful to share needs to become a driving force behind your writing career, if you want it to grow. So share a few tips today. If you leave a trail of tips behind as you go and grow, you will always have an eager audience of readers. You will always be of service to others.

49
AWAKEN YOUR SENSES

Every piece of writing you enjoy contains a lesson for your own writing.

—KIM STAFFORD

I don't particularly enjoy doing the dishes except perhaps during the plum blossom time of year. That's when my slumbering senses are aching to wake up. So when I see the plum tree out the window aflame with blooms, I feel relief that more light and warmth are soon on the way.

We can stir our slumbering literary senses without waiting for the seasons to change. Dipping into a bookshelf (or e-reader) chock-full of high-quality reads can revive our perceptions after a long winter of literary deprivation.

What authors did you adore as a child? How about as a teen? Can you remember your favorite book in college? How about your favorite book when you were in your twenties, thirties, forties … etc.

Our literary crushes can teach us timeless writing lessons, if we let them. I bet you don't have think too hard to remember what your favorite authors did so well on the page. Do you?

Judy Blume is a master of dialogue. J.K. Rowling is pro at creating believable imaginary worlds. Erica Jong's characters are so believable that they seem like real people (maybe they were). Anita Diamant's reimagining of history is alive with contemporary feelings.

Create a special bookshelf with your childhood favorites or collect old faves on your e-reader, and you create a literary lifeline you can draw on over and over.

Don't worry about availability. It's easy to add to your collection these days. Collecting out-of-print books is easier than ever because of the abundance of resellers. If you feel nostalgic about a book, it's probably out there. Create a wish list at your favorite online bookstore for your next gift-receiving time. See what your old favorite reads can teach you today.

Take advantage of easy access to your old favorites by creating a real or digital shrine for your favorite reads of all time. Pick them back up and get schooled all over again by your favorite masters.

Then, next time your mental spirits flag, reach for the writing that is like plum blossoms for your brain.

50 GUARD YOUR TIME

If you don't guard your time, no one else will. It is not enough to simply ask others to respect your "writing time." You must reinforce that request by refusing to drop what you're doing whenever someone interrupts you. Otherwise people will interrupt—not out of malice or lack of consideration, but because you have given them no reason not to.

—MOIRA ALLEN

I think most writers can relate to the feeling that other people are stealing our writing time—the feeling that they are conspiring to keep us from writing. Darn them!

Of course, the truth is that carving out writing time and using it is always our responsibility. If we name and claim our right to write and stay true to it, what's the worst thing that can happen? We might just find ourselves happily productive.

When we don't write, we can become difficult to live with. Anxious. Distracted. Looking for excitement in all the wrong places. We need to face down whatever darkness we are projecting onto others—including the fib that others are preventing us from writing—and become accountable.

And it's not like we face this challenge once and are done with it. We will always meet new people who would love for us to write less and spend more time with them. But you get to set your priorities. My writing time demands the lion's share of my energy and creativity. Spending quality time with my family is not negotiable. Spending some time with our extended family comes next, and they all live thousands of miles away.

So, no, I don't think you should start indiscriminately slashing your social schedule. Nor do I think you should phone up your friends and bid them farewell. But pay attention to the choices you make. You decide what your priorities are and what they are not. Remember, nobody can abduct your creativity without your permission.

5

EXPERIMENT WITH LEARNING

However great a man's natural talent may be, the art of writing cannot be learned all at once.

—JEAN-JACQUES ROUSSEAU

You may be set in the ways you like to learn, or you may be flexible and experimental. Learning styles are not fixed. You can consciously develop any way of learning as well as further develop styles you already use.

Most people use a combination of learning styles. Do you know yours? Generally speaking, there are five types: visual, aural, verbal, physical, and logical.

One cool idea for writers is to try applying all methods of learning to your writing projects to see what happens. Here are several suggestions for each learning method you might try.

VISUAL

Draw pictures or doodle.
List both sides of an argument.
Create a chart or a graph.
Make a mind map on paper spoking associated words or ideas off of others.
Draw the shape of your idea.
Make your writing into a comic strip.
Search for and read a fun, visual blog.

AURAL

Use music to inspire your writing.
Read your work out loud into a recorder or to the dog.
Listen to research in audio format.
Listen to yourself read someone else's writing out loud.
Think of your writing as song lyrics.
Watch the movie *Music and Lyrics*.

LOGICAL

Notice patterns that appear to you.
Classify things.
Use if/then statements.
Set goals and track your progress.
Make a list.
Use examples, stats, and research.
Pose a word problem and solve it.
Make use of a spreadsheet.

VERBAL

Read quality writing to prime the pump.
Use plays on words in your work.
Look up word definitions to spark ideas.
Play with acronyms (make up a story using every letter in one word as the first letter in a part of the story).
Talk your ideas out before you write.
Build an argument for an opinion you feel strongly about.

PHYSICAL

Move through any gestures that are in your writing.
Use storyboarding techniques.
Draw your ideas on large sheets of paper or on a whiteboard.
Go for a walk or a run.
Act out a scene, play all parts.
Get outside and get your hands dirty.

52. HONOR INTROSPECTION

The philosophy of the wisest man that ever existed, is mainly derived from the act of introspection.

—WILLIAM GODWIN

Several years ago while I was teaching writing classes at a local community college, I had a large, enthusiastic class of women writers. By the second meeting, I was convinced it was going to be one of my most productive classes ever. But instead of falling in love with their writing processes, the women fell in love with each other instead.

As social interest in each other waxed, creative self-expression waned. When the six weeks were up, I was disappointed. But I learned a valuable lesson as a writing instructor: The social fun in a group of writers usually will run on its own enthusiasm, but the creative effort of individuals needs consistent support and encouragement to flourish.

Social fun won't necessarily kidnap your creative productivity. Most writers use both social and solitary learning styles to create strong, completed writing. For example, you might find yourself stuck in your writing and bounce ideas off of a friend or partner until you have the aha that you are looking for. The habit of thinking out loud with someone else listening, whether you take input from him or not, is a social method.

If you are a more solitary writer, when you find yourself stuck, you might take your problem for a walk, take a shower, or just take a break from the writing altogether and have a solution "come to you." The habit of working things out without input from others is a habit of solitary learners.

The best communicators combine solitary and social methods of learning to create their strongest writing. Knowing which kind of learner you are can help you make a conscious effort to use both types of learning instead of only using the one you favor.

Introspection, intuition, and faith in your own thoughts and instincts are crucial abilities for writers. Knowing your own mind so you can participate in groups without losing your point of view is also important. Clear thinking, analytical thinking, and good discrimination are important aspects of becoming a strong communicator.

Just be careful not to throw solitary learning out the window because you've caught the current social-media mania. To be overly influenced by any individual, group, or group mind can interfere with your natural creativity and individual growth.

'Keep 13 in Play' tells you where you stand, and keeps you moving forward.

—C. HOPE CLARK

I think it's a good idea for writers to view selling their work as a game. Why not try to make selling fun by creating little gimmicks to motivate yourself?

That's what C. Hope Clark does with her mantra, "keep thirteen in play," which means to always sustain at least thirteen pieces of submitted writing at any one time.

Of course, selling is a game that you sometimes win and sometimes lose. So it stands to reason that the more work you have circulating, the more work you will sell.

Your job is to become willing to learn the rules of the selling game and to master the game so you can increase your odds of success.

If you want to be a selling writer, you need to get in the game. I don't mean "someday," I mean today.

No matter what kind of writer you aspire to become, don't balk. I bet there is a way to start breaking in today so you can join the ranks of published writers you admire.

The key is to participate, not to just sit on the sidelines. Pick and choose whose ranks you will join and then jump in and start submitting.

Writing is an action, but selling is the act that separates the published writers from the wannabes.

Editors like writers to come to them. If you think you might be the writer they are looking for, offer your services persuasively until they decide to start working with you.

I could go back to sleep if I tried, but this is the perfect time to write. The house is quiet except for the omnipresent hum of the refrigerator and the gurgling of the fish tanks. So I get up, feed Jo-Jo and the fish, make a cup of tea, and bring it to the dining-room table where I turn on the laptop or read a few pages of good writing to get my head in the right place, and I begin.

—BARBARA DEMARCO-BARRETT

Since 1966, the United States has consistently upheld the concept of daylight savings time to conserve energy by making the most of natural daylight.

Just as we turn the clocks forward each spring to catch more sunshine in the day, you can change your sleeping schedule to squeeze more writing time out of an otherwise busy day.

Simply by setting your alarm one hour earlier, if you are a morning person, or staying up one hour later, if you are a night person, you can "find" time you didn't previously have and expand your writing time.

Choosing the morning or night hour according to what is the most productive writing time for you is an important part of this strategy. For example, an extra hour of writing time at night would not do me much good since I am a morning person. But if you give me an extra hour during what's already my most productive time, I can amaze myself with how much I can get done.

If you pay attention to the habits of publishing writers, you'll notice that a remarkable number of them already use this technique without thinking about it, especially when under the increased pressure of a deadline.

Often all we need to meet a big deadline two weeks, months, or years away is one quality hour each day of focused writing. If you are like most writers, you can make productive use out of an extra hour on any given day. So why not give this a try? Find the best time to uncover an extra hour and make sure to use it.

With rare exceptions, active language is stronger, clearer, and more interesting than passive language.

—SCOTT EDELSTEIN

The best way to catch the passive voice is by reading your work out loud. If you get in the habit of reading your work out loud to others, or even just to yourself, you will likely hear the past tense and catch the passive constructions when they slip into your work—and, believe me, they will slip in. They slip into mine all the time.

Don't feel badly about any of this. Instead, get in the habit of noticing the passive voice and the overuse of *it* as the subject of sentences. Correct infractions before your draft is finalized.

Passive: *The bike was ridden by Lucy over to other side of town on the gravel road and now the tires were mangled.*

Active: *Lucy rode the bike over to the other side of town and mangled the tires.*

You may also use that little bugger "it" as the subject too often once you slip into the passive voice.

Passive: *It was known all up and down Twin Brook Lane that John had been busted for drinking at the church dance.*

Active: *John got drunk at the church dance and everyone up and down Twin Brook Lane knew it.*

My students have an unwitting habit of mashing up tenses such that a 1,000-word piece can contain up to three conflicting tenses. Naturally this can confuse the reader.

A simpler way to handle tense is to always try and keep your verb tenses present and active. If you keep your writing present and your verbs active, your writing will come across as more immediate, compelling, and universal.

Present: *Lucy rides the bike over to the other side of town and mangles the tires.*

Present: *John is drunk at the church dance and everyone up and down Twin Brook Lane knows it.*

Make your tenses present tense and active, and see if your writing improves. You can always change the wording back in later drafts if necessary.

But sit down you must, and write you will, and if there's one thing every writer learns over time, it's this: The muse is most effectively summoned by the clicking of your keyboard or the scratching of your pen.

—ROBERT MASELLO

Let's say you love tea and have decided to make it one of your writing topics. You have an explosion of ideas because you love tea so much that you feel you could write about it endlessly.

For a piece about wintertime teas, you might focus on hot teas, whereas a piece on summertime teas might focus on iced teas. A piece written about black teas would not contain information about green teas, unless perhaps it included a section that discussed combination teas (black and green teas mixed). You might even write a piece as specific as hot green teas or iced black teas.

A roundup of every kind of tea could work in one piece. This would likely focus on the common denominator of all the kinds of tea. It would offer whatever can be said that applies to all these teas.

A piece on iced black teas needs to contain the kind of depth and detail that is going to enchant the reader, whether the final form is a filler, a feature article, or a book. Regardless of the length, go deep, and take the reader with you. We'll follow you anywhere if the topic is well written.

One important aspect of salable writing is the writer's ability to focus on a topic and stay on track all the way from beginning to end. Articles do this. Essays do this. And books do this.

Focused writing contains depth and tells us everything that's compelling about a topic. It doesn't stray. If your writing goes off on tangents, cut those parts out.

New writers face the constant temptation to trail off in many possible directions. You needn't worry that focusing on one topic will bore the reader. A writer who is a good guide easily hooks and lures the reader into going deeper and learning more.

> *At this moment, more prospects exist for freelancers, in more forms, than ever before, and there are many ways to take advantage of them.*
>
> —I.J. SCHECTER

One of the ironies of the olden days of publishing is that some of the best writing only earned meager wages (or sometimes no wages) for the author during her lifetime.

My greatest hope is that you will not let this happen to you. "I write for love, not money" is the kind of thinking you simply cannot afford.

Instead, how about writing for love *and* money? That's a better way to think and puts money in your retirement account. It pays the orthodontist for your kid's braces and keeps the lights on while you are working.

The easiest and most original way to make a livable wage as a writer is by weaving multiple professional pursuits or income streams into a steady river of earned money. Let's start with a roundup of the shortest basic nonfiction forms that somebody pays for.

SHORT NONFICTION ARTICLE FORMS

- Tips
- List articles
- How-to articles
- Fillers or shorts
- Humor pieces
- Advice
- Personal essays
- Greeting cards
- Interviews
- Quizzes, games, activities
- Sidebars
- Reviews
- Op-eds
- Event coverage/reporting
- Blog posts

If you need to earn money in the short run, I suggest that you pursue writing nonfiction forms either before or alongside writing longer forms or forms where you will not be paid or won't be paid until later.

How can you learn to write short forms? That's easy. You can read books, listen to audio instruction, take classes, or watch videos by folks who will teach you simple forms. This kind of instruction is readily and widely available.

One of the easiest ways to learn, and writers have been doing this for centuries, is by studying strong examples and then trying your pen at the same forms. Thanks to the Internet, samples of strong writing are easier to find than ever. And don't forget to take a look in Google Books while you are searching.

Time is what prevents everything from happening at once.
—JOHN ARCHIBALD WHEELER

Right timing isn't just about you and your topic or the responsiveness of readers. Right timing is a resonance that goes through the entire creative process. And then, of course, there's always how the timing syncs or does not sync with the needs of those who are buying.

Generally speaking, good timing means: 1) It's the right topic 2) at the right time. 3) by the right person. This is always what agents and editors are looking for in writers. And writers can cultivate their sense of right timing in their own work and become consistent at offering the right ideas at the right time.

From a publication point of view, timing is not about right now, or necessarily about you, it's about when the piece will be read after all of the writer's hard work is done.

If you can fast-forward your brain to that time, you can pull together words that will resonate more deeply in the future. Journalists often accomplish this with a news peg, which is the way a story ties into timely events.

Right timing makes your writing relevant when it will appear. Use this table, which represents the seasons and months of the year to "time" your current ideas.

In the "Old Ideas" column, take what you've already written and put it into the table at the most appropriate time to be read next. It's easier to understand right timing vis-à-vis what you've already done.

In the "New Ideas" column, jot down some new time-appropriate ideas. When you are done, you should begin to see how to leverage what you've already published and how to better time pieces you have yet to write. Consult writer's guidelines for specific publications you aim to write for so you can submit your pieces at the appropriate time.

TIMING	OLD IDEAS	NEW IDEAS
FALL		
September		
October		
November		
WINTER		
December		
January		
February		
SPRING		
March		
April		
May		
SUMMER		
June		
July		
August		

I think it's bad to talk about one's present work, for it spoils something at the root of the creative act. It discharges the tension.

—NORMAN MAILER

What's going to advance your writing career faster: talking about writing or actually doing it?

This applies to just about anything in a writing career.

- Do you want to talk about attending a writers conference, or do you want to actually register for one?
- Do you do a little bit of platform development every day, or do you just grouse about all the reasons why you don't think you need a platform?
- Do you want to sell your words or do you just want to let them languish here, there, and everywhere?

Listen to yourself. The things you say you are going to do and don't do are the things you need to stop talking about and start doing.

Anxiety makes writers run at the mouth. And anxious writers would often rather talk than take the preliminary steps that lead to good, solid writing.

Too much talk might exhaust your career potential before it has a chance to get started. And when your talk is not commensurate with your action, you'll notice that others around you don't take your writing career as seriously as you say you do.

Don't beat yourself up if you have been talking about taking steps in your career without actually taking them. Just recognize that talking doesn't get the job done.

So no more jabbering about the writing career you hope to have someday. Show everyone what you can accomplish by accumulating tangible results and then sharing those results with others. In other words, don't tell us what you are going to do, tell us what you did.

I can promise you tangible results for tangible effort. And once you have your daily work in the can, it's time to go out and celebrate with your friends or loved ones. You'll be happier, and they will be happier with you because you feel good about your progress.

Beginning writers, especially, often get caught in a trap—either letting the minutiae of manuscript formats bog down and frustrate their creativity, or throwing all caution to the wind and submitting work so poorly organized that editors can't follow it or summarily reject it.

—CYNTHIA LAUFENBERG

Many writers learned to type in formal typing classes, where they started putting two spaces between sentences. This rhythm became a habit. And as we all know, habits are tenacious and therefore difficult to break.

But even if you learned to type on a typewriter and have never grown accustomed to writing on a personal computer, erratic spacing is an easy fix and something you can easily learn.

If you use Microsoft Word (it's highly likely you will since it's the word processing software most publishers use), compose your document, finalize it, and then go up to the "Edit" tab and select "Replace."

You will see a box that says, "Find and Replace," which contains two fields for you to fill in. Fill in the top box with two spaces (hit the space bar two times) and fill in the bottom box with one space (hit the space bar one time). Then hit the button that says "Replace All."

And voilà! All those years of habitually typing in two spaces instead of one can be remedied without the need for a typing recovery program.

It's important to get into the habit of correcting a document before you submit your work. Don't give editors an easy reason to take a pass.

Writers need to know the difference between a crisp, clear, professional manuscript and a sloppy, halfhearted, unchecked attempt.

While you are in the proofreading phase, be sure to run your spell-check as you read the piece one more time out loud.

6

PRACTICE DETACHMENT

In a sense, what wants to be written is none of my business.

—JULIA CAMERON

I know some writers who are attached to what they write. Some see their words on paper as an extension of themselves—as literally attached to them rather than something released into the world.

You can probably appreciate how this belief can set up a writer for pain, and lots of it. If you are your writing and someone says something careless or negative about what you've written, the remark is personal. If you are your writing how could it be otherwise?

Why not try the attitude professional writers take instead? Professional writers are invested in what they write. They do the best they can on each piece, but by the time they are ready to send that piece of work out into the world, they have cut the cord.

They are not sending out little pieces of themselves. If they did, there would be nothing of them left in a short time. They are sending out a piece of work that's ready to stand on its own. If the work can't stand on its own, they take responsibility for that fact without internalizing the criticism that their writing receives.

Pros do not feel personally injured because someone does not like their work. They trust that some people will like it even as others won't. They calmly stand by the quality of their work, like adults. If they messed up, they can learn something for next time.

Not only are some people not going to like your writing, some people are not going to like you. These feelings might be personal, or you may represent something they already dislike or resent. Since criticism is impossible to avoid as a creative person, become and stay detached.

If you're going to be a successful, creative person, prepare yourself so you will not feel flummoxed by any careless vitriol pointed in your general direction.

A lead is like dressing for an interview: If what you wear turns the interviewer off, it's virtually impossible to get the job however well you speak or what you say.

—GORDON BURGETT

Just jump into your draft without waiting for the perfect first line.

Once you have a complete draft done, decide what the premise of the piece is. Then read it through a couple times and look for phrases that jump out and might make a good hook for the first line.

Once your piece has a solid center, you can think about what makes a good lead and see what you can come up with. Often the best first line is hanging out somewhere in the middle or at the end of what you wrote, and it's just a matter of cutting and pasting it up to the top. Here are ideas for crafting killer leads.

- Condense the entire message of article into a few short, punchy descriptive lines.
- Ask the question the reader might ask and then answer the question.
- Kick off with a story.
- Lay out the most surprising part of your angle.
- Give a detailed description that others can relate to.
- Just jump in. Keep the lead short and melodic and get quickly to the point.
- Start with a quick sketch of what makes the subject interesting.
- If the piece is seasonal, draw the reader's attention to the time of year.
- Find two contrasting ideas in the piece and use them to evoke interest.
- Start with a dramatic anecdote. Something happened. What?
- If the story is about a person, offer an anecdote from the person's childhood.
- Start with a benefit about the person or topic.
- Name a challenge we all face. You'll get everyone's attention.
- Tie the piece into a trend.
- Use a "what if?" statement.
- Gather a list of words or short phrases that make a compelling lead.
- Make your lead parody a well-known saying, poem, line from literature, quote, or lyric.

Advice to young writers? Always the same advice: Learn to trust your own judgment, learn inner independence, learn to trust that time will sort the good from the bad—including your own bad.

—DORIS LESSING

If you have hot ideas but you don't develop them, just watch. Someone else will be brave enough to do the job and then you will feel like he stole your ideas.

He didn't. He just identified a captivating idea and acted on his awareness of the right timing.

You know the saying, *Great minds think alike.* For writers the saying should be, *Great writers act on their hottest ideas.*

Right timing is important to selling your writing no matter what anybody says. And getting the hang of noticing which of your ideas is the hottest takes practice. If an idea seems hot to you, there's a good chance others will think it's cool, too.

It takes a while to get the hang of paying attention to your ideas rather than paying attention to what other people are doing. But once you've been burned a couple of times by other people "stealing" your best ideas and watching them achieve success, you are bound to get the message.

The message is you are not acting. You are letting your ideas languish and other people, having pretty much the same idea, are bolder. They do not hesitate; they just act.

You might think I would suggest that you use outside resources or the Internet to test-market your ideas and find out just how timely they are, but I don't want to do that because I don't want you to start thinking that the litmus test is outside of you. It's inside of you. And it's called your gut.

You knew all along that you had a hot idea. I bet you knew as soon as the idea struck. So, what's stopping you? Don't hesitate next time. Trust yourself.

For writers who have once or twice missed the hot idea boat, having another good idea and calmly acting on it is the best revenge.

SNAP LANGUAGE UP

Words are small shapes in the gorgeous chaos of the world.
— DIANE ACKERMAN

Most beginning writers underestimate the importance of a snappy title. But with more titles than ever competing for our attention, not to mention the subject lines of everything stacking up in our in-boxes, the onus to snap up our titles is heavy upon us.

Every time you present a finished piece of writing, your snappy title becomes its calling card. A killer title draws people right in.

Subheads, when necessary, are equally as important, as they keep the reader's eye cheerfully skittering down the page.

HERE ARE SOME TITLES I FANCY. SEE IF YOU THINK THEY ARE SNAPPY.
- "Green Eggs and Salmonella?" In *Smithsonian* magazine by Abigail Green
- "Finding Binge Absolution in a Do-Si-Do" on NPR by Marc Acito
- *Moonwalking With Einstein* by Joshua Foer

HERE'S A FEW PUBLISHING INSIDER JANE FRIEDMAN LIKES:
- *The 4-Hour Workweek* by Timothy Ferris
- *What to Expect When You're Expecting* by Heidi Murkoff and Sharon Mazel
- *I Don't Know What I Want, But I Know It's Not This* by Julie Jansen

HERE'S A FEW I CAME UP WITH:
- "Hollywood Rx for the Holidays" (article)
- "Rhapsody in Writing" (student anthology)
- "Alive on the Outside" (short story)

Now it's your turn. Use this simple checklist to make sure your title is as snappy as you can get it on your own without becoming overly attached to it (in case your editor decides to change or edit it):

___ Would you read the article, if you read this title?
___ Would the title alone compel people to share the writing?
___ Do the subheads keep the reader more engaged?

Don't be lazy now. If it's not good, make it better. Play around. But don't obsess.

Not feeling so snappy today? Ask your kids. Ask your spouse. Ask your writing group. Conduct an Internet search on the topic. Crack open a thesaurus or dictionary. But don't obsess, even if others can't nail the title.

Your editor might actually be able to come up with a snappy title more easily than you can. Anyone who has written for a newspaper knows that the writer doesn't get to have the final say, anyway. So give your best title three tries and then move on with the best one.

*I feel bad about my neck. Truly I do. If you saw my neck, you might
feel bad about it too, but you'd probably be too polite to let on.*

—NORA EPHRON

If your hand could tell a story, what story would it tell?

How about your foot? Would its story be different than your hands'?

Perhaps this sounds silly, but we have so many memories stored in our bodies, it's
not even funny. Or maybe the stories get funnier in the sharing of them.

Here are some of my examples.

- I remember the time I got hit in the head so hard that I could not hear out of
  my left ear for a week.
- I remember the time a bee flew into my hair and I let go of the handlebars and
  crashed my bike. (That's right, even your hair has stories.)
- I remember how it felt to get my first tattoo. (I might have another by the time
  you read this.)
- I remember how it felt to give birth (although I wouldn't mind forgetting).
- I remember how satisfying it felt to make my first tackle when I was learning
  how to play rugby.
- I remember seeing purple when I kissed my husband for the first time. (Purple
  is my favorite color, so what choice did I have but to marry the guy?)
- I remember reaching out my hand, without speaking or glancing back, and
  having my daughter slip hers into mine.

I remember. My body remembers. And your body remembers things, too.

How much could you write beginning with a physical memory?

A significant body of work, I think. Pun fully intended.

66
COMPRESS TO SELL

Cutting words from writing is like pruning in the garden. When we get rid of the dead, diseased, and ugly, we are left with a stronger, more beautiful, fruitful plant.

—AUDREY OWEN

Another skill of salable writing is the economy of words. Stated concisely, the economy of words means:

- Say everything one time. Don't repeat the same thing over and over.
- Use fewer words to say more. Write long and then cut your prose down to the key phrases.
- Put every pertinent detail in and then squeeze out the extraneous.
- Know what you are trying to accomplish and whom you are speaking to before you start writing, and then you can let the voice, tone, and style of your writing help you get the job done.
- If you don't know what you are trying to accomplish before you start writing, write until you figure it out, and then start writing with a clear topic in mind.
- In fiction, time or history can be compressed into a description of what happens or always happens. Use these summary descriptions to fill in background quickly.
- Use active verbs and specific nouns. Use adverbs and adjectives sparingly.
- List formats are a great way to compress a lot of information in a simple, organized fashion. You can even string lists together.
- The more times you read your work out loud, the more amazed you will be that it still needs to be cut, tightened, and compressed. Therefore, read your work out loud until it rings out as clearly as it can. Then you will know you're done.

You'll be amazed how much meaning you can cram into a few words. Compression takes practice and patience. You will know you have accomplished compression when every single word counts, and only counts once.

Be careless in your dress if you must, but keep a tidy soul.

—MARK TWAIN

Every year, the urge to purge comes around in springtime and we start eyeing the piles of whatnots that have accumulated while we were busy writing. I say go ahead, collect and pile all year long. You can always purge each spring, when the urge is already there.

And don't feel guilty about the mess you might be making. You are not sloppy; you are creative.

Still, it's best to organize your workspace in a way that makes sense to the flow of your work. When we purge, straighten, and organize our external world, we often feel a positive shift in our internal world.

Place copies of your finished, published work in your professional portfolio. Hang the pieces you feel most proud of on a wall. Get all your pens together and refill all the ink. Check the printer while you are at it. Sharpen your pencils. Check your supply shelf. Make a list to restock items you tend to burn through quickly.

Get rid of any office equipment you don't use regularly or at least store it somewhere else if it's in the way.

Clear your desktop, tidy your hard drives, create new folders, sort old ones, throw away outdated tax returns, and just generally purge, purge, purge.

If you suffer from perfectionism and use tidying and organizing as a delay tactic, you might want to lean the other way and muss things up a bit or simply practice letting things get a bit messy.

Spring is only one good time of year to declutter. You might find that you have the urge several times a year. So long as you do it in some kind of regular rhythm, it really doesn't matter when it's done.

Here's the best idea yet: Come up with a sweeping writing project like updating your portfolio or pulling together a compilation of prior work that will require you to tidy up your space and your files. You'll get more done faster, if there is a tangible result as a goal.

68
FINISH EVERYTHING

Listen, being a published writer is a privilege you earn. You're not going to earn it by tooting a horn no one wants to hear. You're going to earn it by knuckling down and writing, and letting the writing itself do the tooting for you.

—JAMES SCOTT BELL

With all due respect, my dear writer friend, if you want to succeed in this biz, you are going to have to start a project … and actually finish it.

Being able to focus and sustain your focus long enough to complete a project is critical to becoming a successful.

For many writers, it's not the coming up with ideas, or the starting, or the expanding, or any of those parts of the process that kick up resistance inside of them. It's the finishing part that is the hardest part.

The solution is to parse out your many ideas so they won't interfere. You can't tackle everything all at once anyway. Keep your other ideas safe and sound in a notebook, a bin, a jar, or somewhere specific where you will know where to find them when you need them.

In the meantime, pick one project and stay with it until it's done. If you have trouble following through, don't work on any other writing projects until you finish the one you've selected. You are allowed to jot down ideas and put them in idea storage. But you are not allowed to work on any other projects at the same time, until you finish the project on hand.

If you have not joined the finisher's club, take heart. You can do it. Use these tips:

- Create a deadline for yourself.
- Offer yourself a reward for finishing.
- Team up with someone who is a good finisher.
- Join a group of people who aim to finish something.
- Have someone be your "catcher" (a person you can send your work-in-progress).
- Take a class or workshop that involves finishing.
- Rest when you cross the finish line, not until.

The most common way people give up their power is by thinking they don't have any.

—ALICE WALKER

Here's what separates "Yes, we'd like to publish this" from "No thanks, this isn't for us."

In publishing parlance, it's oftentimes the difference between the writer receiving a response or hearing nothing but resounding silence.

A lot of books go to great lengths to translate an editor's scribbling in the margins into clues as to what's working and not working in writing. Personally, I think that goes a little too far. I can make it simpler:

SILENCE OR REJECTION MEANS:

- Your work is not an appropriate fit at this time.
- Your work is not publishable at this time.
- Something is off and for whatever reason it's not a match.

SILENCE OR REJECTION SHOULD BE INTERPRETED TO MEAN THE FOLLOWING:

- Nothing. It means nothing about the writer and should not be interpreted as being about the writer.

A WRITER WHO WISHES TO PUBLISH A PIECE THAT HAS BEEN REJECTED OR IGNORED SHOULD:

- Double-check the quality of the piece that was submitted and make sure that it is up to snuff.
- If the work is up to snuff, submit it elsewhere (after re-slanting it, if necessary).

A WRITER WHO WISHES TO WORK WITH A PARTICULAR EDITOR AND HAS NOT RECEIVED A FAVORABLE RESPONSE SHOULD:

- Try another piece with the same editor.

Keep trying different pieces with the same editor or move on to an editor who may be more responsive to your work.

There are so many reasons your work might not be right for an editor. It's silly to count the ways. Just try, try again, try once more, and if your efforts are not met favorably, simply move on.

*No one needs to know that you've shut out the world and are medi-
tating as you stroll down the street. Twenty minutes to a half-hour
every day is a good amount of time to restore a sense of serenity.*

—SARAH BAN BREATHNACH

You can't just sit in a closet all day and write. You're going to need to get out of your head sometimes and restock the well.

Remember that scene from the film *Topsy Turvy*, when W.S. Gilbert is a terrible English bore who won't have sex with his wife but then he goes to the World's Fair and sees the installation from Japan and — ta da! — the inspiration for *The Mikado* is born?

When we feel bored or dull or flat, it's a signal that our output is exceeding our input. We have run plumb out of the good stuff that refreshes us. Or perhaps the demands we place on ourselves are too high and need to be tempered.

The remedy is to find ways to engage your senses instead of increasing your output so you can get back in balance. Here are some ideas for how to restock the well.

VISUAL STIMULATION: Drive. Attend an art exhibit. Lie on your back and stare up at the clouds. Go to the movies. Get down on the floor with a baby. Go for a walk.

OLFACTORY INSPIRATION: Pick and arrange flowers. Visit a perfume/lotion shop. Visit an organic market and smell the fresh fruit. Visit a bakery.

AUDITORY EASE: Visit a music store. Listen to an audio book. Take your favorite audio device on your walk. Attend a free concert.

FEEL BETTER: Dance. Swim. Get a deep massage. Jump rope. Sign up for a workout class. Ride your bike. Hang upside down.

SENSE YOURSELF: Take care of the basics: Make sure you take adequate vitamins and minerals. Drink plenty of water. Get your palm read. Meditate. Sweat. Soak. Do some yoga. Read your horoscope. Watch a sad movie and have a good cry.

Don't become dull from overwork, even if you have deadline after deadline after deadline. Think of something that sounds fun to you and do it. You'll spring back to life and your writing will become livelier with you.

You can be a little ungrammatical if you come from the right part of the country.

—ROBERT FROST

I am not the queen of perfect grammar and punctuation.

I sometimes say "lay" when I should say "lie."

I do not perfectly proofread my newsletters, blog posts, and e-mails. Extra fuss over my nonpaying work would cut into my paying work time.

I write pretty well most of the time and let it be good enough. And when I turn in my work, I do the best I can do and let it be what it is. But there is one mistake I never make, and that's putting punctuation outside of quotations.

For me, putting punctuation outside of quotes is like putting on your underwear outside of your clothes.

Watch.

I can't believe he was there. He told me, "I'm definitely *not* going to Sophie's party".

That period outside the quote at the end of the sentence above is like a white bra on top of a black turtleneck for me. How about for you?

Here's another.

"Every year we get busier and busier", says Johnna Zeigler. "Our name is getting around, and people are starting to recognize us when we do shows."

That comma stands out like tighty whitey underwear worn on top of denim jeans.

Punctuation almost always goes inside the quotes. Punctuation hanging out there in the white space just shouts, "Look at me! Look at me!"

So next time you are unsure about where to place the punctuation in a quotation, remember your underwear. Do you put it on the inside or the outside?

Keep your punctuation on the inside where it belongs. Your punctuation should be enclosed by your quotation marks with rare exception—almost as rare as enclosing your regular clothes in your underwear.

72. PASS UP PLAGIARISM

If you steal from one author, it's plagiarism; if you steal from many, it's research.

—WILSON MIZNER

Doing research is like sticking a funnel in the top of your head.

Sure, it's okay to type a topic into Google, print out interesting writing on the topic, and read up on the topic, conduct interviews, and poll people before you write.

But it's probably not a good idea to look at articles that are very similar to your article idea and recently written by another freelancer. The last thing you want to do is rip off someone else's article idea point by point ... without meaning to.

When I stumble upon something that seems, at a glance, like the direction I am heading with an article, I avoid looking at it any further because I know that if I even read it once, some of those ideas are going to show up in my writing. I want to gather research, but I don't want to copy or imitate.

So look everywhere, as opposed to at just one source, and once you think you have sufficiently expanded your mind enough to spark or build on your original ideas, start writing (or rewriting, as the case may be), and say what you want to say in your own words.

The best way to avoid plagiarism, even if we are only talking about copying yourself, is to not have someone else's work (or your old work) in front of you when you write. When you put research in your own words, put other people's work away. And, for goodness' sake, never copy and paste from other people's work or your own work.

You want to respond to work that has come before you, not copy from it. Therefore when you use other people's words, always use quotations or cite your usage.

REMEMBER:

- Verbatim use requires permission.
- Ideas can't be copyrighted, so after you complete your research simply put ideas in your own words. Attribute big ideas and complex concepts, if they are not your ideas.
- Facts belong to everyone and can be used by everyone. Attribute as appropriate.
- Come to your own conclusions and have your own perspective on what you write about so you can avoid conflicts of interest.

BANISH BLOCKS

Writing became such a process of discovery that I couldn't wait to get to work in the morning: I wanted to know what I was going to say.
—SHARON O'BRIEN

Let's see how you are doing on a scale of "avoiding writing" to "can't wait to get back to writing." Take this writing-block test and see how you fare.

Check all that currently apply:

___ Too much isolation
___ Thinking you need big chunks of time
___ Perfectionism/imposter syndrome
___ Distractions
___ Lack of follow-through
___ Impatience
___ Lack of accountability
___ No set writing schedule
___ Too rigid of a schedule
___ Fear of rejection
___ Fear of success
___ Anticipatory worry
___ Procrastination
___ Not enough skills
___ Not enough experience
___ Not enough practice
___ Not willing to be professional
___ Not willing to work hard
___ Too much talking about writing, not enough writing
___ Heavy on the fantasy, short on the actions
___ Despairing overly about what has not yet been accomplished
___ Afraid of editors
___ Allergic to research
___ Interview anxiety
___ Pitching panic

The more blocks you selected, the more frustrated you probably feel.

But you know what you need to do now, right?

Address each of these frustrations with a helpful how-to resource, supportive resource, or class. And then get back to writing.

SWITCH WORN-OUT WORDS

Substitute "damn" every time you're inclined to write "very"; Your editor will delete it and the writing will be just as it should be.

—MARK TWAIN

Avoid overused words that have achieved cliché status. Thanks to the increased speed of communication, it seems like a word can hit the cliché zenith overnight these days.

I like Sam Horn's advice for how to handle clichés. In *POP, Stand Out in Any Crowd*, she says, "Substituting something unexpected for something expected startles people out of autopilot mode and pleasantly surprises them with your originality."

Here is an assortment of tired words writers and editors shared with me that desperately need to be replaced with fresher ideas, plus a few words I'm weary of myself:

- Trust
- Wince
- Brand
- Wonderful
- Tribe
- Amazing
- Platform
- Leverage
- Connect
- Empower
- Human
- Intersect
- Funnel
- Authentic
- Gazed
- Lucid
- Literally
- Balance
- Peace
- Really
- So
- Like
- Soul
- Seriously
- Impacted
- Signage
- Gifted
- Journey
- Exactly
- Synergy
- Awesome
- Heaving
- Resonate
- Curate
- Actually
- Alternative
- Whatever
- Unique
- Very
- Issue

Of course, clichéd doesn't merely apply to overused words. As author Scott Edelstein points out, "A cliché is anything trite and overused. Clichés are usually phrases (*Look out for number one* or *It's your funeral*). But they can also be images (a cheery soda jerk with a pointed white hat; a cat pawing at a ball of yarn), ideas (war is hell; Californians are laid-back), or even whole scenes (the soldier comes home from the war; the lovers wake up to a magnificent sunrise)."

Pay attention to words that habitually end up on your editing room floor. If you can discover what they are, you are halfway toward swearing off of them. And if you can't train them out of your pen, at least you'll get faster at plucking them out later.

SELECT A CATCHY NAME

If you don't make a name for yourself, someone will make one for you. And it might not be the one you want.

—SCOTT GINSBERG

Let's try a little quiz. I'll give you the real names of eleven famous writers who used pseudonyms, and you see if you can come up with the matching pseudonym.

Ready? No cheating now. Just off the top of your head. Here we go:

1. Richard Bachman
2. Emily Bronte
3. N.W. Clerk
4. Eric Arthur Blair
5. Samuel Langhorne Clemens
6. Dame Agatha Christie
7. Amandine Aurore Lucile Dupin
8. Karen von Blixen-Finecke
9. Pauline Phillips
10. Brook Busey
11. Allen Stewart Konigsberg

What? You didn't score 100 percent?

But you could plug each of these names into any Internet search engine and know who is who in a few seconds, which is exactly my point.

A lot of writers think that the launch of their career is a great time to start thinking about their pseudonym. But since sustaining any kind of long-term hidden identity has become increasingly difficult these days, thanks to the search ability of the Internet, your pseudonym might be more of a headache than a boon to your career.

If you think you can hide behind a pen name, you might want to think again. Or at least think long and hard before you commit to dividing yourself up into multiple identities.

My advice is to come up with one name, plan to use it on all your work, and make it the name you wish to become known by and stay known by for the rest of your life.

Choosing an official name isn't a big issue until you are ready to start promoting yourself, but it's something to start thinking about long before we start seeing your name as a byline.

So what's your writer name going to be again? Make it the one that's going to go the distance.

KEY: 1. Stephen King. 2. Ellis Bell. 3. C.S. Lewis. 4. George Orwell. 5. Mark Twain. 6. Mary Westmacott. 7. George Sand. 8. Isak Dinesen. 9. Dear Abby. 10. Diablo Cody. 11. Woody Allen.

MILK INSPIRATION

An article dealing with "Ten Ways to Deal With Children on a Rainy Day," could trigger an idea for "Ten Ways to Entertain Houseguests," or "Ten Ways to Take a Vacation Right in Your Own Home."

—ELAINE FANTLE SHIMBERG

Think you could have written something you saw recently?

Prove it.

Write it.

I bet you will learn a ton in the process.

Here's how you do it. You see something written you like. Or maybe you read an incredibly compelling essay that moved you to tears. Maybe you loved a novel so much that you just have to write a short story.

For me, I am always fascinated, and have been since I was a kid, by round-up lists that are really long. You know the ones I mean? Like "101 Ways to Enjoy Summer" — when I see an article that starts with "101 Ways ..." I feel giddy inside.

Let what you just read inspire you to write the same kind of form on one of your topics.

I could easily write an article called "101 Tiny Time-Outs for Moms" because this is a topic I've been covering and recovering for years.

Or how about "101 Ways to Bring More Hush Into Your Holiday Rush"?

Another? How about "101 Ways to Say I Love You This Valentine's Day"?

These sound appealing to the reader because of the sheer volume of tips, right?

It all starts with the thought in your mind, *Ooo, I wish I had written that.*

Next time the phrase crosses your mind, don't just think it. Write it.

Develop the habit of dedicating time to reviewing your work with precision in mind.

—JACK HEFFRON

One common mistake my students fall into is overusing the word *it* in their writing.

It is a lazy word. *It* is the word we reach for when we don't want to go to the trouble of coming up with a better, more specific word. It stinks to have to read sentence after sentence starting with *it*. (See? This paragraph proves it!)

But I'll tell you what. I won't hold it against you if you use *it* in your drafts. I won't even hold it against you if you use *it* in your second, fifth, or eighth draft.

But by the time you are ready to hand in a final draft, you need to go through that draft with your "Edit" > "Find" tool and suss out all the extraneous it, its, and it's and make sure they all belong in there.

Here are a few examples. Which do you think is the stronger sentence?

> It's that time of year again.
> Or
> Spring is here again.

> It is a real challenge to find a tasty watermelon in January.
> Or
> Finding a tasty watermelon in January is a real challenge.

> I don't like it when the kids leave their toys all over the house.
> Or
> I don't like the kids leaving their toys all over the house.

Round up it like a usual suspect and come up with better and more specific words you can use in your rewrite process.

78
CULTIVATE CLARITY

When you write something needlessly prolix and convoluted, there's a reason for it, and that reason is usually a lack of clarity and purpose going on.

—ROBERT MASELLO

The reader shouldn't have to do all the work.

Recently I picked up a magazine and read/skimmed through the articles. I was struck by the clarity and excellence of one of the articles in relation to the rambling I-don't-know-what that was passing as another article.

As I was pondering how the editor could have allowed one into print while the other was clearly so much higher quality, I realized something. There are two kinds of writing: good, clear writing that communicates fully, compellingly, and well—and drafts.

And drafts should never be published as final work.

So let's explore what clear writing is and isn't, so you will know when your drafts are done.

CLEAR WRITING

- The idea of the piece is clearly stated and set up in the title and subtitle.
- The idea is introduced by the lead briefly and in a way that makes me want to keep reading.
- The piece is made up of both short and medium sentence lengths.
- Quotations throughout the piece are set up, brief, and relevant.
- Sentences almost never begin with *it*.
- The writer stays out of the way and serves the story.
- The structure of the piece is consistent and has a rhythm.

CONFUSED WRITING

- The idea of the piece is unclear, fuzzy, or too multifaceted.
- The idea is introduced by a long lead that rambles, waxes poetic, and becomes borderline self-indulgent.
- The piece is made up of long run-on sentences followed by long run-on sentences.
- Quotations throughout the piece feel jammed in, go on too long, and don't jibe with the rest of the piece.
- Sentence after sentence begins with the word *it*, even the beginnings of paragraphs.
- The writer can't get out of the way and just say what she needs to say.
- The writer keeps pointing the story back at himself.
- The structure of the piece is nonexistent, free-form, or detracts from the piece.

79

INVENTORY IDEAS

Many writers make elaborate files, spending hours cross-indexing and making notations from these articles. Others let newspapers and magazines stack up to the ceiling and then waste hours burrowing through them trying to find a specific issue. I tend to fall somewhere in between.

—ELAINE FANTLE SHIMBERG

Train your mind to keep tabs on your best ideas and you will eventually use them all. If you are having trouble keeping track of all your ideas because they are popping up all over the place, start a collection method for every worthwhile snippet, scrap, and thought bubble.

CREATE AN IDEA INVENTORY WHERE YOU LIST ALL YOUR IDEAS IN ONE PLACE. This way when you are stumped for a new piece of writing, you can revisit your list or take a few minutes to update it and you will be refreshed and ready to write.

KEEP SIMILAR TOPIC WRITING CLUSTERED TOGETHER. You can use folders on your computer for storing groups of docs. Make the doc titles the same as what they contain and save yourself headaches when you are looking for specific content later.

PIECES THAT DON'T END UP FINISHED CAN ALSO BE INVENTORIED. You'll increase the chance of finishing your work tenfold by printing unfinished work and keeping it handy. Print out your in-progress docs and put them in an in-progress folder so you can keep track of unfinished work you intend to finish later.

PLAY WITH OLD IDEAS. Keep your best ideas in lists that you either handwrite or type up. Whatever works for you. If you covered part of a topic, you might cover it more fully later. If you have covered a topic thoroughly, you might break out and expand a part of the idea.

You are going to be writing for a long time. Over the course of your lifetime, you will have realized hundreds of ideas. Your most compelling ideas will likely stay compelling for you. Years from now, they will still have the same stuff that attracted you to them in the first place.

80
WRITE RICHLY

When you're writing nonfiction, there's no use getting into a writing schedule until you've done the [research] and you have the material.

—TOM WOLFE

Beginning writers often don't understand that writing richly is part of the job description. Or they think writing richly takes so long initially they feel like they will never be able to write quickly enough to make the investment of time worthwhile.

So if you want to compete, you must write richly at the outset of your career and keep striving to write better and better as your career progresses.

Salable writing doesn't usually happen in one fell swoop. Salable writing is well-researched and carefully crafted. You have to care about the details. If you don't care about the details, your reader isn't going to care about the writing.

When good ideas come flooding in, you will want to get the gist of your idea sketched or outlined while it's fresh in your mind. Of course you should get it on the page. And then later, you can come back and add:

- The perfect seasonal hook
- The most timely statistics
- The newly revealed facts
- The most penetrating definitions
- The most revealing anecdotes
- The most appropriate quotes
- The most respected experts
- The most helpful references
- The most illustrative links
- The most necessary details, tools, and resources

Notice in chapter twenty-four, I suggested that you add stats, facts, quotes, etc., but I wasn't pressing you to make sure you dug up the most recent facts or the most appropriate quotes. A beginning writer, who is composing work for lower-paying pubs, can often get away with beginner-level writing.

But as you progress in your career, it's up to you to push yourself to write better and better all the time. Try to include the most relevant, revealing, timely information in your writing, not just whatever pops up at the top of the Internet search or the quote from the first person who gets back to you.

The better you get at enriching your final drafts, the better you will be able to compete.

A good cover letter should be concise, businesslike, and informative. It should give an editor all the pertinent facts—and nothing more.

—SCOTT EDELSTEIN

Publication of your work by someone who can share it with a larger audience is why you go to all the trouble of packaging your words up to make the best possible impression.

Okay, so an editor receives a cover letter from you. Presumably because:

- She might publish your work.
- You know she is open to receiving cover letters with submissions she might publish.
- You are hoping she will write right back and say, "Sold!"
- You are hoping that she will pay you for your polished writing.

And if she is on the receiving end of your best work, and you present it to her in a professional manner, and she has a budget to pay writers, if all of these aspects of the equation are in place, she just might say, "Yes!"

So what do you have to lose? Nuthin', that's what.

The most important factor is to keep your cover letters simple. If all you do in your cover letter is answer these questions, you won't be able to help but write a good one:

- Why are you writing? If you want to get an editor's attention, connect with him and say something appreciative about his publication. Tell him something specific you appreciate about the work he is doing.
- What are you offering? You've got her attention now, but not for long. So can you quickly give her the 4-1-1 on how your words will hook her readers' attention? She needs to be able to read this cover letter in about thirty seconds. If you come up with something that's a perfect fit in topic and form with what she already publishes, you will have a fighting chance.
- Who are you? Can you seal his interest and turn this exchange into an offer? Share only your most impressive credentials. End on a strong note that ties you in with the topic you are writing about and you just might be the writer with the exact kind of writing he needs.

There's a word for a writer who never gives up ... published.

—J.A. KONRATH

Writing success doesn't always come from the places we intend it to come from in the first place. A writer might study fiction writing for three years only to turn around and become a successful nonfiction writer instead.

But what if that writer only stubbornly insisted on fiction success at the sake of any nonfiction success? So she lets a hundred opportunities a day pass her by while she remains stubbornly focused on the one goal. Let's say she's coveting a literary novel—the kind that typically takes most writers a decade or so to accomplish successfully.

While she was working on her fiction, she could have also been writing articles, reviewing books, picking up a little business writing, crafting curriculum, and maybe even writing a nonfiction book or two.

And then guess what happens? After working on a book for seven years and feeling superior to all the writers who work in other genres, she can't sell her novel; she doesn't want to self-publish it, so guess what she does? She quits. What a waste.

You are smarter than this and you will not let your choices be guided by all or nothing thinking. Don't try to write in too many genres all at once, but do take advantage of writing opportunities that are right in front of you that you might otherwise miss because you are so focused on one lofty path.

I just heard from a former student of mine. She wasn't having much luck with article writing, so she decided to open up shop offering writing services. And guess what? It's working well for her. More importantly, she seems excited about what she's doing with her writing.

So she'll probably keep writing. And that's a win because there is no one right path to writing success. There are many choices and many kinds of rewards.

83 UNBLOCK YOURSELF

If tomorrow morning by some stroke of magic every dazed and benighted soul woke up with the power to take the first step toward pursuing his or her dreams, every shrink in the directory would be out of business.

—STEVEN PRESSFIELD

These are the books that have bolstered my creative ambitions and helped me carry on. You can pay full price for them, buy them in digital form, or purchase them used for next to nothing.

If you are stuck, stalled, sucked out, or just slow to get started, these books are going to be good medicine.

CLASSIC WRITING INSPIRATION
>*Writing Down the Bones* by Natalie Goldberg
>*Bird by Bird* by Anne Lamott
>*If You Want to Write* by Brenda Ueland

BLASTING THROUGH BLOCKS
>*The War of Art* by Steven Pressfield
>*The Artist's Way* by Julia Cameron
>*A Life in the Arts* by Eric Maisel

FUN MEDICINE
>*The Pocket Muse* by Monica Wood
>*How Much Joy Can You Stand?* By Suzanne Falter-Barns
>*Living Out Loud* By Keri Smith
>*Write It Down, Make It Happen* by Henriette Anne Klauser
>*How You Do Anything Is How You Do Everything* by Cheri Huber and June Shiver

84
DON'T PEOPLE-PLEASE

Approval cannot be trusted. It can be withdrawn at any time no matter what our track record has been. It is as nourishing of real growth as cotton candy. Yet many of us spend our lives pursuing it.
—RACHEL NAOMI REMEN

Once you become a professional writer, you realize that the world is full of people who will never understand why you would choose such a difficult vocation. Can't you just be like everyone else? Get a real job? Grow up?

Of course, if any of these naysayers are in your close family or circle of friends, you are somewhat obligated to hear them out, nod along like you know they mean well, and then get back to your work when the conversation is over.

Adapt whatever strategy works for you, just be sure not to fall into the temptation of trying to please people who don't get you and may never get you. In other words, don't become a people pleaser for people who are impossible to please. They will waste your valuable time and energy. They will cause you endless frustration, if you let them.

Obviously I'm not suggesting you ignore loved ones who have perfectly reasonable human needs. Nor am I referring to ignoring your children's reasonable needs. I'm talking about when other people's unreasonable needs threaten to eclipse your reasonable need to write.

Author Heather Sharfeddin understands that when she writes it's a gain, not a loss. We were on a panel of writers who are also mothers at Barnes & Noble, and during Q&A, an attendee asked how she could reconcile her need to write with the seemingly enormous needs of having a teenage child—specifically, the way they always need to be taxied around.

Sharfeddin's answer was that she'd made a conscious decision in her life that her contribution to the world is her books. And she has come to terms with what she chooses not to do, like not volunteering for the PTA, for example, because she has made a commitment to what matters most for her.

Win-win-win means that your work makes the world a better place.

*A hero knows it takes hard work and a long time to get published;
a fool thinks it should happen immediately, because he thinks he's
a hero already.*

—JAMES SCOTT BELL

When I was writing my first book, *Writer Mama*, there was a point where I was flailing around trying to find the through-line (which I thought I'd lost). I was expressing what surely sounded like panic to my editor, Jane Friedman, about the sheer volume of the book I was attempting to write.

She referred to a quote that I have since seen invoked by several other writers. It was E.L. Doctorow who said, "It's like driving a car at night. You never see further than your headlights, but you can make the whole trip that way."

Writing is like driving a car at night, and so is growing your writing career. Whether you are reading this book at the dawning of your career, somewhere in media res, or during, sunset years of steady productivity, take a long-term view of your writing.

A lot of people dream of getting published. A lot of people want to see their names on a book. A lot of people would rather have *been* published than enjoy the hard, long work that it takes to get published over and over. And a lot of folks won't stick it out in the long haul.

Writing success is daily. Meet the goal you need to meet today. You can't see what it will all come to down the road.

A collection can't become a collection until there is a collection to collect. A book is written one chapter at a time. An article goes through many drafts before becoming the final version.

So commit for the long haul. Don't seek short-term gratification. If you are expecting supersized results from a short-term commitment, I can almost guarantee that you are going to be disappointed.

86
EXORCISE ANXIETY

A wounded deer leaps highest...

—EMILY DICKINSON

Writing serves many purposes, and one that should never be overlooked is writing as a way to release your fears, frustrations, and falling-down places. The mechanics of writing for release are easy. Have one place, a specific notebook or file where you keep these kinds of writings, and pull this virtual venting room out or up when you need it.

If you want to get to writing with substance sooner, experiment with a venting practice that works for you. Sometimes just scribbling one page will open you up and get you ready to write. Other times, you might go on for pages and hit upon some realizations before you feel ready to write for the public.

If I've noticed anything over the ten years that I've been teaching, it's that anxiety is part of writing career growth. I have never encountered a writer whose professional development was not accompanied by a certain amount of heightened nervous energy. And nervous energy always needs an outlet, otherwise it becomes destructive.

Just remember that writing to heal or for release is not writing for public consumption because as soon as you put this kind of public expectation on your writing, it will become self-conscious. We are not talking about writing for others. We're talking about the writing you do for self-disclosure, for self-discovery, and to get through whatever feelings are stalling you, so you can get back to the writing you intend to make public.

Later, if you want to use process writing as material, you can if you wish. But I suggest that you look at it for insights into the human condition rather than as personal secrets you need to divulge to the world.

If you want this practice to become a helpful tool for you, play around with it. Then hang on to the aspects that work for you.

If you keep the focus on clearing the pipes when they are blocked, you will have an easy, quick, and cathartic way to get back to work whenever you stray off course.

From self alone expect applause.

—MARION L. BURTON

When you submit your writing for publication, you are not asking, "Do you like it?"

You are asking, "Does it *work* for you?"

If it works for an editor, she will say, "Yes, this works."

And that's it. Your writing either works for the editor or it doesn't.

If it doesn't work, she will likely say nothing or "No thanks," or maybe, "No thank you."

And she still won't likely shower you with praise. Because it's either a fit or it isn't a fit.

It's your job to praise yourself when it's a fit. And it's your job to say, "Next!" if it's not a fit, without being overly hard on yourself or feeling desperate for a response.

Professional satisfaction comes from doing the best you can. You don't need an editor to tell you whether you did your best or not. You need to experience a clear sense of good enough yourself, before you submit.

And then if you submit and you hear back good news and that your work is well done, you should feel good. But you should also feel like you already knew it was good—not like you can't believe it's any good.

If you hear back that an editor needs a rewrite or you see a piece published and notice that it has been heavily edited, don't head straight for the box of shame. See what can be learned from the experience. Become curious about where and how you might improve—without excessive guilt or self-rebuke.

Praise may come from a job well done. But praise needs to come from you first. So make sure you do your best and give yourself some strokes for all of your hard work. Then you won't be so surprised by the compliments about your work when they come.

88

CELEBRATE FRUGALLY

My husband and I spend little on clothes and dining out. Our son goes to public school. We get deals on travel. We have never had a nanny. And for the first time in our eleven years together, we only recently bought a new car.

—BARBARA DEMARCO-BARRETT

I believe that if you write what you love, the money will follow. However, the operative word here is *follow*. I can't tell you when to count on any particular check's arrival on your calendar.

So when good things happen in your writing career, by all means, celebrate, but frugally. I have learned over time with more mini celebrations than I could possibly count, to keep my celebratory expenditures to scale.

- Instead of developing a spending habit more lavish than you can possibly sustain, pick and choose a couple of inexpensive pleasures like buying yourself a latté or a package of your favorite colorful pens or an e-book that was on your wish list.
- If you are the kind of person who prefers one larger reward rather than multiple little rewards, consider a ritual reward. If you meet your monthly goals, you can get a pedicure, go out to eat, or purchase something you will cherish in the twenty-five to fifty dollar range.
- If you are a person who is rewarded by taking care of the future, consider starting an IRA, investment portfolio, or college fund for your kids. Every time you send in a contribution you will have the satisfaction of future payoffs from your current earnings.
- If you are motivated by giving to others, consider tithing a percentage of your income to your favorite causes or charities. What cheers you won't be the recognition from giving, although you can publicize your generosity if you like, but the feeling of contributing to the common good.
- Keep in mind that you can have good things happening in your career without much cash in the bank to show for your work. If you are still waiting for the profits to catch up with your efforts, consider the win-win-win reward of a twenty-minute daily walk or of spending time on a hobby that has nothing to do with writing or of making a phone call to supportive friend.

GROW A GARDEN: PART ONE

Nature is whole and yet never finished.
—JOHANN WOLFGANG VON GOETHE

If you conceptualize your career as a garden, you'll be able to manage the growth process better, as well. The first time I experienced the feeling that my writing career was similar to a garden, I felt a tremendous amount of relief. I was juggling a lot at the time and also learning a lot, as usual, and the concept of "garden" made me realize that no matter how wild and unwieldy my career seemed to be growing, I'd be able to handle it if I just kept nurturing it and stayed focused on the moment.

PROCESS CLAIMED

If you have gotten this far in this book, you have actively claimed a space for your writing both internally and externally. You have gotten into the habit of creating fertile ground for your self-expression on the page. Once you have this habit down, plant an idea, nurture it, and flesh it out fully, the habit is yours for good.

RITUAL AS CREATIVE CONTEXT

Just as a garden may be a raised bed with copper wire to discourage slugs and a tall fence to keep out deer and other animals, you are cultivating a space that nurtures your most high-minded aspirations, because once you activate your creative "place," whatever comes into it will be amplified. Therefore, treat your real and virtual creative spaces as you would sacred spaces. Recognize that if you stop showing up, everything will grow wild with neglect. Visit your creative garden in a committed, devoted fashion.

PREPARATION AS FERTILE SOIL

You recognize that your mind is only as fertile as what you put in it. Therefore, be particular about what will fertilize your best ideas. You are methodical, yet selective, just as you would be in nurturing a child. You keep your mind receptive and enriched along the entire journey because you understand that your creative process needs healthy choices. You read books, take classes, and participate in events that will give you the key growth ingredients your garden needs.

IDEA PROTECTION

You have learned that talking about and dissipating your ideas only weakens them. You've noticed that premature exposure may pollute your ideas and make them become what others conceive instead of helping you exercise and develop your own perceptions. You want to take your ideas all the way from seed to result. The same way slugs are not welcome in a garden full of fresh sprouts, keep your mental space clear of "predators" that would mow down your dreams and make a feast of your hard work.

TRUST YOUR GUT

If we had to say what writing is, we would define it essentially as an act of courage.

—CYNTHIA OZICK

Writers take risks every day. It takes guts to put your ideas out in the world.

Maybe we spend too much time glorifying all our little fears, when really we should spend a lot more time talking about our guts. Guts are when you dig down deep and pull something out of yourself that scoffs on your self-manufactured fears.

Now, guts may come more easily to some of us than to others. However, I believe that we are all born with guts. A certain amount of fearlessness must be innate … so long as it has not been systematically bred out of us in favor of perfectionism or some other unachievable behavior ideal.

What's the best way to get some guts if you don't feel like you have any?

- Test-drive the little things your gut tells you to. Not just the big things—listen to your gut better on the fly, too. If you have a hunch, follow it. Turn one direction instead of the way you usually go. Give yourself choices and enjoy every choice you make.
- If your gut says write a novel, take a fiction class or participate in NaNoWriMo (National Novel Writing Month).
- If a hunch says go to a writing retreat, apply for fellowships or concoct your own getaway. Why not?
- If you feel gross from watching trash television, stop. If your gut says start watching a little television for a mental break now and then, then start.
- What is your gut saying right now? Go to a bookstore and let your gut steer your attention around the store.

Instead of following someone else's marching orders, you're going to need to tune into and follow the lead of your instincts. You will feel so much happier when you are in sync with yourself.

You already have guts. Don't let anyone tell you that you don't. But if you don't feel a sense of your own creative autonomy, remember that creative power comes from tuning in to your gut and learning to trust it over time.

If writing novels is like planting a forest, then writing short stories is more like planting a garden. The two processes complement each other, creating a complete landscape that I treasure.

—HARUKI MURAKAMI

If you have the impulse to apologize for how much you love writing, just think of all of those passionate gardeners out there who don't feel like they have to apologize for digging in the dirt. Nobody needs to garden perfectly to produce fully formed results. If you claim your space, plant your ideas, nurture your ideas over time, microprotect your fledglings, and guard them against predators until they can stand up for themselves, you will eventually create splendid results. Here are a few more reminders:

DETACH FROM DRAMA

Recognize that even if you set clear intentions to keep what you don't want out of your creative space, some distractions are going to get through. Develop healthy responses to interlopers, responding in a friendly but firm manner. Trustworthy types who won't rip out your fledgling ideas and tromp on your young plants may visit so long as they are respectful. If you are focused and productive, you will quickly notice the difference between others who are focused on becoming prolific and those who are just mucking around.

BE PATIENT

As you work on a few focused projects, you begin to set aside and reserve ideas that may work later but can't have your attention now. Compost as you go along and add what is pruned to the pile to come back into your process enriched and transformed. Fertilize your projects and do what it takes to keep them healthy and growing.

STRONGER MEASURES

Just as a garden will become more alluring to those who would devour the harvest prematurely, take whatever measures you must to physically, mentally, emotionally, and spiritually protect your creative space. You can employ a fence, netting, or whatever it takes to preserve your hard work without apologizing. It's your responsibility to protect your work. Don't expect anyone else to do it for you.

ACKNOWLEDGE THAT MORE IS BETTER

At some point, you realize that if you plant ample seeds, then thin them out to the most flourishing prospects and run with what's working, you are going to yield better results in the long run. Only take on as much as you can creatively handle, but keep in mind that some of your projects probably won't flourish.

If your writing career is clearly delineated, protected, and nurtured, it will grow. But if you are too sloppy and cavalier or not industrious or consistent enough, it won't. A little preparation goes a long way in a writing career, and you will need to tend yours concientiously if you want to realize the future harvest you have envisioned.

SUMMER:

FIND YOUR STRIDE

Victory in anything, from war to football, is founded in training and discipline. Nothing worthwhile is gained by sloth and wishful thinking. It's not the will to win that counts but the will to prepare to win.

—JAMES SCOTT BELL

During the summer phase of writing career growth, you improve your skills, start writing faster, develop resilience, test your determination, rack up clips, accumulate credits, and learn to ride the joys and disappointments that come part and parcel with the writing life. Writing gets easier the more you do it, but this intermediate phase of your writing career brings new challenges and new impatience. You may become discouraged and wonder why you are not farther ahead than you think you ought to be. At this stage, impatient writers fall away or run off in pursuit of shortcuts that may slow or delay their professional progress in the long run. In the meantime, if you want to keep making strides, stick with what works for you. The more you dive back into your work, the more you will appreciate the benefits of a deeper, more resilient creative process. Steady, serial success helps you burn off residual angst and impatience so you can focus on your work in a grounded way. Writing blocks that initially feel like deal breakers can become stepping-stones to your success once you learn how to write through them.

Every artist was once an amateur.

—RALPH WALDO EMERSON

Remember, nobody is born a professional. So this stuff has to be learned and practiced.

Stephen King used to just be some guy who had a traumatic experience in his childhood.

Janet Evanovich did not always have her face plastered across a bus.

There was a time when no one knew what a *muggle* was, not even J.K. Rowling.

These writers and indeed, all writers, were once simply somebody's baby—a mother's son, a father's daughter, and then, eventually, they became writers.

At some point thereafter, they became darn good writers, and then even farther down the road they became the writers we know and love today.

Writing is work, just like many other kinds of work that require a certain amount of artfulness and intuition. And the more willingly you acknowledge the more well-rounded qualities of the writing life, the better you will fare.

I teach people how to approach writing as a business because I find this approach works well for practical people who have practical demands in their lives.

I don't teach how to get really, really inspired and then, POOF! create a writing career out of nada, because I have never seen that work.

Luckily there are no prerequisites. You can aspire to be just as famous as Stephen or Janet or J.K. But don't latch on to pipe dreams that distort the hard work it actually takes to make that scope of success possible.

Success always starts with a calling to write. But after that, the difference between the famous and the anonymous comes down to how many buckets of sweat you have produced up to this point.

So don't tell me how much you want fame and success the likes of which only a select few have seen. That's not going to impress anybody. Take me to the closet where you keep the buckets of sweat. Then I'll be impressed.

Because these writers, and most successful writers, are not focused on how impressive they are. They are focused on what they are going to write next. And they've got the buckets of sweat in their closets to prove it.

AIM TO EARN

I don't know much about being a millionaire, but I'll bet I'd be darling at it.

—DOROTHY PARKER

I know other writing instructors who suggest that writers go for the highest paying gigs right out of the gate, but I think that's bad advice.

When overeager writers pursue opportunities beyond their confidence and their experience, they sabotage themselves. Aiming too far over your head can keep you in the land of second-guessing. It's uncomfortable not knowing if you are ever doing things appropriately, and it causes inexperienced writers a lot of stress.

I try to teach writers a quiet confidence, not wishful thinking. I try to teach *Yes, I nailed it*, rather than *Geez, I hope I am doing this right*.

So instead of going for the highest paying markets right out of the gate, I suggest you aim just one step higher than the targets you can hit right now. Increasing your pay rate as you increase your skills is the key to increasing your income level.

Once you are writing consistently, assess whether it's time to ask for better rates from the folks you already write for. See if you can also increase the volume of submissions you make across a range of pay.

If you continuously raise your rates and continually widen your income streams as you become proficient at juggling more tasks, you can become quite prosperous as a writer in only a few years.

The easiest way to raise your rates is to commit to asking for a pay raise once a year from publications you write for regularly. I teach my students the golden phrase: "Is this the best you can offer?" Which also comes in handy when you are negotiating your first payment amount.

But don't become greedy. If you outprice yourself, there will be another, hungrier writer ready to take your place. Make the most of the skills and services you have to offer across a wide range of clients and you will never run out of cheerful work.

LENGTHEN AS YOU GO

If we're growing, we're always going to be out of our comfort zone.

—JOHN MAXWELL

I always suggest that writers hold off on writing longer pieces until they have written a goodly number of shorter pieces and gotten them published. This helps you learn how to respond more fully, deeply, and widely before you embark on longer projects that still need to be written in a detailed manner even though they have a high word count.

Fortunately, something cool that happens once you write short pieces for a while is that you start to have a lot more to say. Earlier, I suggested that you write as a way of responding to what you notice. After you have been writing short pieces for a while, you will be in the habit of noticing more, which will naturally lend more authority to your writing.

This strategy applies to other forms the same way it applies to nonfiction. Here's a list of various forms by length. Does it give you any ideas of how you might be able to structure a workout plan for your writing within one genre or by combining forms within genres that are most important to you?

SHORT FORMS
- Haiku/short poetry
- Fillers/shorts
- Flash fiction
- Blog posts
- Sidebars

FEATURE-LENGTH
- Profiles
- Travel pieces
- Columns
- Roundups
- Personal essays

MEDIUM FORMS
- Personal anecdotes
- Poems
- List articles
- Op-eds
- How-to articles

LONG FORMS
- Memoir
- Epic poem
- Novel
- Nonfiction book proposal
- Nonfiction book

The bottom line is this: If you have not written the short forms first, the long forms are going to be very difficult to get published. But if you start with short forms and write your way up, you will increase your chances of success.

BEFRIEND TIME

I find it impossible to divide my life into neat compartments. I enjoy my work, so it's hard for me to say, "Hey, it's five P.M.—I'm outta here!"

—DIANA BURRELL

Time is much more malleable than we know. Anyone who operates on a strict timetable might not believe it. But creative people know that you can actually coax time to come on over and be on your side instead of fighting it. Here's how it's done:

JUST START

If you can't get started, let go of the future and just ask, what is the single next most important thing I need to do? Once the immediate pressure lifts, you can plan to move forward in a measured way.

MAP OUT THE STEPS

List every single step that needs to be taken, figured backwards from the deadline, and broken down into a tidy to-do list. Let it be long, if it must. As long as you break it down into steps and check them off as you complete tasks, you win.

RUT BUSTER

Stuck? Take advantage of pauses to switch gears. Either do something totally different like take a walk, watch a movie, or relax, or do more work that is something different to help you switch gears.

UNCONSTRUCTIVE THOUGHT REPELLANT

Worry, fears, and anxiety eat up time and keep us distracted from the work at hand. Keep the constructive thoughts, and assess and ditch the rest: Write two columns. Put distracted thoughts on the left, constructive thoughts on the right. Then back to work you go.

RELINQUISH PERFECTIONISM

Anne Lamott calls it "The voice of the oppressor." I call it a great excuse for procrastination. You can't write the final draft until you have an almost final draft to polish. Better get back to work.

WRITING IS A HARD, WONDERFULLY REWARDING WORK

But hard work just the same. Once you accept that writing is work and lots of it, there really isn't much to talk about, only progress to make.

PUT EXCUSES TO WORK

Don't wait until you have big expanses of time in your schedule. Grab writing time in the nooks and crannies. Nothing else will bring you closer to your dream. Every time you catch yourself making an excuse about not having time to write, make yourself do some work anyway.

96
STACK UP SUCCESSES

Whatever we learn to do, we learn by actually doing it: Men come to be builders, for instance, by building, and harp players, by playing the harp.

—ARISTOTLE

Everything you create is complete and concrete. Every project you finish becomes something solid, tangible, and permanent. Each product of creativity is something that can be combined with other products the way stones mixed with other stones create something mighty like a wall or a chimney or a house.

What if every piece of writing is like a stone? Not that stones can't become worn down or weathered. But when you've invested the proper amount of work into your writing, it becomes like a perfectly smooth river stone or a shiny piece of granite or a jagged piece of red rock. It becomes substantial.

And if you can create stone after stone after stone, just think of the potential. You can use all of your stones to build something more substantial in your writing career. But this only happens if you finish projects. A bunch of incomplete stones are gravel, which is something that gets tread upon, not built up.

We often hear infopreneurs speak of leveraging what they have already written. I don't think of it so much as leveraging , rather I think of writing as building. The solidity of the work is what makes it a stable part of a foundation for future work. And the mastery of the skills comes from doing solid work over time.

Mastery is what enables a writer to continue well and happily with a writing career. Not some secret formula or borrowing someone else's formula for success.

How will you become a master writer in your own right? By building what only you can build.

The house that you eventually build will represent your life's work and will not look like anyone else's.

So build it slowly and steadily, stone by stone, with intention and purpose. The career you leave behind can last as long as a house made of stone, maybe even longer.

97 BE AN ORIGINAL

Be a first-rate version of yourself, not a second-rate version of someone else.

—JUDY GARLAND

If you can simply be yourself, you'll write like yourself. If you write like yourself, and write as best you can, you will never suffer in comparison to another writer because there will be nothing to compare. Your true voice and style will shine through.

I think this also explains why, even though I have been teaching writers for ten years—and even though I've been teaching the exact same forms, class after class—no two writers ever sound the same to me. Each piece that is written has a distinct tone and style that reflects the individual.

In five years of teaching hundreds of writers in one particular class, only one or two topics have ever been written on multiple times by different writers, with the all-time high for one topic being repeated three times.

This demonstrates how rare it is for any two writers to tackle the same topics. Even though I teach writers who are very similar in their roles in life and the types of publications they are targeting, they still don't write on the same topics, never mind in the same way. Given their shared similarities, the sheer volume of variety in my students' work is amazing.

And yet, when I go online and follow folks from the same field, they all seem to be carrying on the same conversation. How can one environment (the classroom) breed so much creativity and individualism, while the other (the online writing conversation) seems to breed so much regurgitation and echoing of the same information?

Every writer is unique and has original ideas and a fresh way of writing. But in an echo chamber environment, this same writer can be reduced to a parrot in a very short time.

Banality is contagious. Creativity cannot be imitated. And apparently creativity can be taught and banality can be imitated.

Remember: Be yourself. It's you the readers want, not your best imitations of someone else.

98
PEN A SHORT BIO

If you're just beginning your career, a short bio may be all you need to describe your background, education, awards, publications, and so on.

—GIGI ROSENBERG

One of the most common questions my beginning students have when the time comes to compress their experience into their first professional bio is, what are you supposed to compress if so far you haven't really had any professional experience?

I tell them to take the say-it-until-you-make-it approach. For example, if you are starting out as a freelance journalist, just say that. For example:

> Susan Johnson is a freelance journalist from Missoula, Montana.

Of course, if you write a variety of forms, your statement of purpose might look like this:

> Susan Johnson writes articles and personal essays in her hometown of Missoula, Montana.

Then add absolutely any writing credentials you already have. For example, let's say you were the secretary of the PTA for three years and this job included editing the monthly newsletters. You could say:

> Susan Johnson writes articles and personal essays in her hometown of Missoula, Montana. She has three years of newsletter editing experience and ...

And what? Well, how about something related to what you are submitting now? For example, if you are submitting an article about how to keep your bathroom sparkling while only cleaning it once a month, you could say:

> Susan Johnson writes articles and personal essays. She has three years of newsletter editing experience and is the proud owner of the cleanest bathroom in her hometown of Missoula, Montana.

Now see? Susan Johnson was formerly a mystery to us readers. And now she sounds like someone interesting, skilled, and funny, all of which increases her odds of getting the gig.

Your turn. Gather up several clever, short bios and then write your own. Keep it flexible, and update it on an ongoing basis as your writing career grows. You may wish or need to customize your short bio based on the published work it will accompany.

99 ENJOY YOUR EFFORTS

> *Success is not the key to happiness. Happiness is the key to success. If you love what you are doing, you will be successful.*
> —ALBERT SCHWEITZER

If you have been at this writing game for a while but you are not seeing the kinds of results you'd like to see for your efforts, you may not be working as hard and in as focused a manner as you may think.

Because if you were, you'd be piling up the proof, so let's keep things in perspective. Here's how a writing writer experiences the world vs. how a not-writing-enough writer experiences the world:

A WRITING WRITER'S EXPERIENCE

- Someone is trying to get your attention and is having a hard time doing it.
- Hours have flown by and it seems like you just sat down.
- Your file cabinets and hard drives are overflowing with things you've written.
- People want to interview or quote you about your writing.
- You earn a living or make money writing.
- You are familiar with the sound of your fingers moving across the keys.
- You have burned through all excuses not to write.
- You have a university degree hanging on the wall that says you are a writer (and you are writing to pay it off).
- You have an ever-growing portfolio of published work.

A NOT-WRITING-ENOUGH WRITER'S EXPERIENCE

- You are reading about writing.
- You are dreaming about writing.
- You are caressing your imagined future book.
- You are grousing about how so many writers who get published should not get published so often or at all.
- You sit in cafés killing long periods of time.
- You drink and smoke and drug and engage in lots of juicy relationship drama instead of writing.
- You spend a lot to time deciding whether or not to go back to school to write, and then don't.
- You think all the drama in your life might make a good story some day.
- You are frustrated, blocked, and generally too ticked off to get out of your own way.

Read about writing, then do it. Sit in the café, relax for a few minutes, and then do some writing. Clean up your relationship dramas so you can meet your deadlines.

Once you make your way into an editor's stable of freelance writers, you won't have to pitch as often because they'll come to you with assignments—and as a bonus, you'll know what they want from you and be used to their editing process.

—LINDA FORMICHELLI

Of particular importance as you look for a bigger yield from past writing gigs are what I call "warm leads."

Warm leads are the editors you've already worked with who like and publish your work. Continue serving these editors.

This is your bread-and-butter writing and can bring you more money if you can stop castigating yourself for not publishing somewhere else each and every time, and publish where you used to publish more at the same time you continue to expand your publishing horizons.

Who should you write for? Keep an ongoing list of your top ten editors and cultivate stronger relationships with them. Make the most of each and every relationship by listing their editorial calendars, keeping their writer's guidelines handy, and supplying them with a steady stream of articles.

PUBLICATION	EDITOR NAME / TITLE	E-MAIL ADDRESS / WEBSITE URL	GOT EDITORIAL CALENDAR/WRITER'S GUIDELINES?

Do something. If it works, do more of it. If it doesn't, do something else.

—FRANKLIN D. ROOSEVELT

Of all of the creative inspiration I've been exposed to over the past few decades, no advice is more prevalent than "Do nothing, then you'll become inspired, and then you'll know what to do."

But this advice is misguided. Because doing nothing without intending to accomplish something will yield you nothing. If you want to accomplish something, you have to clarify your objectives and take concrete actions toward your goals.

When we are heading steadfastly toward a goal and we take a break and do nothing, that's when we are often rewarded with inspiration or just the right solution to a problem. But earnest focus needs to come before inspired epiphanies.

So if you want to become more productive, don't do nothing; do something. And if you don't know what a good direction might be, ask someone who knows.

Temper any advice that suggests constant pursuit of doing nothing with a larger amount of doing focused work. After you break the tension, that's when the epiphanies will come. Between the tension of doing and not doing, breakthroughs happen, not from a life of careless aimlessness.

Therefore, if you are a doer, or an over-doer, you may need to take a break. Plan regular breaks and vacations that will help you balance not doing with all of your doing.

But if you are not doing enough, your remedy is going to be more intentional action. There are some people who have no trouble whatsoever doing nothing. They tend to gravitate to that set point without the pressing structure of obligations and responsibilities.

If you are already productive and you want to stay productive, intersperse more breaks in your workday. And if you are not productive enough, set more concrete goals and work toward them. And don't take breaks until you have earned the reward.

Referrals are very powerful. When I refer you, I give a little bit of my reputation away. If you do a good job, my friend that hired you is pleased. But if you do a bad job, that reflects badly on me. People forget that.

—IVAN MISNER

Okay, let's not pretend it isn't helpful to get a personal introduction—it is!

However, if you are not as professional and poised as you can be, even a personal intro won't get you a gig.

But I'm going to assume that you are taking care of your side of the street. You're reading the books, taking the classes from people in the know, and not just scanning blogs and then demanding attention and respect you have decided you deserve.

Referrals tend to happen in casual ways when you are open to them and prepared to act on them. Let's say your friend Susan shares that she is working with an editor you'd like to work with. You think about it for a moment and decide you're really not ready to work with that editor. You could still say, "Hey, do you think you could give me a referral some time, when I'm ready and I've done my due diligence?"

Your willingness to do your due diligence is what every person who can give you a referral wants to hear.

Here's what they don't want to hear:

"Hey, wow, you are really making some good money from that editor. Can you hook me up so I can get in on some of that? I could really use the money."

Yikes. Now you sound like a desperate person who is going to stalk my client.

So, sure, consider who you know, and who they know, and whether it's wise for you to approach them for a referral. But don't go referral crazy and don't lean on any single one of your professional colleagues too much for referrals.

Anyone can write someone else's name at the top of a cover or query letter, but a personal referral from a writer the editor already respects can carry a lot of weight and cut through the slush. The connection you use is doing you a big favor—and one day you will be that connection for someone else.

DIG UP CONTACTS

> *Successful people—whether freelance writers or professional atheletes—have one thing in common: focus.*
>
> —ROBERT LEE BREWER

If you are going to be pitching frequently, it's always a good idea to keep market guides handy. *Writer's Market*, *Writer's Market* online, and *Wooden Horse* Magazine Database are good choices for starters.

Not only do market guides contain most of the pertinent info that you need organized in a way that makes sense to freelancers, they summarize writer's guidelines and sometimes even editorial calendars, which can be extremely helpful.

Wooden Horse Magazines Database is more expensive than *Writer's Market* so you may want to try the nickel tour, which costs $1.99 for a twenty-four-hour subscription. Even if you only pop in a couple of times a year, that's less than five bucks for helpful, up-to-date information.

If you are not finding contact info that you need in your usual market guides, go straight to the source instead.

> **Step One:** Find a phone number that reaches the publication (whatever one you can find is fine; people don't usually mind transferring you or giving out the correct extension).
>
> **Step Two:** Write down your questions and get your pitch notes in front of you (just in case you are asked to pitch verbally!).
>
> **Step Three:** Dial the number, get the right department, ask for contact information, and take detailed notes.

Keep your phone interactions brief and professional. The more prepared you are, the more professional you will feel. Avoid "winging it" until you feel confident enough to do so. If phone pitching is not your strong suit, that's okay. Just get the info you need and send your work via e-mail.

SOME BASICS QUESTIONS TO ASK SWIFTLY:

- Editor's name, correct spelling of name, and gender (if unclear)
- Editor's title and correct spelling of title
- Address, e-mail, and phone extension (if they'll tell you)
- Other pertinent questions you might have like, "Do you have writer's guidelines available? Do you have an editorial calendar for freelancers?"

104
BULLDOZE THE IVORY TOWER

A pedestal is as much a prison as any small, confined space.
—GLORIA STEINEM

If you are in this writing game for literary greatness, maybe you need to come down out of your ivory tower and start fraternizing with the rest of us.

We all have to accept, sooner or later, that writing is not the only art involved in the writing life. There is an art to all aspects of the writing life: writing, selling, focusing, lifelong learning, and self-promotion.

There is literary appreciation and there is literary snobbery. The former is cool. The latter is distasteful. If you are such a snob that you won't even think about selling, focusing, learning, or self-promotion, you are likely blocking yourself from potential growth.

On the other hand, don't go overboard. If you are so busy selling, specializing, learning, and networking that you can't create and sustain solid writing, you are cutting off one foot at the sake of the other.

Have good taste. The world benefits from good taste. Create quality art. But don't lord over the rest of us.

The art of the writing career is when quality writing is crafted for the sake of integrity and shared, promoted, and discussed among an expanding audience. You can't participate in the process if you are looking down from up on high.

So don't just come down from your ivory tower, avoid the stairs leading up there in the first place. You can write without being superior. Snobbery is not a professional career requirement.

And remember when you encounter someone who is swimming in snobbery, she is probably just nervous or afraid of what might happen if she lets down her hair.

So prioritize writing, value your writing especially, and put your career at the top of your priority list. But don't forsake the rest of the mundane roles writers play in life. Or you may wake up one day, peer out the window, and discover it's a long way down.

QUERY WELL

In today's Zeitgeist, pitching skills are crucial to the business of writing. Yet few writers know how to pitch.

—KATHARINE SANDS

Much can be gleaned from a quick read of a professional sales letter. Everything you don't say is there between the lines. What's evident is: your level of professionalism, your attitude toward gatekeepers in general (and this one in particular), the sophistication of your past professional experience, the appropriateness of conducting business with you, and your established status beyond this exchange.

To illustrate what I mean, here's the rundown on what a typical query letter communicates.

GREETING

The way a query letter says hello is with simple, professional-quality formatting. If an agent or editor can see at a glance that you have sent a long, rambling correspondence, that's it. Your time is up. Your inquiry will go unread. Open your query with a strong, clear, brief greeting instead.

CONNECTION

If an agent or editor is going to decide to take the time out of a busy day to review your inquiry, you will want to make a quick, sincere connection. You can do this by dropping the name of a mutual acquaintance or complimenting the recipient's recent work (something you like about his publication(s), past acquisitions, or his track record).

MEAT

Make your pitch in context. The meat of your offer contains a quick thumbnail description of the specs (length in words, form of writing, and where/how it fits in the scheme of the publication/portfolio of the recipient). Give a sample of the work, either in summary form or by sharing an excerpt.

EXPERIENCE

If everything is in alignment thus far, the agent or editor will look at your bio to confirm what she has already decided: that you either have or don't have what she is looking for.

CLOSE THE SALE

The best sales letters assume the sale will be made—without sounding arrogant. They end on an up beat, with the expectation of a positive conclusion. A sale should never be closed on a pushy or inconsiderate note. The appropriate attitude is always being of service without coming off as servile.

TRY HARDER

I like skin that is just about to break out in glistening sweat.

—TWYLA THARP

I've noticed three consistent qualities of writers who get their words into print. Here are the three *F*'s of writing-for-publication success (which have worked just as well for me as they have for my students).

FOCUS: Do you think homing in on one goal at a time will be the death of your creativity? It won't. I've found that the discipline it takes to focus on one goal at a time is the key to every single writing success, large or small. You can't write well if you can't or won't focus on one project at a time.

FOLLOW-THROUGH: Nothing is finished until it is delivered. You've got ideas galore and you can finish publishable work, but if you let fear stop you from hitting "Send" your words won't get into print. Get better at putting your words in front of decision makers and letting go of the outcome. You will increase the odds of a favorable outcome if you do.

FORGET ABOUT TALENT: I don't prefer working with "talented" writers because I find they are more focused on getting strokes than motivated to work hard on to the next piece of writing. Show me an industrious writer who knows how to keep moving forward and I'll show you a writer who is going to get published.

If you focus, follow through, and forget about talent, you will succeed as a writer. It's that simple.

If you can't focus to save your life, can't ever finish projects, and just know you are more talented than everyone else, you're going to try the patience of others. On the other hand, everyone enjoys working with a humble, thorough finisher.

Do what you need to do to make those words describe you.

PROSPECT FROM YOURSELF

Writing becomes real when it has an audience.

—TOM LINER

The first thing we need to ask ourselves is this: *What is the richest well of material for me to draw on in seeking publishable ideas?*

Before you try to nail down a specific market, have a broader direction in mind. Do you want to write for parents, travelers, or budget balancers? The trick when you want to speed up the time from writing to publication is to write for others who are most like you.

Why? Because if you don't already have clips from national publications to demonstrate your writing abilities, you may still be a good person to execute original and timely ideas that match the publication because you are a member of the tribe.

You can use keywords to drum up the best publications to choose from.

My four keyword roles from chapter twenty were: writer, mother, wife, teacher.

What are some keyword roles for you? Go back to chapter twenty and redo the exercise, if necessary.

1. Write one keyword in the center of each box in smallish print. Around each word jot down any pertinent credentials, published clips, education, professional experience, and personal experience you have to back up that expertise. Write small and squeeze in as much as you can.

2. Brainstorm four different ideas at one time to see which of your keyword roles has the most potential. Use the four boxes like the ones below for four keyword roles.

Example: Mother	Example: Wife
Example: Writer	Example: Teacher

3. The boxes that end up jam-packed with credentials are your most persuasive topics. Those are the ones you'd want to write first because you have the most experience to back them up, even if the experience is largely personal experience.

I must govern the clock, not be governed by it.

—GOLDA MEIR

Time is elastic.

If you think it controls you, you lose.

When you can make time fly by with your ability to serial focus, you can focus on a project, take a break, then focus on another, then focus on another and another. When you can spend a day this way, you'll be writing successfully.

Everything falls into place when you sit down, clear your mind, and focus your attention where you need it to be.

- Set a timer. If you are having trouble getting started, set a timer to kick you into action. Use a timer on an ongoing basis if it helps. If you have a lot to do in a short time, reset the timer over and over and get the writing done in short, timed bursts until your daily work is completely done.
- Kick up some dust. Put your sneakers on and take a ten- or twenty-minute jaunt. The ideas will be flowing in no time. Then, quick, get back to writing.
- Use the other side of your brain. If you are feeling stuck and glum, pull out your sketchpad and some colorful markers and start doodling. Your inner child probably needs a hall pass.
- Say anything. Get out your smartphone and record yourself talking your way through an idea. You can babble until you come up with the point. Or try interviewing yourself. Once you know the point you are trying to make, record it.
- Answer this question. When you are stuck or the writing isn't going the way you'd like, ask yourself, "What am I really trying to say?" Then answer that very question in your writing. "What I'm REALLY trying to say is _____." Fill in the blank. Then run with it. Next time you are stuck, ask the question again. It works every time.

I learned that we can do anything, but we can't do everything—at least not at the same time.

—DAN MILLMAN

Organize your published clips in a notebook using clear plastic sleeves separated with section dividers by month or season. This can help you visualize the best timing for your reprint submissions. In other words, if it's summer now, take a look at your winter clips. Could you brush any up and resubmit them? Could you come up with new ideas based on old ideas?

Once you have an article published, ask your editor how far ahead he likes to receive new pitches. Incorporate this into your calendar so you can send regular pitches, possibly even a few ideas at a time.

Remember, when it comes to pitching and submissions, it's always better to be early than late. For example, Mother's Day comes around once a year, so if you miss the boat on a Mother's Day article, you'll have to wait until next year or try to find another tie-in or rewrite your article to take out the tie-in altogether. Plan ahead!

Use these timing rules of thumb to note when to submit articles you published last year as well as new work, and you will make most efficient use of past and present article ideas.

NEWSPAPERS (AND NEWSPRINT MAGAZINES)
- Daily papers: Pitch one month ahead, especially if you are a new writer to that editor.
- Weeklies: Pitch two months ahead, ditto above.
- Monthlies: Pitch three to four months ahead, as these editors often carry over articles that almost made the cut from the previous year. You want to get their attention with something fresh before they pull that file back out.

MAGAZINES (GLOSSIES)
- Regional: Pitch six months ahead.
- National: Pitch one year ahead, no matter how dreadfully early that feels. Or strictly follow the advice given in *Writer's Market*. Remember to err on the early side.

ONLINE PUBLICATIONS
- Pitch one quarter in advance (or three months ahead). In other words, look ahead to the next season and pitch for that, unless guidelines specify something different.

10

DIG DEEPER, SAY MORE

Quality is never an accident; it is always the result of intelligent effort.
—JOHN RUSKIN

A scattered mind has trouble going deep enough to write anything worth reading. Therefore, it's very important to get in the habit of creating quality every time you write. And the key to quality is depth. So get ready to dive deeper.

A lot of times when we study a topic and get very immersed in it, we leave out key persuasive points until we talk about it to other people and all the key points come tumbling out. So, before you start wondering if your story is finished, put on your editor hat and answer the questions below.

WHY THIS IDEA?	KEY POINTS IN MY QUERY:	POINTS TO ADD/EXPAND:
WHY NOW?	KEY POINTS IN MY QUERY:	POINTS TO ADD/EXPAND:
WHY SHOULD I WRITE IT?	KEY POINTS IN MY QUERY:	POINTS TO ADD/EXPAND:

TOSS A CRUMMY HEAD SHOT

You don't want the look of an amateur—you're a professional all the way. A great head shot is key to presenting exactly the right image to the world—whatever you want that image to be.

—RACHELLE GARDNER

Let's demystify head shots. They don't need to be intimidating. What is that member of the media or program organizer really asking for when she asks for a head shot?

A head shot is simply a picture that is mostly composed of your head, from the middle of your chest to the top of your head, with some space all around your head and shoulders.

The background should be simple, abstract, or out of focus to keep the attention on your smiling face. And you should be looking at the camera. If you want to keep a few photos where you are looking away from the camera, that's fine. But keep one where you are looking directly at the camera on hand, too. The viewer wants to look you in the eye.

Your photo does not have to be taken by a professional. But it does have to be professional quality. This means good-quality light, saturated colors, and nothing distracting going on.

Getting a professional-quality head shot is the best course of action. It means that you respect the people you work with enough to deliver what they ask you for. It means you consider yourself a professional and you take yourself and your career seriously.

Sure, a professional-quality head shot costs a couple of hundred bucks. But at some point, that's going to be money well spent because of all the ways your smiling face can expand your visibility and further your writing career.

It's important to respect other people's time. If someone asks you for a head shot, will you be able to send one they can actually use in the next five or so minutes? I hope so.

As a journalist, the details always tell the story.

—JAMES MCBRIDE

Here's a query-ready checklist for you. When you can say "yes" to all of these, you are ready to query!

___ Did I read the magazine, notice where my idea and experience connect with a current issue, and point this out explicitly in my query?

___ Have I checked my bio against the bios of those who already write for this publication and found my experience is a good match?

___ Do I feel a strong sense of "Yes" about this idea, at this time, with my experience, for this editor, in this publication?

___ Do I believe that there is an absolutely perfect publication out there for my story, and I just haven't found it yet?

___ Am I calmly confident that I can pitch, write, and fulfill this assignment?

___ Is that confidence clear from what is written on the page of my query?

___ Have I found a natural audience for my expertise with the possibility of future gigs?

___ If my initial idea isn't accepted, would I be open to another assignment from this editor?

___ Is my choice of publication a writing-career builder (the next logical step up)?

___ Do I know someone who can give me a personal referral?

WRITE MORE THAN YOU READ

For most artists, words are like tiny tranquilizers. We have a daily quota of media chat that we swallow up. Like greasy food, it clogs our system. Too much of it and we feel, yes, fried.

—JULIA CAMERON

If you tend to read a lot and not say much yourself in the way of writing, why not make an effort to carve out more writing time?

Thanks to the Internet and blogging, the temptation to spend too much time in the shallows of quasi-thinking and quasi-conversation is omnipresent. The only way around this in the modern world is to stubbornly increase your insistence on quality reading experiences, intelligent conversations, and a firm, unyielding grip on your own thoughtfulness.

Deep thoughts come from deep processes. On occasion, superficial thought or conversation may provoke something deep within our thinking, but too much time spent splashing around in the shallows will cause you to think shallowly as well.

Admire deep thinkers of the past. Make a study of how the deepest thinkers today continue to plumb the depths even while participating in online media. The first thing I notice about these people is that they have a strong sense of what is theirs. They do not blithely hand over control of what goes on in their brains to peer pressure or social tyranny. And neither should you.

Like most things in life, balance is the key to maintaining deep thoughts in everyday life. Go ahead and participate in the every day; just because something is happening now doesn't make it shallow. However, be extremely choosy about what you read, the company you keep, and the quality of the conversations you have. If you do, you will never run out of profound thoughts.

And of course, remember that it's a good idea to take breaks from too much deep thinking and just hang out sometimes, too.

14

ASSESS THE REALITY

Four basic premises of writing: clarity, brevity, simplicity, and humanity.
—WILLIAM ZINSSER

When you look at your credentials, do you see a working professional writer or a beginner hoping for a shot at the big leagues? If you see a beginner, an editor will, too.

So it's important, once you start angling, to pitch the publications that are most appropriate for your level of experience.

Beef up your bio with solid credentials until you are as professional as the writers in the publication you are targeting. If you don't have clips to back up your skills, you may be able to write the story first and submit it in its entirety. If you are clipless, but convinced you've nailed your idea and publication, admit you are green and ask the editor to take your article "on spec"—another way of saying you'll write it and let the editor decide whether she wants it (with no obligation to buy).

If you conclude that you are simply aiming too high for your level of experience, consider daily newspapers or regional specialty or trade magazines. The editors of these magazines are always in need of fresh ideas and good writers to carry them out. You'll work your way up to the nationals, probably sooner than you think.

Consider pitching fillers instead of features at the outset. Seek out the short stuff written by freelancers or consider whether any of your feature ideas could be adapted as fillers.

There's one exception to all of these strategies: When you have a fresh idea and you know you can knock it out of the park in a query letter, an editor will likely say yes, despite your lack of experience.

Initially, though, think in steps: *First* I'm going to land an assignment for the daily newspaper, *then* a national trade publication, and *then* I'm going to use those clips to take my idea national.

Many writers would love to land an assignment for *O, The Oprah Magazine* or *Real Simple* magazine (at least this is what I've learned from my student questionnaires). But most of the folks who write for these publications are either established authors or seasoned professional journalists.

15

BUILD BETTER BOUNDARIES

I don't know the key to success, but the key to failure is to try to please everyone.

—BILL COSBY

Wouldn't it be great if all of the important people in your life were happy and healthy with impeccable boundaries and perfect manners?

As your writing career progresses, how you relate to others is an important consideration in accelerating or sidetracking your productivity.

So let's say you have a person, or maybe even two or three, who tend to drain your energy or ask more than you can give of your time. How are you going to handle this?

The best way to deal with this is to develop good boundaries while maintaining solid manners.

Among my students over the past ten years, I've noticed a pattern. Those who cultivate a happy, healthy life for themselves (and for their families, since I work mostly with moms) don't seem to have trouble getting their writing done. They give themselves time to practice the skills they wish to build and they naturally improve over time. They are also not impatient. They relax and enjoy the process.

Their focus isn't on pleasing or caretaking others. Why? Because they are busy tending their own lives. Pleasing and caretaking others can become an energy drain for writers. And writers who lose energy pleasing and caretaking can lose their focus to an inability to prioritize their own desires.

Respectful boundaries are an important part of a happy, healthy writing career. If you feel like you might be weak in this area, or that you could use some improvement, I recommend the following books:

- *Anxious to Please* by James Rapson and Craig English
- *Toxic Criticism* by Eric Maisel
- *How to Avoid Making Art (Or Anything Else You Enjoy)* by Julia Cameron
- *Better Boundaries* by Jan Black and Greg Enns

UP YOUR BEAT

A great attitude does much more than turn on the lights in our worlds; it seems to magically connect us to all sorts of serendipitous opportunities that were somehow absent before the change.

—EARL NIGHTINGALE

Something I've always noticed about experienced writers is that they have mastered what I call the "selling voice."

The selling voice is very distinct, and you can tell it comes easily to those who have mastered it. This convivial voice takes you warmly by the hand and pulls you along through a sales offer (or whatever) and doesn't let go until the close.

And by the way, the selling voice knows how to close. In fact, the selling voice bounces all the way from the beginning to the end of the communication until the sale is closed.

The selling voice uses phrases like:

> Sure I can.
> No problem.
> I'd be happy to.
> I can do that.
> Just let me know what you need.
> Thanks for the opportunity.

Most importantly, the selling voice is not phony. The person behind the selling voice is genuinely confident, upbeat, willing, flexible, and grateful. You can't fake these qualities!

You are not going to find your "selling voice" right away unless you have had some kind of sales training or selling experience.

But once you start finding it, how happy you will be. Because from there on out, every time you sit down to write an e-mail or a pitch, you will just bounce your voice right through it.

Which is a pretty far cry from the way most beginning writers approach any kind of selling experience.

Try it next time. Put some bounce in your voice and watch the acceptances pour in.

TRANSFORM IMPATIENCE

A garden requires patient labor and attention. Plants do not grow merely to satisfy ambitions or to fulfill good intentions. They thrive because someone expended effort on them.

—LIBERTY HYDE BAILEY

All writers become impatient at some point. They decide that they should be farther along than they are. Then they start looking around for people to blame. It's common for writers to want to be farther ahead than they actually are. So if you have ever felt impatient or you feel impatient right now, welcome to the club!

Let's say you are impatient right now. You've taken some classes. You've learned some skills. You've put them into practice, and you are just not getting the results you'd hoped for.

Here are some constructive ways to deal with impatience:

- Whatever you just did that didn't work, do it again, only better.
- Whatever you just wrote that wasn't strong enough, edit it and make it better. Then submit it to someone else.
- Accept that you are going to spend your entire career getting better whether you think you are already the best or not.
- Then set about getting better, whatever that looks like for you. If you are not sure what better should look like, get a review or consultation with someone who can advise you wisely.
- Get faster at recognizing your impatience and put it to work faster every time.

Whatever you do, be leery of surrounding yourself with other impatient writers who like to grouse and moan about how unfair the professional writing world has been to them.

You'll be better served by surrounding yourself with flourishing writers who are continually writing and continually pushing themselves to get better.

The remedy for impatience is always the same: Focus on process, not product. You can't take your frustration to the bank. The bank won't let you cash it in for a retirement account today or tomorrow. But the creative process you are investing in today just might be worth millions down the road.

18
HIT A RANGE OF TARGETS

Don't wait. The time will never be just right.

—NAPOLEON HILL

I have a student who started writing a neighborhood column for a statewide newspaper four or five years ago and has been hitting that target ever since. In the meantime, she has worked her way up to writing for regional and national publications and now has a book published. Yet she continues to hit that weekly target because it's always nice to get a frequent paycheck. And they really do add up!

When it's time to move on to the next most likely to publish your target market, don't shoot your arrows straight up in the air or they will come crashing back down on you. And don't aim your arrow straight down at the ground because I'm pretty sure anyone can hit a target that close. Lift your bow and point your arrow not as far as your eye can see but as far as you can still hit your mark.

Once you've looked at what you've published thus far, make a list of editors who have published your work and determine what the next, most-logical target is. Then fix your eye on the center of that target, take aim, and shoot. Continue to do this all the way down your list of warm leads.

Once you've got all of those offers out, you are ready to aim for a target a bit farther than those you usually go for. You will be hitting those faraway targets in no time, and still hitting all the targets you already know how to hit.

Don't use up all your valuable pitching energy on targets you are not likely to hit. Conversely, just because you start hitting big targets doesn't mean you have to stop hitting the smaller, easier targets. Develop a knack for hitting a range of targets regularly instead, and keep hitting them all until it no longer makes sense to do so.

19
CULTIVATE CONFIDENCE

Confidence is contagious. So is a lack of confidence.

—VINCE LOMBARDI

You can be confident without being overconfident. Behaving in a confident manner will help you find self-assuredness. It will help you become more certain of your own abilities. When you let your creativity flow, your self-expression will inspire others.

Every writer I meet is looking for creative confidence. I wish I could get my students to believe that the confidence will grow commensurate with their creative experience. I wish I could pull out a crystal ball and show them what their confidence will look like in ten years. That way, when I tell them to go ahead and write their way there, they would believe that there really is a place that they are writing toward.

But of course I can't. All I can do is encourage those who are brave enough to go for it to work hard and stay with it and not give up. And of course, the students who can summon their faith on a regular basis succeed.

Confidence comes from the word *confide*. The prefix *con* means *with* and the root *fidere* means *faith*. Therefore, confidence means *having faith in yourself*. For most successful writers confidence comes from and with experience. Even those who demonstrate more bravado than others often need reassurance when it comes to their writing. Of course, bravado is not the same as confidence. Bravado is confidence's little punk sibling, who can only gain true confidence with years of effort, not merely imitation.

Therefore, the key to becoming a confident creative is to act with faith until the initial fear and hesitancy you have felt starts to be replaced by confidence. You can't really be defensive or modest. You need to be bold. You need to write confidently in the direction of your dreams.

If you don't have anything at the end of the day to show for your efforts, you won't have anything to share, and you won't have anything to offer, and then you are going to feel frustrated.

But you can't move toward your creative goals unless you trust yourself and act from that trust. So don't fake it until you make it. Tap into your creative confidence each day and live from it instead.

Make the most of yourself, for that is all there is of you.

—RALPH WALDO EMERSON

Think of one topic you have a lot of passion for.

- Write down every single personal anecdote you can think of related to a topic.
- Write down every possible audience that might be interested in the topic.
- Write down every single tip you can come up with on the topic.
- Tweak the tips for each audience you came up with.
- Write down every single list of tips on the topic.
- Tweak the list of tips for each audience.
- Write down every single how-to possibility on the topic.
- Tweak the how-tos for each audience.
- Write down every single filler possibility on the topic.
- Tweak the filler for each audience.
- Write down every single essay possibility.
- Come up with more essays for each audience.
- See how many quizzes you can come up with on the topic.
- See how many checklists you can come up with on the topic.
- See how many exercises you can come up with on the topic.
- See how many startling facts you can dig up on the topic.
- See how you can connect the topic to time, money, life, death, success, love, friendship, self-worth, popularity, health, savings, learning, travel, career, group events, and personal contentment.

You can now write dozens of pieces for dozens of markets with dozens of slants on one topic and modify them for various audiences. Good job brainstorming.

2
ENLIVEN YOUR WRITING

If you can't play all the instruments in the orchestra of story, no matter what music may be in your imagination, you're condemned to hum the same old tune.

—ROBERT MCKEE

You are writing, and the piece is no longer thrilling you. Here are some ways to shake things up.

SHIFT FROM WRITER TO READER MODE. Read the piece out loud. Imagine you are reading it for the first time. Pretend, as much as possible, that someone else wrote it, so you won't take the fact that it may be thin and lame personally.

ASK PROBING QUESTIONS. Read each paragraph and ask questions about what else you might like to know if you were the reader. Write or type these notes in your draft to answer later.

POLL PEOPLE. Maybe your writing is suffering because your opinions are narrow. Are there other perspectives on this topic? Poll some people and find out. This is easy to do on social media. Just post your question on your profile pages and let people respond.

SPARK A DISCUSSION. If you really want to dig deeper, start a discussion. Get on a conversational social media site and toss questions out there and then respond to the folks who respond with more questions. Be sure to thank everyone for their time.

QUICKIE INTERVIEWS. Informal and yet effective, e-mail interviews can get you quick input from savvy people. Just be as formal or informal as the situation merits. Interviews can be as simple as an e-mail introducing yourself, explaining the purpose of your inquiry, and then asking a few questions.

SEARCH THE WEB. Try popping some of your questions or article keywords into a search engine. Just remember that this is only a small part of research—being able to search the Internet does not make you a journalist.

USE EXAMPLES. Examples bring your statements to life. They offer authority and proof. They provide illustration. They build your case. They are the picture and not the thousand words.

TRY AN ANECDOTE. A brief personal story is often a great way to get a piece of writing rolling or to keep it rolling. If your anecdotes tend to run away with you, try taking a personal essay class, which will help you channel that urge to share personal stories.

22
STREAMLINE YOUR SYSTEMS

I love being a writer. What I can't stand is the paperwork.

—PETER DE VRIES

Over the years, I have tried to become motivated by tidiness so I could enjoy the benefits of such an attitude. But I can't seem to overcome the natural way my mind works. That is, my mind honors creativity and process over tidy systems and careful mechanics.

I suppose all I have done is flip the left-brain rules on their head. Instead of trying to force my right brain to serve my left brain, which it won't anyway, I expect my left brain to serve my right brain, and somehow this works.

Instead of creating systems and then slavishly following them, I write first and then let the project drive the way I organize the results. And so it has gone over the years: I start each project with a real folder and a virtual folder, where I collect all the important pieces, so I can access the project when I want to work on it.

This keeps everything I need at my fingertips. I can "Save As" my drafts as I go in Microsoft Word, thereby saving the old drafts, in case I am concerned about losing anything to cutting and editing. I can proceed unhindered by system constraints and follow my instincts instead. Without any marching orders to get in the way, I am free to simply develop projects from wisps of an idea to completion.

As a result of this workflow over the years, I have several overstuffed hard drives and back-up drives. But it would never occur to me to drain them or even to spend time decluttering or organizing them. Unless I'm mining my own past work for fresh inspiration, there is always going to be the next idea, the next project, and the next gig to keep me moving forward.

You have to find your own project-to-project system of flow. The one that best works for you. Develop the habits that make you feel safe and supported in your writing process so you can continue toward your next gig without worrying what's going to happen to the last one.

GO FOR JUICY

The best advice on writing I've ever received is "Write with authority."
—CYNTHIA OZICK

One day I read an entire article standing halfway up my front walk. By the third paragraph of the profile, I was in love with the writer. He had done an amazing job getting out of the way and letting the subject shine through. The writing was like butter, melting on hot toast, only in words. I wanted the experience to last forever.

How do you create writing that captivates a reader's attention like this?

Here are a handful of ways:

- Pick a juicy topic. Fascinate us.
- What about the way you approach the writing is going to make an old slant gripping? If the topic has been written about often or widely, crack the topic open in a new way for us.
- Pick a topic that is already juicy. If it is something we almost know or think we know, take it farther, wider, deeper.
- Say something dripping with suspense. "I had to tell this story … It's the gift a writer waits for her whole life," said Heather Sellers in *Poets & Writers* Magazine.
- Include action. A slow motion car accident. A long kiss. A mysterious whack to the side of the head.
- Include critical moments. List them. Get them all in there.
- Include a great photograph, a superb title, and a compelling subtitle.
- When appropriate, consider personal disclosures to move the telling forward.
- Write until the entire piece feels perfect. Get every word to stand up straight and deliver for the overall impact.

Nothing exists in itself.

—HERMAN MELVILLE

The simplest way to match your article ideas to what editors want is to break your work into two columns: What the Editor Wants vs. What I Am Offering.

First, after you read and digest the writer's guidelines, fill in the column describing what the editor wants.

Get the guidelines and check the editorial calendar, and pull out a sample article from the publication that is similar to the kind you wish to write to use with this exercise.

After you have determined the kind of article the editor is looking for, fill in the column describing what you are offering. Break down what you are writing by content, form, benefits, and length. You can use this form either before you brainstorm your article or as a way toward brainstorming your article.

Once the two columns are similar enough, you can eventually make a sale. If you can't get the columns to line up, try to match your piece elsewhere.

Their published article/what editor wants:	My article idea/what I am offering:
Pub. Title:	Pub. Title:
Article Title:	Article Title:
Subtitle:	Subtitle:
Synopsis sentence:	Synopsis sentence:
Lead:	Lead:
Body of article:	Body of article:
Format:	Format:
Tone:	Tone:
Topic:	Topic:
The Five W's:	The Five W's:
Who is it about?	Who is it about?
What is it about?	What is it about?
When is it taking place?	When is it taking place?
Where is it taking place?	Where is it taking place?
Why is it taking place?	Why is it taking place?
How is it taking place?	How is it taking place?
How many quotes/experts/sources?	How many quotes/experts/sources?

HEAL THYSELF

With sixty staring me in the face, I have developed inflammation of the sentence structure and a definite hardening of the paragraphs.

—JAMES THURBER

One of the best parts of summer is that it inspires us to get outside and get some fresh air, which can be a boon to our writing.

Joyce Carol Oates is one of the most prolific writers of all time. But writing and teaching are not the only things she is passionate about. She is also a prolific runner.

In an essay in *The New York Times* she wrote, "Running! If there's any activity happier, more exhilarating, more nourishing to the imagination, I can't imagine what it might be."

Here's a list of simple activities you can do outside that are complementary to writing because they allow you to think your own thoughts while moving your body at the same time.

GARDENING: You don't need a garden of epic proportions. You could always start with a window box.

WALKING: A twenty-minute walk is a good way to exercise your dogs (if you have any) and get your heart rate up for twenty minutes.

HIKING: Don't feel like you have to go too far afield. Ask at your local visitor's center for a trail guide to your area.

BIKING: Don't have a bike? Check out Craigslist or swing by a neighborhood garage sale. So long as the tires hold air, you can get some good mileage out of any type of bike.

RUNNING: Running might be easier if you have a goal, like a 5K, 10K, or half-marathon and work your mileage up gradually.

Writing typically involves sitting, hunched over for long periods of time. When you change your posture you also change your mind-set. When you expand your horizons, you also expand your mind.

No matter what kind of physical activity you do, whether inside or out, getting up and away from your desk is not only good for your mind, it's good for your body, too.

WRITE FASTER

You don't write because you want to say something, you write because you have something to say.

—F. SCOTT FITZGERALD

Sometimes it's harder to write on a topic you already know well. When you "know too much," it can be difficult to know where to begin and how stay on topic.

On the other hand, specialists who can regularly mine their expertise and provide a steady stream of articles on the cutting edge of their topic will always be in demand. This worksheet can help get you started:

My great idea or topic:

The main points of this idea according to me:

Three specifics other people *don't already know* about this topic:

Which audiences would most like to hear about these insights?

Which specific publications could you target (that serve these audiences)?

Look for three shocking aspects of this idea that might provoke a member of the audience to say, "Holy cow, *really*?"

Three (real, live) expert sources you will consult before you start writing (don't skip this):

This idea would make a great ... (brainstorm possible titles or angles):

Tip:
List of tips:
Fillers/factoids:
How-to:
Short essay:
Mini interview/mini profile:
Quiz:
Table (e.g., dos and don'ts):
Photo:
Other idea:
Possible sidebar resources for this topic:

MONITOR YOUR ATTENTION

The best time for planning a book is while you're doing the dishes.

—AGATHA CHRISTIE

Downtime becomes a powerful productivity ally after you are already productive. The writing can show you the way, when you let it.

Strive for focus. Focus comes from repeated writing practice. Learn to love the state. You'll know you are focused because time will fly by. You will be immersed in your work. You will love it or hate it but you will be doing it.

When you are focused, and working, all is well. Green light. Full steam ahead.

When you are hung up, you are getting either a yellow light or a red light. You can't make decent progress. You might be spinning your wheels or wasting your time, which might be better spent on another project or paying bills or making a grocery list, for that matter.

When you are focused, your attention is one place only: on your work.

When you are distracted, your attention is everywhere and anywhere else. It is looking for things to get hooked on and tangled up in that don't involve your work.

Stop staring out the window and write. A walk in the woods might sort out where and how you are stuck. But then again, it might just be time you could have used writing.

Focus is a relaxed state. Distraction is an anxious state.

The difference between a focused writer and a distracted writer is this: When you are focused, you are able to move forward on a project in a loose, laid-back fashion. When you are distracted, you can't get out of your own way.

The way many writers talk about writing, you'd think all writers do all day is stare out the window, lollygagging their way through life, and somehow—magically, perhaps—the writing gets done.

That's a nice story. And it would be great, if it were true. But it's not the whole truth.

Work first. Stare out the window afterwards. Rest when you are not working. Come back to the work refreshed. And focus once again.

REWRITE FREQUENTLY

Half my life is an act of revision.

—JOHN IRVING

When you are a professional writer, you spend at least half of your time rewriting, likely even more time than you spend drafting new work. But the process of rewriting needn't be tedious and nitpicky. So go ahead, draft, cut, rearrange, review, tweak, tighten, and then work your way down this list.

Here are some general tips to getting to your best drafts quickly.

1. USE YOUR SPELL-CHECK, GRAMMAR CHECK, AND CHECK YOUR SPACING. Run all three of these checks a couple of times, once right after your first draft and once right before you turn your work in.

2. KEEP YOUR FORMAT SIMPLE. Single space. No all-bold or all-italic. Justified left. Put your title and byline in bold. Use Times New Roman, Times, or Helvetica as your font. Never use tabs or insert manual spacing. Forget any fancy formatting. Sidebars go at the bottom with the subhead, "Sidebar." That's it. No box or special bullet points. Remember that you will often submit in an e-mail, which would mess up any formatting anyway.

3. READ YOUR DRAFT OUT LOUD ONCE OR TWICE BEFORE YOU TURN IT IN. The places where your tongue trips and your voice doesn't flow indicate that you need a few more tweaks before your draft is really done.

4. HAVE SOMEONE ELSE READ YOUR PIECE BEFORE YOU TURN IT IN. Ask them if the article is clear and error-free. Ask them if they have any questions after reading it. (Your article should answer questions, not prompt them.) If the reader's concerns are irrelevant, that's okay. Jot them down if they spark any ideas for you. Get in the habit of thanking others for their help, whether you agree with their suggestions or not. A good standard response is, "Thanks, I'll think that over." When you are ready to edit, revisit the notes or suggestions and decide which ones you want to incorporate.

No matter how many drafts it takes you to get to crisp, clear writing, don't judge yourself. You will improve with time and practice. Who cares how many drafts it takes? Just get the job done. You'll get faster over time and with practice.

29
INTRODUCE YOURSELF

The amount of good luck coming your way depends on your willingness to act.

—BARBARA SHER

Once you have an established track record, one technique you can use to get assignments is the letter of introduction.

The letter of introduction is not ideal for every writer. For example, let's say you are basically an unknown writer without much of a track record and no specialty. In this case, I would suggest using a cover letter and eventually a query letter to place your work because your credentials are going to have a hard time standing on their own.

However, if you already have a long list of publications and a thick portfolio of clips, a letter of introduction can be a great way to get your pen in the door. If you have been writing regularly for national publications, but then you took time off to have a baby or two and you are getting back in the writing-for-publication game, you are a veteran writer who is looking for new gigs. So why not put that information in an e-mail and send it to some regional editors? Simply let them know that you are experienced and local and happy to take assignments. Then see what happens.

If the editor needs a better idea of what you can do, she will ask you for samples or specific pitches. The letter of introduction will get communication between you and an editor rolling.

What goes into a letter of introduction? Some of the same components that go into a cover letter, only in this case your credentials are the primary focus.

- Introduce yourself. Why are you interested in creating a working relationship with this editor? What do you like about his publication or work?
- What makes you a perfect match for assignments from this publication? Can you lay it out in a few sentences in a persuasive manner? Mention past experience that supports your case.
- Can you end the message on an upbeat note that convinces the editor to work with you? Can you highlight your availability and willingness to take assignments? Always close on a strong note.

If the answer to all of the above is yes, expect a response.

The successful and the newbie, the seasoned and the student, have days that dip down so low that the negative feelings can entice someone to pivot, make a change, leave writing, and pursue another life.

—C. HOPE CLARK

Prolific writers produce pages despite their circumstances. How do they do it? You can uncover the power of your own writing rhythms and routines in the daily schedule you already have if you really want to. You don't have to sacrifice sanity to find more time to write. You just have to be willing to surrender to the processes that work best for you.

Try approaching all of your writing projects in five distinct steps that spell PAPER:

PREPARATION
The curation process comes first. Toss everything you think you'll need into a folder, folder pocket, box, or plastic tub. Get your head into your topic by handling the material. Read, stew, ponder, and review. Accumulate material and play around with it until your aha moment comes. That's when you are ready for the creative process.

APPROACH
Consider the means of getting the project done that will work for you. Is it sitting and writing each day for a certain amount of time? Does it mean taking a walk with your phone voice recorder? What does getting this project done look like in the schedule you already have? You can make it work if you give it some forethought.

PROCESS
What do you want to say? What do you need to say? What wants to be said? What does the reader need and want to know? Journal or interview yourself on the topic to get initial thoughts down on the page.

EXECUTION
Organize what you want to say into a quick working outline or list. Having a working outline is good for your momentum and makes it easier to pick up where you left off. Working outlines change as your thinking changes. Let them.

REVIEW
What do you have so far? What do you need to do to get this project to the next level? When will this project be complete? How many more times will you need to pick it up and work on it to get to that point?

I imagine that yes is the only living thing.

—E.E. CUMMINGS

Your "inner yes" is that feeling you have when you have just the right idea for the right publication and you know, deep down in your gut, that you are going to get the gig if you handle it appropriately and take things one step at a time.

Often when I have this feeling, things pan out. Recall all the times you just *knew* that you had a great idea for the perfect publication and your instincts turned out to be right on the money.

You know what I'm talking about, right? Hold on to that feeling, because you're going to use it again and again and again as a writer.

If you feel a genuine sense of green light after green light as you ask yourself the following questions, go for it! Your aim is right on target.

- Do you feel an "inner yes" about the query you are working on for this publication, or are you just feeling lukewarm?
- Are you overly optimistic about your chances, rather than aiming for a target you know you can hit?
- Do you feel like you have a slim chance, but you are proceeding anyway?
- Do you feel like you might be targeting the wrong publication?
- Do you feel an "inner yes," but you are having trouble communicating why you are the right person with the right idea at the right time?
- Is it time for a rewrite or to share what you are trying to say with a supportive listener, so you can get it down on the page more clearly?
- Do you feel calmly confident about writing for this publication and able to articulate clearly and logically why you are the best writer for the job?

Yes begets yes. When you feel the yes, move steadily toward it and close the deal.

REPEAT SKILLS

That is never too often repeated, which is never sufficiently learned.

—SENECA

Every day, in schools all across the country, teachers are introducing new skills to students in the form of lessons that the kids will attempt and eventually master.

Usually, the repetition of practicing a skill is what leads to mastery. But somewhere along the history of education, repetition got a bad rap. The public started calling it "rote learning," saying this with distaste and making sputtering sounds, as though describing war crimes.

However, what I see in my writing students is that repetition is the path to success. And in my own career, repetition has been a boon, accounting for a considerable amount of my income.

If a writer never repeats a skill, she probably won't hang on to that skill.

If a writer repeats a skill, whether it's a writing skill, a sales skill, a specializing skill, or a self-promotion skill, he gets to keep the skill.

It's that simple.

So regardless of where you come down on "rote learning" for kids in school, I sure hope you will give yourself the gift of repetition when it comes to mastering any skill you need in your writer's toolbox.

Once a skill is yours, you can do something creative with it whether on the page, in making a sale, in creating a service, or in promoting yourself in a memorable way.

People ask for criticism, but they only want praise.

—W. SOMERSET MAUGHAM

When I have to respond to folks who are angling for praise, I try to remember something author Eric Maisel once said to me when I approached him to review one of my books.

He said, "The topic interests me, so I'll read it."

I thought this was an amazingly empowered statement. He would read it (I had asked him to read my first book) because he wanted to read it, not because he felt any particular obligation to read it, even though I had a referral from a mutual professional colleague? Brilliant.

What makes this attitude so empowered is that this arrangement is the opposite of the "I'll scratch your back if you scratch mine." It's also the opposite of "I'll swoon over your writing whether I like it or not, so long as you will swoon over mine." A lot of people experience both of these kinds of social pressure, and a lot of people have trouble dodging them.

But when Eric Maisel demonstrated the power of choice to me, I noticed it. And I wanted that much detachment myself.

Today, I live by his example. I have to because I get many requests for my time and energy on an almost-daily basis.

Reading on account of guilt is no fun whatsoever. In fact, for me, it's torture. And feeling pressured into being supportive or encouraging or generous, if you feel none of these ways, is draining.

If you feel needy about your writing, if you crave praise for it, if you hope your writing will redeem you, or make you feel whole, or worthwhile, you might be stepping on other people's toes trying to get them to respond in a certain way.

Even a writing instructor or an author or any other person who works in the biz should be allowed to decide what writing to read, enjoy, and admire.

I've learned to say no to peer pressure from other writers—even my former students. I like what I like. I read what I want to read. And that's a gift I give to myself.

Be generous with your time when you feel generous. The rest of the time, I hope you will give yourself the gift of honest discretion—otherwise known as the truth.

34
PRIORITIZE THE BOTTOM LINE

Don't be a time manager, be a priority manager.

—DENIS WAITLEY

If you want to be most efficient, keep things simple: write, earn, and prosper. An efficient writer is a profitable writer.

The best way to take care of your bottom line as a writer is to prioritize your time and spend the lion's share of your day on profitable projects. Here are six prosperity-increasing tips that put more money in the bank in the same number of hours you spend working:

1. MAKE A LIST OF PAID WORK VS. UNPAID WORK, AND UPDATE IT MONTHLY. For example, paid work is an article assignment or book deadline and unpaid work is bookkeeping or portfolio updating. Keep it on your computer or jot it down by hand monthly in retrospect. The point is to become aware of the percentage of time you spend on each.

2. PRIORITIZE PAID WORK OVER UNPAID WORK. This doesn't mean the unpaid work is not important or doesn't need to get done; it means that you get the paid work done first and then tackle the unpaid work. Do the paid work at your most productive times and the unpaid work at your least productive times. Or do unpaid work as a break from paid work—whatever works for you.

3. SPEND TIME WITH WRITERS WHO MAKE MONEY WRITING. Observe their work habits and mimic their professionalism. If they are too busy (making money) to spend time with you, sign up for their newsletters, read their blogs, or connect with them via social networking. When contacting successful writers, keep your expectations realistic. There's a reason they make the big bucks, and it's not because they hang out all day.

4. WHY NOT TAKE ON THE SURE-THING ASSIGNMENTS THAT PAY DIRECTLY FOR COMPLETED WORK? Tackle the assignments that pay directly. Forget about any kind of writing job you "might" get paid for later. Don't pursue writing for exposure alone. If someone offers you future money for today's actual work, carefully consider the offer. If you earn for your work, you are more likely to prosper in the short and long run.

5. SPEND TIME DOING WHAT YOU DO BEST EVEN IF THAT MEANS DOING A FEW DIFFERENT THINGS AT ONCE. For example, I don't only write, I also teach, speak, coach, train, and allow these efforts to feed each other and increase my overall value. I know another writer who writes, ghostwrites, and speaks. Another might write articles, books, and edit anthologies. Cobble your energy into whatever kind of work weave is going to serve you best. Your best choices will become apparent as you go.

Forget the lottery. Bet on yourself instead.

—BRIAN KOSLOW

Gather the following query components in a folder. You will need them not only to write your query, but also to follow through with the eventual assignment once you get it. This list came from a list I use to organize and inspire myself.

1. Choose a target market (get a copy of the magazine or photocopy pertinent pages).
2. Check guidelines (put in folder).
3. Study the market for freelance articles with bylines (mark them with sticky notes).
4. Choose an idea to pitch.
5. Develop that idea through comparing and contrasting with existing article(s).
6. Gather appropriate research, contact experts, etc.
7. Draft query (in a Word doc).
8. Ask at least one person to read your query and ask you questions that pop into her head.
9. Place folders where you keep queries in progress, preferably somewhere visible, like in a stacking file folder holder, in a designated spot.
10. Work on revisions and proofing over the course of a week.
11. Send.
12. Make a follow-up note on calendar two weeks after submitting.
13. If no response, send query to another market (re-slant, as needed).
14. Plan to query a new-to-you editor at least three times with three different ideas before you give up, even as you keep your unplaced queries moving on.

Revise a copy of this page to suit your own process, and keep copies handy to use as a checklist for your query-writing process. Perhaps you work in a different order or combine steps. Perhaps you have other steps you forget that need to be added. Perhaps you'd like to add words of encouragement. Whatever will help you query better and faster, add it to this list!

36

AIM FOR ESTABLISHED

Everybody wants to be somebody; nobody wants to grow.
—JOHANN WOLFGANG VON GOETHE

When will you *arrive* as a writer?

Never. I hope.

Or maybe when you are dead. That would be a good goal.

However, you will know you are *established* when certain things start to happen. I see them happening for many of my longtime students. Here's what *established* looks like.

- You present yourself as a professional; others treat you like a professional.
- You feel like a successful writer, and you can provide recent clips to verify that this is indeed the case.
- When you approach an expert for an interview, you get the interview granted even without a prior assignment because you are such a pro that you inspire confidence in others.
- You have dozens of pieces in print. You are starting to reprint your old work.
- Editors jump on your work when you submit it.
- Editors are quick to let you know that they would like you to stick around.
- You are starting to think about one or several specialties to cultivate over time.
- You have an eye on ramping your career to the next level, and you keep it there.
- You invest steady energy and a percentage of your profits back into continuing education.
- Your career growth excites and motivates you but doesn't prevent you from keeping your focus on serving others.

TEMPER YOUR DISAPPOINTMENT

How many cares one loses when one decides not to be something but to be someone.

—COCO CHANEL

The worst thing a writer can do is wear his disappointment like a badge of resentment. That is the first thing other people notice about you and the last thing they forget. You want, instead, to become the writer who bounces back from disappointment, stronger and wiser. Respond to disappointment with poise and dignity and remember that no one can take anything from you that is truly yours.

For writers, disappointments exist on a spectrum. You may become disappointed as a writer because you had unrealistic expectations and those illusions were dashed. Maybe you are having trouble getting published, or you got published, you thought, but then something went awry along the way. You could lose your agent or your editor, or your publishing company could go under or get reorganized.

Disappointments can be avoided in the future by staying detached from any outcome. Let's face it, if you could change the outcome of a major disappointment you would. But when you can't, and usually you can't, there is nothing else to do but accept the loss, put it in perspective, and move on.

Just because something unfortunate happens, you are not a bad person. Bad things happen to good people all the time. Just like with anger, a major loss is something that needs to be processed emotionally. You'll need to be able to talk about your feelings freely with folks who respect your privacy and are supportive. Trust that with time and adequate support you can get through anything.

I have seen writers experience disappointment and then bounce back so strongly that it makes you wonder if a little disappointment now and then might not actually be good for us. What you want people to remember is what you did next. You don't want them to remember your temper tantrum. Speak up for yourself, act in your best interests, but respond with class and dignity, as best you can, no matter what happens.

The five essential entrepreneurial skills for success are concentration, discrimination, organization, innovation, and communication.
                                        —MICHAEL FARADAY

At some point in every writer's life, solid organization skills come into play. And woe to the writer who thinks she can thrive without methods of managing the constant stream of information, data, trends, news, gigs, deadlines, and contacts.

Let your systems emerge from the way you work. Don't try to impose a system on yourself. These simple systems work for me:

PROJECTS

Once an idea or topic has some momentum, break out a folder or container for the material you collect on it. This could be a manila file folder or pocket, an accordion file just for ideas in progress, or even a plastic tub for each collection of material. I prefer file pockets to file folders, as they hold loose bits together better.

PROJECT CALENDAR

Get a wall or desk calendar just for your freelance work and goals. Make sure you also pencil in any commitments that take you away from your work day.

ADDRESS BOOK

Whether you use the old-fashioned kind or an electronic version, get in the habit of keeping tabs on editors, publishers, agents, and fellow freelancers.

SUBMITTED WORK

You need to keep track of your queries for tax purposes, so print them out and file them away. Check this file occasionally to see if editors need a follow-up e-mail reminder. Sometimes queries get lost or misplaced, or never make it to the place you send them.

ASSIGNMENTS/CONTRACTS

Print and file the e-mails that offer you assignments. Ditto a copy of every contract you sign. Keep these files for tax purposes. Rule of thumb: If you make over $1,000 a year freelancing you graduate from hobby to business. Keep track of expenses before this happens. It's good practice.

BACK IT ALL UP

If you are writing and selling articles, you are making a goodly portion of your livelihood from the stuff inside your computer. Back up your computer regularly, and you'll have one less major concern to worry about.

ACCUMULATE CREDIBILITY

The first goal of writing is to have one's words read successfully.

—ROBERT BRAULT

There are no shortcuts to lasting writing success. Once you start to experience consistent publication success, it's time to think about sharing your success with the world. Let your clips accumulate for a while and then begin sharing them and highlighting your professional strengths.

In their enthusiasm to succeed, writers often become confused about the timing of building an online presence. I don't think writers should rush into building an author platform before they have the writing and pitching skills they need to succeed as writers. When they rush in instead of first patiently accumulating clips, they often muddle their writing momentum. This is because creating work worth selling, selling what you create, promoting yourself, and building a platform are all totally different skills.

I have heard a lot of theories about how novice writers are going to upset the payscale apple cart for professional writers by gaining skills by writing for online markets ,and if your paying markets are online markets rather than print markets that's fine. Most writers work with a variety of types of clients.

I have seen content mills and online markets take gross advantage of naïve writers. I have also seen a preponderance of poorly written material that nobody would want to read online. Basically what I'm saying is: No matter which medium you write for you still need to write well. You will also need to write well when you build your platform and promote yourself.

Skillful writers are still getting read and paid. And as long as this is the case, I am going to continue to recommend that aspiring writers focus on the writing and selling strengths needed to succeed in this business before the development of specializing and self-promotion skills. The bottom line is that writers who can sell themselves will always succeed more than writers who cannot sell themselves.

Faced with a multitude of ways to spend our time on a daily basis, writers need to take the slower, steadier, more lasting road. Build credits, gain professional experience, and become trusted service providers to those who buy quality content first, then start thinking about how to specialize and position your online presence.

Success is a ladder you cannot climb with your hands in your pockets.
—WILLIAM JAMES

Not every writer needs or wants a writing instructor or coach. Some writers are excellent at taking what they've learned and applying it to test-drive new skills. When they get stuck, they seek answers to their questions. When they are ready to learn beyond what they already know, they are proactive about taking steps.

But don't judge yourself if you need more accountability and more support to grow. Some folks might say that writers who like support don't "want it enough" or shouldn't pursue writing if they can't "make it on their own." Yet, we are all wired differently. You can have similar goals to other writers and reach them in the ways that work best for you.

If an instructor, coach, or school is offering an experience that you think will help you achieve your goals better, sooner, or more professionally—and what they are offering matches what you specifically need and want at this juncture in your career—you can serialize learning experiences to help advance your career.

Approach mentoring relationships like a matchmaker for your professional needs and the experience will be win-win for everyone involved. Get as much as you can out of every learning experience by investing yourself fully in the experience, then integrate what you've been taught into your own process and put the skills to use.

Keep in mind that just as writers have personalities, writing teachers and coaches also have personalities. The best writing instructors and coaches put their own personalities in the backseat in the service of their students. They are not hoping to get students or clients addicted to them or to jack themselves up on a pedestal; a teacher's job is helping writers learn how to accomplish something in a more creative, expansive, or professional direction that will meet the student's goals.

If you stick with a series of teachers who are sincere, focused, and conscientious, you will make longer strides in the shorter run. Be sure to thank them for it.

4

STOCKPILE RESOURCES

If you stuff yourself full of poems, essays, plays, stories, novels, films, comic strips, magazines, music, you automatically explode every morning like Old Faithful. I have never had a dry spell in my life, mainly because I feed myself well, to the point of bursting. I wake early and hear my morning voices leaping around in my head like jumping beans. I get out of bed to trap them before they escape.

—RAY BRADBURY

If organizing is cutting into your writing time, stick with finding your writing rhythm instead. Go ahead and let the papers pile up around you, let the sticky dishes accumulate and the dust bunnies gossip about what a lousy housekeeper you are. You don't care—you are happily writing, racking up pages, and discovering your rhythm.

Take the money you will earn from selling all of your polished writing and hire a cleaning service. Then get back to work.

You don't need perfectly arranged office furniture. You don't need labeled file folders tidily arranged, standing ready for papers that may never land. You don't need anything on the calendar except items reminding you to show up elsewhere as you've planned.

Don't schedule writing time. Just write. Don't decide too far ahead what you will do, just do what you need to do now. Let the words for your next deadline grow. Keep writing until you meet each goal. Deliver your work and move on to the next assignment.

Here's a list of things that will start to grow around you as your writing career progresses.

- A growing file of reliable source materials you've used so far (article clippings, quotations, blog posts, tweets—sources that can all be reused)
- A growing address book or access to a targeted freelance forum (providing access to real-life people in the know)
- Class materials, notes, and assignments on whatever topics you have learned (leaving you with helpful resources for the future)
- A few magazine subscriptions (trade publications and those that serve the audience you serve frequently to keep you in the mood)
- A growing personal library of books on topics you often write about (actual and digital books)
- Association membership to the groups you belong in (writing professionals like yourself or groups of folks you serve)

Sameness is the mother of disgust, variety the cure.

—FRANCESCO PETRARCH

I am certain that focus helps new writers move forward, complete projects, and follow through with goals. But I'm also sure that variety is what has kept my writing career going, when it would have crumbled right alongside me, if I'd had to do the same exact thing every single day.

Ask any professional writers you know, and I can bet this is what they spend much of their time doing: updating databases, buzzing upcoming events, pulling old content into articles, creating a new presentation, and brainstorming their next book. They are also likely communicating with other writers, editors, agents, and publishing insiders. They are probably making decisions that will affect their future, running a business, and keeping themselves entertained while they do busywork.

Writers rarely do the exact same things every day. Writers today are cottage industries, of sorts. You are the talent, the idea person, the troubleshooter, the coach, the taskmaster, the producer, the trainer, the accountant, or whatever else you need to do on any given day.

The mutable quality of a writing career allows it and you to grow and thrive in directions that may have otherwise gone unexplored. If you only do one thing, you might feel crabby if the economy starts to tank in a way that tips income away from you. Change is inevitable; very few people write and only write in the present world. We are living in the gig economy now, we may as well face it.

But the good news is, you don't have to be merely a freelancer. You can be a *creative*. You can script your own career. You can write the soundtrack, the promos, and the copy. You can write talks, curriculum, bios, blog posts, and workshops. Despite how it may appear from the outside, you can be fairly consistent in the variety of things you do over time, in any combination that works for you.

Author Marc Acito embraces the "What do I want to do next?" kind of quality in his career that I think we all need to embrace. His career is growth-oriented. So far, he has been an opera singer, a novelist, a playwright, and a songwriter.

I was born to be Christina. Marc was born to be Marc. And you were born to be you. What kind of unique trail are you going to blaze?

43

EXPAND ON WHATEVER FLIES

The older I get, the greater power I seem to have to help the world;
I am like a snowball—the further I am rolled, the more I gain.

—SUSAN B. ANTHONY

Over the past twelve years, I have gotten the hang of certain forms—specifically, short list and how-to articles—simply by doing them over and over. I can crank one out in a couple of hours from start to finish, including the various drafting and rewriting phases, letting them cool off in between drafts, and sell them to regional parenting publication editors. The crazy part is that I still enjoy the whole process.

I teach other moms how to do the same thing. So what have I done that you can also do? I have mastered basic writing forms (list articles and how-tos) and from just those two skills, I can earn thousands of dollars a year.

I have maintained productivity in this area for the past twelve years. I have expanded on my old systems of writing and submitting, and learned things from other people's systems to create systems that work for me.

Any writer can use systems like those I use to create personalized writing habits to sell specific kinds of writing to specific kinds of editors. It works for short story writers, personal essay writers, or any other short form. Heck, it's really not that different than the way novels and memoirs are sold, if you're in the habit of writing longer forms.

Why don't you try to do the same thing with the kind of writing you'd like to publish?

1. You start by learning the basic mechanics of the writing forms that editors often publish.
2. You practice the forms until you become swift and skilled at writing them (at least on your good days).
3. You build up published articles and editor contacts over the years.
4. You keep circulating your work to get it in front of noncompeting editors who have not seen it yet.
5. You become happily, repeatedly published.

This is such a simple, straightforward approach, and it takes about a year for a seasoned writer to get the hang of it, and usually a couple of years for an unseasoned writer to get the hang of it.

44

STAY STRONG, CARRY ON

*I guess I started collecting rejection letters because I couldn't think of
any better way to organize a record of those to whom I'd submitted.*

—DAVID MICHAEL SLATER

You can't let rejection get you down. In fact, you need to get in the habit of barely letting it throw you at all.

When you get a rejection, it should register as just a little pinch, just enough to get you to take a closer look at what you are doing and what you did, but no more painful than that.

If you can see rejection as a waving flag trying to get you to refocus your energy on your work (instead of a slap across the face), you will be in great shape. Of course, it might take you a while to get from wherever you are to here.

If this is difficult for you, just try to keep rejection in perspective. If you can, you'll see that rejection of our writing falls into the high-class problems category.

Somewhere else in the world, someone just got killed in a war, someone else is experiencing the excruciating pain of chronic hunger, and a mother lost a child or a child lost a mother.

So keep rejection in perspective. Once you experience it, you have two choices: You can bounce back or you can quit.

I prefer the first course of action. Can you bounce back from rejection and get on with your next writing project? The people who succeed in the long run are those who do not quit in the short run.

So you got rejected? Bummer. I'll give you twenty-four hours to get over it. Next time I'll give you twenty-three. Until eventually, you won't even blink before you resubmit that sucker.

Do you have a roof over your head? Food in your belly? Are you surrounded by loved ones?

Then, so far so good. Be thankful for the privileged life you lead that allows you to write. Then get back to work.

In the grand scheme of things, rejection is just a speed bump on the road to your next publication. You might go over ten or one hundred before you succeed. Don't make a speed bump into Mount Everest. It's practically nothing. Carry on.

Put your ear down close to your soul and listen hard.

—ANNE SEXTON

Creativity is powerful. It can grow from something small into something very big. But don't be in a big rush to get there. Don't try to skip steps. Don't constantly try to be ahead of wherever you actually are.

If you get in your writing process and stay in your writing process, you will grow creatively. If you are willing to learn from your mistakes, you can become a more empowered person by learning from the ways you fail or flail.

But if you are constantly off and running, chasing down the latest "how to get rich writing info product," your head is going to constantly swim and your creativity is going to become tainted by other people's desire to turn you into sheep for their flock.

Focus on your writing, not on the ego benefits of writing. Create a body of work that others can appreciate. Get published as you go along so that your growing body of work will gain exposure to potential readers. If you want fans, act like a writer with a high quality of work and a strong work ethic who deserves fans.

As Tim O'Reilly from O'Reilly Media says, "Make good things happen." This simple phrase can apply to life in so many ways. You can make good things happen in your writing, or even when you are not writing. Try it out and see.

Make good things happen in your career, certainly make good things happen in the lives of those who are closest to you, and make good things happen to help others you meet.

Hopefully your work will also make good things happen in the world.

Will my work make good things happen? is a good touchstone question for writers. If whatever you are devoted to will make good things happen, go forward and prosper with it as best you can.

If your work does not make good things happen in a win-win-win kind of way, you may wish to choose a different course.

Let the beauty we love
Be what we do.

—RUMI

If you don't keep tabs on your writing history, who will?

I encourage writers to keep two portfolios: one as an official version for the public, the other as a more personal version that contains your early starts (those that might have indicated greater things to come, but which were not yet visible).

Compile everything you've written that has been meaningful, starting way back in the beginning, including a few precious or precocious pieces you wrote when you were young and foolish. Don't let anyone tell you that keeping track of your writing history is foolish or unnecessary. Simply compile your personal portfolio alongside your professional one.

If the task seems overwhelming, start with two large tubs, larger than you think you could possibly fill with stuff you wrote, and start sorting into them. When you are done sorting, you can decide the best way to showcase your work. For now, just sort. Enjoy the process but be quick about it, too. Don't get bogged down. Use journaling if a lot of old feelings overwhelm you or if important observations come up.

You may also need a third container for incomplete projects. You may find bits and pieces of incomplete projects and think they're unimportant. But I would suggest otherwise. I have noticed that writing projects that come around, go around. You may not have heard the last from projects you never finished. Keep them in their own container.

When you are through, put your personal portfolio aside for the time being and focus on your professional progress. Keep an updated portfolio of everything you have had published; include only those projects that you have followed through to completion.

I bet you learned a few things about yourself as a writer from this process. Take the time to write down for future reference everything you learned or noticed. Where do you want to go from here? Keep both of your portfolios updated as you go.

47

ABSTAIN FROM ENTITLEMENT

Strive not to be a success, but rather to be of value.

—ALBERT EINSTEIN

In life, I've learned that humility will get you everywhere and entitlement will get you nowhere. I'll describe two scenarios in each example. You decide which is an entitled move and which is a humble move:

1. You are an unpublished writer. You decide that you need to hurry up and make some money, so you don't pay attention to what editors want and need from writers. Instead, you decide to mass e-mail your query letters. Through a small number of positive results you determine that it will never be worth your while to serve individual editors and proceed to pursue a career based solely on mass mailings.
2. You learn in a class from a seasoned professional writer that in certain situations, editors don't mind being mass-mailed quality material. You research the appropriate methods of correctly mass e-mailing the group of editors, taking care not to include anyone who would not be a good fit. A few article sales later, you decide to make mass selling certain types of articles to certain types of editors a regular part of your writing business.

1. You are the high school intern for a monthly author series. You've put in six of your committed eight Sunday afternoons. You have some college scholarship deadlines approaching, so you decide that it's time to ask for formal recommendations in writing. So you send a gracious e-mail requesting a letter of recommendation.
2. You are an enrolled college student with a B- average in a writing class. Rather than ask your instructor for a written recommendation, you let her know that you used her name in an application and tell her thanks in advance for giving you a good recommendation if she hears from a potential employer.

1. You hear through the grapevine that a published author is recommending your e-book in his private classes. You decide that the world needs to know this bit of information, and so you publish the news in your blog without soliciting a quote, endorsement, or permission from the established author.
2. You are a recently published author. You hear directly from an author you've long admired that she is recommending your book in her classes. In your excitement, you are tempted to copy the words from the author's e-mail and post them directly onto your book's website. But after sleeping on it, you decide to write back to the author and request a formal testimonial as well as permission to use it to promote your book.

The world of reality has limits; the world of imagination is boundless.
—JEAN-JACQUES ROUSSEAU

One mistake I made when planting my last garden was not thinning the seeds adequately so that each seedling would have the sun, nourishment, and space it needed to grow. What ended up happening in the long run was that overcrowding caused the plants to become stunted. So I ended up with more, technically. But ultimately I ended up with a half-realized harvest because of overcrowding.

I think this is something for writers to keep in mind when building a portfolio of clips. It's great to grow ideas to the point of publication. And to do so we must sow ideas vigorously in the short run. But until we have more experience, we don't really know which ideas are going to flourish. And we never will know if we are continually trying to carry through too many ideas at one time.

So although I suggest that writers cultivate and nurture many writing projects from the idea phase, I think it's a good idea to recognize at some point that it's time to thin your projects so that each one has enough breathing room, support, and space to expand.

If you jam too much in, you might find that you are stunting the growth of the projects you pursue and that, in turn, your productivity is affected.

Sequences of projects are great because they come with deadlines to keep us moving along to the next project. But variety is also important for most creatives, and this is where time management can become more like a juggling act.

You may have a whole row of projects lined up and that's fine, but if you plan to juggle projects, each individual project is going to need to eventually stand on its own.

Keep each project manageable in size and scope so it won't drag you down or spill over into the time you need for your other projects. Whenever you have a project that is not on track to stand on its own, you might consider skipping it entirely in the short run.

And just keep putting enough energy into each project steadily over time and you will get them all done.

49

SUCCEED EVENTUALLY

If you're skilled, your wallet will be filled.

—YIDDISH PROVERB

No matter how challenging it is to find your momentum as a professional writer, you will know when you have gotten the hang of working in this business.

No matter how many times you have to train yourself not to take either no or silent rejection personally …

No matter how many times you have to catch yourself from slipping into discouraged thinking because you feel like you get one publication forward and two rejections back …

No matter how difficult it is to finally figure out how the shifting playing field works …

No matter how many times an editor you like working with leaves her position just when the two of you have achieved a rapport …

No matter how many times you meet a deadline, get an article proudly in print, and then discover a typo that you are sure you did not include, in what you hoped would make a great addition to your portfolio …

None of your journey is going to be perfect or happen perfectly. And besides, none of us are perfect, either.

No matter what happens throughout the ups and down and the many years of a writing career, the day when you get to the point where you truly feel like a freelance professional is a great day and a big accomplishment.

When you get there, I hope you will take at least a day to celebrate all the hard work that got you where you are.

I hope you will pull out your portfolio, pour over your best work, forgive yourself for less than perfect attempts, and find concrete ways to pat yourself on the back. Whatever you have accomplished thus far, let it be enough.

Most beginning writers (and I was the same) are like chefs trying to cook great dishes that they've never tasted themselves. How can you make a great (or even an adequate) bouillabaisse if you've never had any?

—DANIEL QUINN

If you have gotten this far in this book, I bet you are writing, even if you were not writing regularly before.

What's the recipe for your life that will get you writing and keep you writing?

How about sketching out a recipe you can improvise and update many times? Here's one I wrote many years ago.

WRITING CAREER

> Ingredients:
> 1 cup of great determination
> 1/2 cup of joy from the writing process
> 2 cups of stamina
> 3 dashes of empathetic spouse
> 1 heaping tablespoon of trainable kid
> 2 teaspoons of rolling with the flow
> Optional: Sleep, babysitters, and writing buddies
>
> Mix well. Beat around and around and around. Then beat some more. Pour into pan and bake at medium heat.
>
> Remove from oven while still hot and gooey on the inside.
>
> Let cool. Serve with ice cream. Enjoy!

Now you write your writing recipe.

FURNISH A HOME OFFICE

—DESIDERIUS ERASMUS

Sure, you can launch a writing biz for next to nothing. But if you have the resources at your disposal, launch yourself in style for under five thousand dollars. Here's what you will need to get down to business.

A RELIABLE COMPUTER. If you are going to be a professional, get the most reliable equipment you can. Buy a Mac because you can get about five years from an Apple computer with less crashing and therefore less lost content even with constant use. (Or buy a PC, but do your homework on its reliability first.) Most computers come with a hard drive large enough for any writer. However, if you go multimedia, you probably will want to purchase a larger hard drive and faster operating system. Get the low-glare screen to ease wear and tear on your eyes. To save money, purchase a refurbished computer.

A SOLID BACK-UP SYSTEM FOR YOUR WORK. Keep multiple backups of your work in multiple locations, so if one source falls through you'll have another. I use both an at-home automatic backup to a hard drive (the software to do this comes on a Mac) and an automatic backup to a remote location, but there are plenty of options out there. In a pinch, you can always e-mail a doc to yourself, assuming it will be auto-saved by your e-mail software. Make backing up simple and do it regularly.

A MULTIOPTION PRINTER. Every time I buy a new Mac from Apple I get a one hundred dollar rebate for purchasing a printer at the same time. You'll need to make copies once in a while, so go for a printer that also serves as a copier. Multioption printers also typically include a fax machine for when you need to turn around a contract quickly.

MICROSOFT WORD. Word is the most-often used software in the industry. Microsoft Office Suite comes with Excel, PowerPoint, Messenger, and Entourage, which can help you track your submissions, give presentations, collaborate, and manage your in-box.

A RELIABLE INTERNET CONNECTION AND E-MAIL PROVIDER. Think long-term when choosing a provider and go for the company with the best reputation that will likely be around for years.

ALLOW FOR SURPRISES

A good style should show no signs of effort. What is written should seem a happy accident.

—W. SOMERSET MAUGHAM

When I was a graduate student in fiction writing, one of the things we were told to expect, indeed to hope for, were the ideas that come through the writing process but are not preconceived.

These "surprises" tend to be the moments in a story that galvanize eyeballs. They are the parts of the plot that readers have to tell their friends about. They are the reasons that readers read: to be woken up.

And when we are writing, we know when we have stumbled on a surprise because it wakes us up, as well.

These surprises that arise from writing are not merely confined to fiction. Writers should be surprising themselves in every drafting process. But don't despair if no surprises come during the drafting process; they may come during the rewrite or editing process. In some cases, the surprise idea may not be yours, it may come from a first reader.

And when surprises don't come, something is wrong. Perhaps we need to loosen up our choke hold on the process and see what wants to come out. By the final draft, there should have been plenty of revelations that take the writer and the reader in new, unexpected directions. Don't resist the possibilities or you might miss your biggest opportunities.

But don't confuse muddled rambling with artful storytelling. Your editor doesn't want the job of correcting well-meaning confusion. Muddled ramblings are a draft. Artful storytelling is the crisp result you hope to eventually treasure.

A seasoned writer takes the reader firmly by the eyeballs and leads her along a primrose path of storytelling. The pathway of the story, no matter what the genre, should be crystal clear. The writing should positively drip with clarity. At no time should you mislead the reader and then call it art. Never keep readers hanging or leave them dangling just for the sport of it.

Surprises do not confuse. They delight.

TACKLE THE GIG ECONOMY

> *Gigs: a bunch of free-floating projects, consultancies, and part-time bits and pieces they try and stitch together to make what they refer to wryly as "the Nut"—the sum that allows them to hang on to the apartment, the health-care policy, the babysitter, and the school fees.*
>
> —TINA BROWN

There's a huge mythos around writing for a living. Rumors commonly heard about successful writers, which are true but irrelevant, include:

- You can work in your pajamas.
- You can hop on over and grab a coffee in the middle of the day.
- You can set your own calendar and make your own hours.

However, none of these benefits actually make a writer any money. So I would not dwell on them. And steer clear of people who try to lure you in with offers baited with such hooks.

The truth is that writing for a living is hard work, long hours, constant juggling, and a steady parade of deadlines to meet. If this does not sound like pressure you would enjoy, think twice before you give up your day job.

Writing is probably not for people who like a steady paycheck, set benefits, and a retirement plan. The biggest pitfall is the constant need to hustle to keep bringing in consistent pay.

Yet despite more former employees thrust into the existing freelance pool, most of the established writers I know are doing just fine. I think this is because freelancers are accustomed to adapting and evolving to stay viable.

Before the economic downturn, writers who were at the top of their games, earning six figures and making sure everybody knew it, were initially complaining the loudest. Prosperous times continue for rising writers, established freelancers with more moderate earning ambitions, and established niche cultivators and authors with loyal followings.

To a certain extent, the freelance life is survival of the fittest. All of the advice in this book is geared toward helping you run with the pros. If you want to grow a solid, steady freelance career in the gig economy, you will fare better with less stress if you can give yourself a year or two to ramp up to earnings you can live on. And even then, you will still always have to hustle.

I live in a small mountain town, Taos, New Mexico. Writers here hold readings. They get together in living rooms and small ca-fés and read to each other. They hold open mikes and poetry slams. They run off copies of their stories at Copy Queen, our Xerox establishment, and they mail them out and hand them out. They post their writing on the Web. Not coincidentally, Taos has spawned quite successful small presses, carrying the "just do it, just print it" philosophy one step further.

—JULIA CAMERON

Would your writing career take off if you lived in a more literary location?

How about if you visited one of the most literate cities for a writers conference or literary event?

What would it feel like to visit a place where the literary arts were better valued? Where newspapers were abundant, bookstores still proliferated, library resources were stellar, magazine circulation was high, and Internet resources were excellent?

Sounds like heaven to a writer, right? Actually it sounds like a city on the list of America's Most Literate Cities, which is created annually by Dr. John W. Miller for Central Connecticut State University.

Dr. Miller says that his study tries to capture a critical index of our nation's social health–the literacy of major cities. My writing career has taken off since I have lived in proximity of two of the most highly ranked cities in the study: Seattle, Washington, and Portland, Oregon.

Coincidence? I doubt it.

In Oregon, we have major literary events such as Wordstock and an arts and lecture series called Literary Arts. We have the world-famous Powell's Books and a statewide writers' association called Willamette Writers. All this literary love seems to ripple out across Portland and spill over the edges, where you will find literary happenings happily occurring in towns of all sizes.

Surely a writer can write anywhere, and should write anywhere and everywhere. But I think you should Google "America's Most Literate Cities" and check them out next time you plan a move. Certainly consider them when you plan to attend a writers conference or envision your future book tour.

STEER YOUR CAREER

The secret of health for both mind and body is not to mourn for the past, worry about the future, or anticipate troubles, but to live in the present moment wisely and earnestly.

—BUDDHA

If you balance what I call the big three—your accomplishments, your goals, and your to-do list—you will not only have a clear idea of where you are going; you will be able to get there faster.

WHAT YOU'VE DONE

What you have accomplished tells you not just what you have done but also what works. If you can take what works and duplicate it, this is one of the easiest ways to expand your success.

WHERE YOU'RE GOING

If you know where you want to go next in your career, you can figure out how to get from where you are currently to where you'd like to be next.

HOW YOU'RE GOING TO GET THERE

If you know what your goals are, you can break them down into doable steps and work those steps into your current schedule.

Build new goals on top of past successes. Create extra time for new goals by becoming more proficient at the tasks you already do that have become habitual.

The only time to drop strategies that are working is when you need to make space for a new activity and you just don't have room in your day. When this happens, drop the lowest priority and lowest paying opportunity to make room for a new higher paying goal.

It's pretty simple, really, though you may get bored sometimes continuing what you've been doing. You may feel frustrated that you are not getting where you'd like to be as fast as you'd like. But you may not yet possess the skills to get where you'd like to be. You certainly don't want to let go of any old profit streams until you have replaced them with new higher paying profit streams if you can help it.

Try to be patient. Meanwhile, think of it this way: You are building the staircase as you walk up it.

Action expresses priorities.

—MAHATMA GANDHI

What's at the center of your writing career?

I call it your "espresso." Your espresso is what you are innately good at, how you do things, and ultimately, what you contribute.

And how many different drinks can one person make with an espresso shot? Plenty.

For example, *instruction* is at the center of my writing career. That means the part of my work that I value most is the *instruction* part (often this is in written form but not always because I instruct in other ways, too).

If I were Starbucks, *instruction* would be the beans, and I would grind them, tamp them, and squeeze energy through them. The resulting espresso would be something I could teach.

I have instructed with articles, stories, books, workbooks, curricula, websites, e-books—the list continues to expand. Since my ability to instruct is limited only by my imagination and choices, I have pretty wide options of how to proceed.

My espresso is instruction because I am primarily a how-to writer. I am not saying I will never write anything else in any other way. I'm simply saying that I have a tendency to offer instruction. Know what I mean?

The onus is always on you to make good choices with what you offer—to mix the best of what you offer with other things that make what you offer more substantial.

You are looking for the best ways to serve up what you offer vis-à-vis your topics, your audiences, your time, and your publishing partners.

Long story short, when you start to offer something specific repetitively, things in your writing career start to become very interesting.

> *It's my experience that very few writers, young or old, are really seeking advice when they give out their work to be read. They want support; they want someone to say, "Good job."*
>
> —JOHN IRVING

After twelve years of writing for publication, I treat my writing a lot less preciously. I don't believe that every word I write is somehow sacred. I take pride in my work without feeling offended if it is edited.

I'd rather work with others to make my work better rather than merely pressing on alone. Why write mediocre prose when you could write better with editorial support?

Some writers may want to feel that they did it all by themselves. But we can all get farther faster with a little help from our friends, and those friends are often editors.

I love to see how much better my writing is in the long run after it's been through the content editors and copy editors mill.

I have an ego, certainly, I do. But my ego is not tied up in my work. I take pride in writing I have done well, but I also know that my writing is as good as it is because of having editors involved in the process.

If you want to write, you don't need to be a prodigy. You don't need to be a genius. You don't need to be revered by your readers. I am sure you will like having readers. You will likely appreciate it when they say that your work is _____ (whatever the intention is behind your writing).

I think it's smart to decide what a true compliment is for you. A true compliment is what you are hoping to hear. Hopefully it isn't that you are a prodigy, genius, or a literary god. Hopefully it is something real and true about how you express yourself that reflects your natural dynamic.

Learn not to take compliments too seriously. Say thanks and carry on. Certainly never let praise or flattery distract you from the work at hand. There's always going to be the next project to write, no matter how many rave reviews you received for your last project.

58
GO GENERAL

A human being should be able to change a diaper, plan an invasion, butcher a hog, conn a ship, design a building, write a sonnet, balance accounts, build a wall, set a bone, comfort the dying, take orders, give orders, cooperate, act alone, solve equations, analyze a new problem, pitch manure, program a computer, cook a tasty meal, fight efficiently, die gallantly. Specialization is for insects.

—ROBERT A. HEINLEIN

Writers' brains seem to work in one of two ways: They want to write about everything and anything, or they want to dive deeply into one topic.

Some writers are just generalists at heart. If you are one of them, you will never run out of paying opportunities, because there are always going to be publications and businesses that need excellent communicators to carry out a wide range of assignments.

A generalist concentrates on writing in a lively and engaging manner on any topic, for various audiences or a general audience. A generalist will write for any market, but typically for those that offer paid assignments consistently.

Since I am a specialist, I asked Gretchen Roberts for her insights into how generalists can make the most of their penchant for variety.

Here are Gretchen's tips for getting started as a generalist:

- **BE A PRO.** "If you're generalizing, you need to write well and be professional in order to stand out. Otherwise, you're just one of a slew of writers. Always answer the 'Why me?' question in queries."

- **DON'T START AT THE BOTTOM.** "Start at the top and work your way down market. If you start querying the bottom rung, how will you know if *The New Yorker* would have taken it? If your top market says no, go to your B-list, then your C-list."

- **PROMOTE YOUR WORK.** "No one can toot your horn like you can. Give us the details on your website. Spread the word with social media. Make sure editors can find you and your writing without a hassle. These days, they're busier (and more inundated with queries) than ever."

59
WORK-CATION WIDELY

As writers we do most of our work in the privacy of our own minds, but at some point all of us need to take a vacation—a working vacation—in order to recharge the batteries and open our minds to new perspectives, new experiences, and new landscapes.

—KEVIN LARIMER

What's a work-cation? A work-cation is when you combine work with pleasure. Since continuing education is a tax deduction for profiting writers, you can work, play, and write off at least a portion of the resulting expenses on your Schedule C.

One of the best things about becoming a professional writer is that you get tax write-offs. What this means, to a growing writer, is that you can deduct your continuing education expenses, which allows you to grow your business from your annual profits.

There are writing conferences in Hawaii, Vermont, and Iowa. Are any of these places you would like to visit? There are book festivals in Chicago, Washington D.C., and San Francisco. Do you have friends or relatives in these areas you'd like to visit?

Writing workshops with publishers, authors, and industry insiders take place all over the world, and often in exciting and exotic locations.

If you choose to be a hobby writer, you won't receive the same tax benefits. According to the IRS, the difference between a hobby and a business is the answer to this question: Is your hobby really an activity engaged in for profit?

If you intend to profit, and you actually profit, you can take tax deductions. If you don't intend to profit, and you don't actually profit, you should not consider your writing a business that is entitled to tax write-offs.

If you treat your writing as a business, you should make increasing amounts of money from your writing over time so you can prove to the IRS that you actually are in business and not just taking deductions with no real plan to grow your business.

So plan to earn and plan to grow your business over time. And be sure to schedule a work-cation regularly for education and pleasure.

Generalists should be the upbeat, positive people in the profession while specialists should be their grouchy, negative counterparts.

—KARL WEICK

Editors usually appreciate a generalist's flexibility, willingness to take any assignment, and ability to turn around a story on a quick deadline.

Generalists are by and large quick, flexible, and deadline-oriented. They are excellent time managers because they work on a variety of topics at one time. They break down multiple goals into complex to-do lists and manage to get everything done on time. Generalists are, for the most part, not as attached to their ideas, writing, and audiences as specialists.

A generalist typically has a restless mind, which means he becomes easily bored, and therefore likes to exercise a variety of interests and skills all at the same time. Generalists like to multitask, check things off a to-do list, and make deadlines and meet them. They strive to earn more money in the short run by working on many pieces at once. And they are good at pitching themselves and their skills. For sure, generalists know how to hustle.

In the beginning of your writing career, like a generalist, you will want to keep your options open. Even though I'm a big proponent of specializing in the long run, I've noticed that writers who try to specialize too soon have trouble finding and staying with one specialty, even if they can come up with a good, viable specialty topic.

The reason has become apparent over the years. There are so many reasons to write, and so many topics to write about, that when you are just getting started, it's natural to want to explore as many of them as possible and it's also good exercise for your writing skills.

But don't be surprised if, along your merry generalist way, you discover a specialty topic or two or three. Others may have a similar idea, but the person who writes on the topic most is going to end up being viewed as the more knowledgeable expert on the topic.

Hang around any generalist long enough and I bet you'll start to notice that she is hiding a specialty or two up her sleeve, even if she adamantly denies it.

16

SHAKE OFF A SLUMP

Don't agonize. It slows you down.

—ISAAC ASIMOV

Let's say you've been published. Perhaps you've even been published quite a bit. Maybe you have up to twenty clips, when at one time you had none. Hey, this is great! Congratulations.

And now, here comes the sophomore slump. The sophomore slump is caused when writing for publication is no longer new. Gone is the challenge of figuring out all the how-tos required to get your words into print.

You've been there. Done that. Ho-hum. This is getting kind of, oh, boring.

For many writers, the end of being a beginner can mark the beginning of the "not knowing quite what to do next" phase. I have been through the sophomore slump and have seen plenty of students face the sophomore slump, so I have two ideas to hopefully help you through it.

IDEA NUMBER ONE: CONTINUE WITH THE SUCCESS YOU'VE ALREADY ESTABLISHED. I know. It's hard. Because jumping through these hoops becomes rote. That's okay. If you don't repeat the momentum you've established, you will lose your writing rhythm and maybe even some of your confidence. So keep writing, keep submitting, and keep getting published, even if you are starting to feel that you should be beyond this stage (whatever stage it is) by now. Keep in mind that you are not alone. Many writers feel the exact same way.

IDEA NUMBER TWO: PITCH THE PLACES YOU'D RATHER BE. One of the pitfalls of the sophomore slump is not making enough time to reach out to the places where you'd rather see your work published. But if you work in a focused way on where you'd rather be, you are going to get there.

Stretching is a necessary discomfort for most writers. Seek challenges and let the freshness of each challenge energize you instead of throwing you. View a steady diet of doable challenges as invigorating you, not something to throw you off track.

Get a new rhythm that combines comfort first then stretching yourself. Repeat this virtuous cycle of mixing new challenges with old. Keep at it. Don't stop the old work as you wait for acceptances at a higher level. That's the kiss of death for freelancers. You may lose your momentum and your confidence.

IDENTIFY YOUR DYNAMIC

Happiness is that state of consciousness which proceeds from the achievement of one's values.

—AYN RAND

When I ask writers what is at the center of what they offer, some become confused. They think I am referring to their passion, mission, or purpose.

What I mean is: What is the *dynamic value* you continuously offer without straining yourself or thinking about it much?

The dynamic value that you offer can be perceived and sensed by others. Other people may be able to describe it better than you can.

It's not merely the value you deliver; it's also how and why you deliver whatever you offer.

And I mean what you already consistently deliver naturally and authentically, not what you hope to deliver someday.

To go back to my Starbucks analogy, it's the sheer variety of what Starbucks can do with a shot of espresso that makes them so brilliant as an enterprise.

They can give you espresso hot or cold. They can give you espresso with milk (or variations of milk). They can give you espresso with chocolate or caramel. They can give you espresso big or small. They can give you espresso straight, with hot milk, steamed milk, or just foam. They can give you espresso iced, iced with milk, or whipped with ice and milky stuff in a frappe.

Clearly, when it comes to what Starbucks can do with their espresso, they are not messing around. Right? They are going to give espresso to their customers exactly the way they want it, and this *concept of espresso customization* is built into their business model.

What you offer to others makes a big impression, too, or at least you hope it does.

What did you say your espresso was again? And what is the uniquely dynamic way that you customize your espresso to create value?

If you are not in business yet, or you are not successful in business yet, it's going to be difficult to answer this question because you do not have the results to draw on. But once you have been in business for a couple years, you will likely start to have some ideas.

BATCH RESPONSIBILITIES: PART ONE

For me, it's making a regular effort to work when I'm working, and not think about work when I'm not.

—KELLY JAMES-ENGER

What prevents you from reaching the goal of writing enough each day to accumulate enough pages to reach your goals over time?

Let me guess: the rest of the responsibilities in your life?

Here is a roundup of typical adult priorities. Start thinking about how to contain and batch them so you can write when you are supposed to write and do other things you need to do when you need to do other things, and not spend energy trying to do two things or more at once.

FAMILY & EXTENDED FAMILY

If you know that sit-down dinners matter to you, plan on having sit-down dinners most every night. If you feel seeing your family a certain number of times a year is not negotiable, plan your year around that. Think of quality family time as part of your daily, weekly, monthly, and annual rhythm, and then you can let go of family commitments during writing time because you know you have set priorities that take care of the most important people in your life.

PETS

Animals are a big responsibility in our house and they may be in yours as well. Since they can't care for themselves, think about your time with your pets in the big picture of your life and then weave their care into a typical day. A daily dog walk or time playing with smaller animals can become a relaxing, anticipated daily pleasure or stress release instead of just another to-do.

BILLS

Touch bills as infrequently as possible. I touch them once, when I open and pay them. I only pay them once a month, which saves me loads of time during the rest of the month. Whether you opt for paper or e-pay, streamline the process so that all bills can get paid in less than two hours per month and in one sitting, if possible.

APPOINTMENTS/HEALTH

You probably know off the top of your head what appointments need to happen annually, semi-annually, and intermittently, so go ahead and create a list of just health appointments for you and your family members for one year. Then take a look at your calendar. Does it make more sense to spread them out, or tackle them all in one week, when you don't have much else going on? Schedule accordingly.

Hard work's a good distraction.

—SCOTT WESTERFELD

Remember that song from the movie *The Sound of Music*, "So long, Farewell"?

Louisa sings, "I flit, I float, I fleetly flee, I fly."

Louisa is not the only one who does this. Writers do it, too.

We flit. We float. We flee. And we fly away to the next more attractive-sounding opportunity.

But what we need to do, if we really want to put down solid roots and grow our careers, is hold still and put the skills we have already learned into action.

But a lot of writers don't want to do this. So off they run to the next offer that appears on the horizon. Anything rather than actually hold still and work.

And I can tell you one thing from watching enough writers do it over the years, flitting will get you nowhere. Floating will get you lost. Fleeing will become a bad habit. And flying away to wherever the grass seems greener is an endless pursuit.

It's one thing to vary your work habits for variety, but it's another to habitually flit away from the work that is right in front of you. It's also one thing to float around when floating will expose you to potential opportunities. But fleeing just means running away because you are scared or overwhelmed. And flying is better when you have a destination. Preferably a tropical one.

In today's consumable knowledge economy, it can be easy to become addicted to restlessness and distractibility. Mind that you don't.

A better strategy is to put the skills you have learned into practice. Learn and apply what you've already absorbed. In this way, you will grow.

Or, at least, if you do get off track, come back quickly. I have one student who is a mom, who was completing a Ph.D. then took a full-time job at Sesame Workshop. She continued to work on her writing career on the side, never gave up, and kept coming back. No matter how busy you are, just keep coming back to your commitment to write.

We save the world by being alive ourselves.

—JOSEPH CAMPBELL

Here are a few more of those pesky adult responsibilities you might want to batch up.

EXERCISE
Join a fitness club or get a trainer if you are not motivated enough to stay fit on your own. But don't turn fitness into a major time waster. Keep it simple and you'll get in and stay in shape. According to the Centers for Disease Control and Prevention, adults need two kinds of weekly exercise—aerobic and muscle-strengthening—to improve physical health. Writers might need to add a bit more to balance out the ill effects of a sedentary lifestyle.

HOUSEWORK
Hire it out. There's already enough to do with dishes, laundry, and seasonal chores. If money is an issue, find an up-and-coming cleaning service that will accept copywriting services to reduce your costs. This strategy will save you a bundle and do wonders for your productivity.

VACATION/TRAVEL
Plan to get away no matter what your budget. Think through your year and consider not just the seasons and holidays but the way your work and lifestyle naturally create preferable times for travel and visits. Balance togetherness time with alone time, if you need it. Forget what the Jones family is doing and create a recreation plan that works best for you.

VOLUNTEERING/COMMUNITY SERVICE
Again, plan to do it, but make it as pleasurable and manageable with your busy schedule as possible. Even if you are a busy parent writer, you can fit in some community service, but only if you get on top of it and stay on top of it. I donate about four hours each month to hosting my local author series, and I chaperone my daughter's field trips as much as I can. All other donations I currently make are in money, not time.

CONSIDER SPECIALIZING

As soon as you connect with your true subject, you will write.

—JOYCE CAROL OATES

A specialist concentrates writing-for-publication efforts on a specific niche topic, usually one with a large audience. For example, a writer might decide to create a specialty in home, garden, and décor topics.

Specialists produce themselves and grow more visible over time. They are typically not just writers; they are also entrepreneurs, media spokespeople, and service providers. That's what specialists do today.

So when you're thinking about a specialty, think long term. Editors usually appreciate a specialist's ability to understand the subtleties of the topic, the jargon, and how to adopt that information for various audiences.

SPECIALISTS:

- Are typically experts on a topic or body of expertise
- Value depth of understanding combined with thoughtful expertise
- Focus on one topic or one specific audience
- Sustain a long-term relationship with their audience
- Are not necessarily quick turn-around writers

A SPECIALIST:

- Has a focused and probing nature
- Likes to spoke one topic into many formats (written, visual, audio, digital)
- Can adapt content to a variety of situations
- Earns more in the long run from one topic than a generalist
- Becomes adept at matching expertise to opportunities

EXAMPLE: DEEPAK CHOPRA

Started his career writing books on spiritual topics like *Ageless Body, Timeless Mind* (Harmony, 1994) and *The Seven Spiritual Laws of Success* (Amber-Allen Publishing, 1994).

What's interesting about specialists isn't what happens to their careers in the short run but over time. Today, Deepak Chopra does a heck of a lot more than he used to. Today he is his own media company and online superstore. Check out all that he has built:

- Deepak Central website
- The Chopra Center for Wellbeing
- Over fifty books
- Audio, video, and CD-ROM titles
- Training Programs
- Live Tour
- Classes
- A blog
- A radio show
- A newsletter
- Teacher training

Remember, your professional portfolio is not going to resemble Deepak Chopra's in the short run, but over time, just imagine what you might create!

FIND YOUR STRIDE

Don't go through life, grow through life.

—ERIC BUTTERWORTH

Let's talk about what it *feels* like to have momentum. How do you know when you've got it and when you don't?

YOU ARE COMMITTED. You have to make a commitment to your writing process just as you would to anything else that's important in your life. The promise you make to your writing is as daily and regular and certain as any other major commitments you make. You kiss your writing career good morning when you wake up and you kiss it good night when you go to bed. Writing becomes the norm.

MANAGING YOUR WORK FLOW IS LIKE GALLOPING ON A HORSE. Riding a horse is bumpy and takes a while to get used to because a horse's natural gait jostles the rider all over the place. A writing career is like this. It forces you to maintain your center of balance over the horse even as your career momentum wants to throw you off your center. You have to learn to stay focused on your goals and stay centered despite the bumpy ride. When you start feeling momentum in your writing career, it's easier to stay on. Just like riding a horse.

YOU MAINTAIN STEADY DEADLINES. There's two ways to get steady deadlines: You impose them on yourself, or someone else imposes them on you. If you are going to have a writing career, steady deadlines are going to be an important part of it. Give yourself some deadlines and achieve them or get some deadlines from someone else. Hit your deadlines as best you can, and make sure you always finish your work.

YOU START RACKING UP PAGES. As you meet steady deadlines, something wonderful happens. You start to accumulate pages. When you start to accumulate pages that have been put through the editing mill a few times and have achieved a level of publishable quality, you will develop a body of published work.

YOU ACHIEVE PUBLICATION SUCCESS. Remember that it's not quantity that gets you published; it's quality. When you get to the point that you can craft and match your best writing to the needs of those who can publish it, you are succeeding as a writer.

YOU ENJOY WRITING FOR ITS OWN SAKE. When you get to the point where writing well is its own reward, you have found the gratification of a career writer, who writes from a sturdy center of solid skills and always produces her best work.

68

EXPRESS YOUR SPECIALTY

Writing is an exploration. You start from nothing and learn as you go.

—E.L. DOCTOROW

One thing I've noticed over the years is that most writers with specialties found their focus by writing about a topic first and then writing about it over and over. And each time they wrote about it, they noticed something more. They were engaged and interested and excited about the topic and every idea that followed. And that's how a specialty is born.

Writers who consider a specialty in the abstract but haven't yet explored the topic through writing have a much more difficult, and much less exciting, time because abstract specialties are based on untested ideas, not a concrete track record. You want to find your specialty and build it from an established groove, not a far-fetched idea.

Writing is the momentum that gives your specialty liftoff, because you know from experience that the topic is not only compelling but also a great subject to write about.

And when you feel compelled to write more widely and deeply about a topic, something natural happens: What is interesting and compelling to you becomes interesting and compelling to others. You start to notice and trust your strong response.

Maybe editors really jumped for a particular idea of yours. Maybe a radio producer became interested in one of your published articles. Maybe one of your editors selected your topic to mention on a television show. All of these strong response are signals to the writer to go deeper and write more on a topic.

It doesn't matter if other people write on the same topic. They won't write about it the same way you do. If you are going to establish a bonafide specialty, you'll want to eventually check out what other people are doing. But in the beginning don't worry about it too much.

When your work starts to have an impact on others, you'll know you have hit a rich vein of writing material that you can mine for a very long time. I'm still republishing articles that I originally wrote a decade ago.

Things could be worse. Suppose your errors were counted and published every day, like those of a baseball player.

—AUTHOR UNKNOWN

A lot of beginning writers experience imposter syndrome. Imposter syndrome is a form low self-esteem experienced by people you would not imagine have low self-esteem. When accomplishments bring up feelings of unworthiness or of being a phony or a fake, these are the internal signals of imposter syndrome.

If you experience imposter syndrome, it doesn't mean you aren't writing well, it means you think success is for other people, not for you. Maybe you can't give yourself credit for your own hard work or maybe you simply believe you are not deserving of feeling proud of yourself.

But success is for anybody who wants it. Once you've earned it, you deserve to feel good about what you've accomplished. If you have imposter syndrome, you can address it in a variety of ways. Keep writing through it. If you don't let it stop you, it will eventually go away, but probably not overnight. You may need to outwrite the negative voices for quite some time before you can reconcile them. The roots of imposter syndrome seem to run pretty deep.

I believe that imposter syndrome is a hallmark of perfectionism. It whispers to you that no matter what you have done and no matter how well you have done it, you and your efforts will never be enough. The solution to perfectionism, which only honors outcomes while insisting at the same time that they are never good enough, is to honor process, baby steps, and progress more than products, results, and other people's opinions of your work.

Making mistakes and making them daily is an important practice for perfectionists. If you are afraid to make mistakes, your compulsion for perfect behavior will inhibit your ability to move forward. So set a goal to make at least one mistake a day and watch how much better a day you have when every move you make no longer requires the appearance of absolute perfection.

You have achieved exactly what you have achieved and not more or less. When you can embrace this and own it in your writing career, imposter syndrome and perfectionism will abate. And then you can start having more fun in your work.

The little needle always knows the North,
The little bird remembereth his note,
And this wise Seer within me never errs.

—RALPH WALDO EMERSON

Write your way to a specialty. Try it on for size. See how it feels. Notice how the topic engages you. Notice how it changes you. Notice how it impacts others.

Here are some questions that will help you write your way to a specialty:

1. What one topic could you write about for many years without becoming bored or burned out?
2. Now, pick *one* of your specific audiences that you communicate with naturally and easily (you did this in chapter twenty).
3. Give *three* reasons your topic is hot right now.
4. Name *three* recent trends (with stats, if possible) related to your topic or audience, if you can.
5. Describe the intersection of your topic with your audience and the timing over the next couple of years.
6. Look into the future possibilities of your topic. What needs to be written about it but has not yet been written?
7. What written form lends itself to your topic, audience, and timing best (fiction, nonfiction, articles, books)?
8. How does this all add up to a juicy-enough topic you could write about for a long, long time?

Scope is an important part of a specialty but, fortunately, scope is something you can play with and adjust over time, as needed.

ESCHEW BRANDING

A personal brand is a little package you make of yourself so you can put yourself on the shelf in the marketplace and people will know what to expect or look for when they come to buy you.

—MAUREEN JOHNSON

The second you put "my brand" at the center of your writing career, is the second you suck all the air right out of your creative process. Many may preach the gospel of branding for the benefit of creating fans, but from the perspective of creating, branding is the kiss of death.

What should go at the center of your creative thrust, instead of brand, is a simple verb that describes *the dynamic you create in the world with your work.*

For most writers, you might think that verb would simply be *write*, but that's so generic. If we have a million writers and all we all do is write, how do you tell any of us apart? You can always choose other, more specific, words like *create, inspire, thrill,* or *empower.*

Empowering writers is at the center of my platform. Mostly what I create are empowering tools for instructing writers. That's not just a verb; it's a dynamic. A dynamic involves more than just what I do on a daily basis (instructing), it also includes whom I serve and how I serve them (in an empowering way).

Being a brand is like having to walk around wearing a sandwich board. No sooner do you become a brand and it's going to get old, bring you down, weigh heavy on your creativity, and potentially even hurt business.

So don't let those who insist that writers brand themselves take the expressive, evolving pleasure of your natural dynamic away from you and turn it into something packaged, phony, and forced.

As soon as you feel like you can't follow the dance of your creative spark, you are going to wonder why all the branding baloney being served up all over the place ever sounded like a good idea.

Put your natural creative dynamic at the center of your writing career and you will soon wonder how you became so engaged, prolific, and productive. Your career will evolve naturally, unhindered by phony labels. Most importantly, you will be able to serve your audience and grow in a most natural way.

CONCENTRATE SPECIFICALLY

I specialize in murders of quiet, domestic interest.

—AGATHA CHRISTIE

Specialists are made, not born. Don't let a lack of fame or knowledge stop you from making a beginning. Every specialist you have ever heard of was once completely unknown and didn't know a thing about his forthcoming specialty. Factor time into the equation and don't try to rush your specialty.

Here are nine more things to keep in mind as you begin the somewhat daunting task of establishing and growing a specialty.

1. **BUILD YOUR SKILL SETS.** Journalism skills come in very handy. It's not all about you and your thoughts and discoveries on a topic. There is reading, research, polls, interviews, and partnering with other experts.

2. **STAY CURRENT.** Keep up with trends on your topic while staying true to your particular audience.

3. **DON'T ISOLATE YOURSELF.** Get out and about. Forget your focus occasionally so you can keep it over the long haul. Take a broad view once in a while. Beware of tunnel vision.

4. **REDUCE, REUSE, RECYCLE.** Transform comments, questions, and criticisms into fodder for more content on your topic. Just keep growing your information base.

5. **KEEP YOUR COMPETITION CLOSE.** Pay attention to your competition—those who do what you do. Keep your contribution to the field relevant and desirable. Position yourself to stand out and get noticed.

6. **MINT YOURSELF.** Coin your existing expertise into multiple forms and media. Produce yourself. Choose the media formats that best match your message.

7. **ESTABLISH YOURSELF, THEN EXPAND.** Once one audience likes and respects you they will help spread the word to a larger audience. Don't think about expanding too soon, or you may risk spreading yourself and what you offer too thin.

8. **JUST SAY NO.** Learn to say no to opportunities that won't make the most of your strengths (leave them to the generalists).

9. **DELEGATE.** Learn to pass along tasks that don't need to be performed by you (housework, bookkeeping, etc.) to others, to free you up for new growth opportunities.

In the immortal words of Gold Five, "Stay on target." You may or may not be the one who destroys the Death Star. But you're a hero if you get out of your own way, put it all on the line, and try.

—CYNTHIA LEITICH SMITH

The goal of the writer is to be centered and be at the center of her own career without being self-centered. The most masterful writer is the invisible writer who can shine a spotlight on her presence in the story without so much as casting a shadow.

But the minute you-you-you is all you focus on, you go from being centered to being self-centered. Yet, if you don't focus on your responsibilities, they won't stay in the center of your focus.

The solution is to keep your eye on the prize: your writing career progress, while aiming to grow in a calm and steady fashion.

Try to focus on making good things happen (in the inspiring words of Tim O'Reilly of O'Reilly Media). The way I have always taught writers to succeed is by asking them to shift from a focus on themselves to a focus on service.

Serve your readers. If you are a pen for hire, before you can serve readers, you serve editors. Staying centered is lot easier when you know whom you serve and what you offer and why.

What happens when a writer shines the spotlight on himself is that the service to the reader stops. When your self-consciousness gets in the way, the reader stops reading.

Remember, you have a choice to shine the light of your prose on the topic at hand in a way that serves the reader, or you can shine the light back in your own eyes, which will have the same unfortunate effect on the reader that it has on you.

You want people to follow what you write. You want them to enjoy your work, and you want them to want to read more of it. You want to provide high-quality reading experiences. You want what you offer to be consistent with the dynamic specialty and excellent reputation you are becoming known for.

DITCH THE OUTLINE

Good writing is formed partly through plan and partly through accident.

—KEN MACRORIE

In a recent issue of *Writer's Digest*, I read that Ken Follett is an inveterate outliner, often spending six months to a year on a fifty-page outline for a book, while David Morrell says that he likes to think of writing a book as an adventure. He has only a general sense of the beginning, the big scenes, and the ending, and other than that he tries to "Serve the story, listen to the story."

If both of these approaches work so well, why not simply do both? Start by figuring out your beginning, big scenes, and ending, and then leap into the adventure. If the adventure starts to get away from you, you can always pause to outline. You may choose to see if using Follett's technique of writing an outline and then going back through it backwards and writing a one-line chapter summary of each chapter works for you. He says that in this way he can see "where the final scenes are not fulfilling the promises raised by the early scenes."

Most nonfiction books are outlined in advance. But I always have trouble following a plan once I've set it down in ink—even if it was a sound plan to begin with. The reason, I think, is because I get bored following a stringent outline. I also learn so much from the process of writing that I want to integrate what I learn as I go.

For me, brainstorming a plan and then feeling tied to that plan is too limiting. I like to be able to act on the ideas that are being inspired today. I don't want to feel like I can't act on them because they were not part of the original plan.

But here's the quirky part. A lot of times I will deviate from the plan for the sheer fun of following a good idea in the moment. And I will be very pleased with myself for not letting that good one slip past me in favor of following the boring old plan … and then, later, when I look at the plan again, I discover that the supposedly brilliant inspiration I'd thought I'd had was actually in the plan the whole time!

So make a plan but don't feel bound by it. In this way, you will create the best writing and have the most fun doing it.

TAKE TWENTY-FIVE ACTIONS

The big question is whether you are going to be able to say a hearty yes to your adventure.

—JOSEPH CAMPBELL

Remember the board game Chutes and Ladders? There were one hundreds squares and lots of images of kids sliding and climbing? You spin the spinner and go forward or back on the board depending on the outcomes depicted in the squares you land on.

No doubt, your writing career will follow a similar pattern of either climbing ladders or sliding down chutes. There are no guarantees or certainties. Other days, you'll just progress square by square.

The typical writing career is made up of a lot of normal, steady days in between breaks and setbacks, small and large. What I have noticed over the years—and I am sure this will not surprise you—is that up days tend to follow the smart choices and good preparation.

There is no such thing as luck in publishing. There is only the fruition of cumulative efforts. And if you have a habit of calling things luck, you might be depriving yourself of credit that is rightly yours.

I'm not suggesting that you take all the credit; I am suggesting that you acknowledge you are going to win a few and lose a few, and possibly even split a few.

But despite any ups and downs in the short run, your writing career will flourish according to the positive, proactive steps you take. Why spend time worrying about the chutes when you could be climbing up the ladders?

Here's a board game for you to fill in with twenty-five constructive actions you plan to take for your writing career. Taking everything you've learned about finding your writing momentum so far, fill in the twenty-five blanks with twenty-five concrete actions you know you need to perform (even, or especially, if you don't want to do them). And make sure that each one is the kind of step that will move you up the ladders, rather than sending you sliding back down the chutes. Cross off each action completed and watch the result. No luck, just payoffs for steps taken.

PUT YOUR NEEDS FIRST

I felt resentful about helping to make others successful yet never getting around to doing what I wanted to do. I also had to face the reality that too many of my relationships were one-way streets. Some of my friends were extremely needy, yet I kept them in my life because they made me feel safe, in control, and significant.

—CHERYL RICHARDSON

The best way to monitor your writing career health is to keep your finger on the pulse of your own energy. Make choices, not because someone else told you to, but because you think for yourself, trust your instincts, and make decisions accordingly. Cheryl Richardson discusses this determination in *Make Time for Your Life*; I've adapted this material from her.

Keep tabs on your energy and trust what it is telling you. Here are a few areas of life, which if left unattended, might cause your energy to dip. They are important parts of life that sustain and support you, so be sure that you don't neglect them—or yourself.

ENVIRONMENT

Do you live where you'd like to live? Does your living environment sustain you? Does it boost your energy? Does it help you feel cradled in a rocking world? Are your closets and storage areas overcrowded? Do you need to sort through or update your wardrobe? Are your pets well attended? Does the place where you live feel like home?

HEALTH

Is everyone in your home happy, productive, and playful? Is everyone getting their needs met? Is your home stocked with healthful, delicious, and fresh food? Do you sleep well and wake refreshed? Do you exercise, garden, or walk? Are you up-to-date on your checkups? Do you attend spiritual services or have a way to bring positive inspiration into your life regularly? Do you have enough down time? Do you feel healthy?

MONEY

Can you pay all of your bills on time? Do you plan for a secure future? Have you stashed away some savings in case of an emergency? Are you well insured? Do you have a financial advisor or source of good financial advice? Do you pay off your debts and maintain a good credit rating? Do you have flexibility?

RELATIONSHIPS

Are you on top of personal correspondence and phone calls? Do you have a few really good friends you can say anything to? Are you in a happy, healthy, mutually supportive relationship? Have you distanced yourself from needy, draining people? Do you feel like you are part of an extended, supportive network of support? Does anyone in your life cause you anxiety? Is there something you need to address with someone and you are afraid to face it? Do you rejoice in your friendships?

77

DON'T RUSH RIPE

Nature, time, and patience are the three great physicians.

—HENRY BOHN

Ever feel like you are the victim of the publication process?

Because let's face it, the way publishing works is fairly absurd. For example:

> Editors rarely get back to you right away—or at all.

> There is no guarantee that you will be able to earn six figures or any other amount of money writing.

> Even if you land a book deal, there is no guarantee that it will reach its intended audience and sell.

> Sometimes the most successful authors are not the most charming or well-behaved people.

But this is the business model we inherited, so we may as well just deal with it as it is and do the best we can with it. Sure, you could just go self-publish at this point, but I'd prefer you hung in there and learned what you need to learn first.

The publishing business is impeded by a lot of legacy practices. However, you can still work with the system to learn a ton. Rather than throwing the whole old system out with all the new theories of publishing Nirvana coming down the pipe, I'd suggest you get as much out of the old system as you can.

You are not a victim. Nothing could be further from the truth. But this means you have to act like you are not a victim and learn the skills you need to succeed instead.

It takes time for writing careers to ripen. They take effort and nurturing and constant care. And there's no way around it.

Do the best you can with whatever opportunities you can find today. There is no such thing as publishing perfection today, and there will likely be no such thing as publishing perfection tomorrow.

Knowledge is of two kinds. We know the subject ourselves, or we know where we can find information upon it.

—SAMUEL JOHNSON

A specialist was often first a generalist who stumbled on a good idea, a natural proclivity, or a personal fascination and ran with it. Sometimes a generalist, especially one who is not very successful at generalizing, will decide to become a specialist in a particular niche and stay in that niche. But successful professionals often juggle the qualities of generalizing and specializing over the course of a career and can do either or both when either skill set is needed.

So should you generalize or specialize? If you are just getting started writing as a professional, start with generalizing. You can sample an array of topics, develop your writing skills, experiment with different forms, and learn your strengths—as well as what you prefer.

You can test-drive ideas and see if you might like to write on them in more depth. You can build the two foundational skills all writers need: writing well and selling your words.

If you have been in the game for a while, I can almost guarantee you that you are sitting on a bunch of potential specialties. I help people discover their specialties, but if they haven't been writing for very long, it is difficult to find any specialties. A specialty focus typically comes from the actual experience of what you are good at, not your best guess at what you might be good at.

So don't feel badly if you are frustrated because you know you have a specialty in you somewhere, but you are having a hard time identifying it and making the most of it. This is a very common dilemma and it will solve itself the more you write, and the more you pay attention to how you feel about what you write, and the better you get at understanding the marketplace.

For those who juggle both generalizing and specializing, the two can help keep the income stream flowing. When one ebbs, the other can flow. The hallmark of success in the gig economy is not only having professional instincts but also knowing how to consistently use them to navigate your way to the most successful paths for your career in the moment.

BALANCE DEPTH AND VARIETY

A full one-third of our respondents are now working either free-lance or in two jobs. And nearly one in two of them report taking on additional positions during the last six months. Just as startling, these new alternative workers are not overwhelmingly low-income. They're college-educated Americans who earn more than $75,000 a year. Welcome to the age of Gigonomics.

—TINA BROWN

In the long run, the most balanced strategy for this new gig economy is maintaining a balance between generalizing and specializing.

As a writing professional you are striving to become:

- Focused and flexible
- Curious and quick
- Facile at conducting research in depth and hitting your deadlines
- Good at staying on one track and still staying open to new topics of interest
- Practiced in developing expertise and moving from paying project to paying project
- Able to spend time on self-promotion and pitching yourself to new-to-you editors
- Known and influential via your expertise and audience awareness
- A go-to source for a variety of clients, including big ones
- The creator of revenue streams from a few consistent sources and a variety clients
- Able to vary the amount of content and media that you sell and share

Being a writer is like having homework every night for the rest of your life.

—LAWRENCE KASDAN

Right after a major leap forward, like a book deal or a column in a major publication, it's easy to forget there are still many strides ahead, all of which you are unlikely to accomplish in one fell swoop, no matter how many successes you've already had.

So in the spirit of keeping things in perspective, this list of lifelong accomplishments by other esteemed writers (as of the time of this writing) may help refocus your long view, as well as help you become more patient with yourself as you aim higher and increasingly higher.

Name: Paul Auster
Born: February 3, 1947
Books published: 23
Novels published: 16
Best known for: the search for identity and personal meaning

Name: Meg Cabot
Born: February 1, 1967
Books published: 50+
Novels published: 50+
Best known for: romantic and paranormal fiction for teens and adults

Name: Louise Hay
Born: October 8, 1926
Books published: 27
Best known for: self-help and new-thought books

Name: Alice Walker
Born: February 9, 1944
Books published: 34
Novels published: 14
Best known for: economic hardship, racial terrorism, and folk wisdom of African American life and culture

At the end of the day, after you complete one project, maybe an article or an essay or a story, remember there's always going to be the next one and the next one and the next. Too much emphasis on how your first efforts are received or how much they increase your literary standing is self-destructive. This kind of self-consciousness is not going to help your professional progress in the long run.

Writing is not a competition. It would be far better to write a few books well, if that's the best you can do, than try to compete with a Walker or an Auster. Try to keep the big picture in mind. Do not become so enamored of your own success that it interferes with continuing to move slowly and steadily forward.

8 | ENCAPSULATE YOU

Since you must sell yourself even before selling your goods, it's important to sell yourself on yourself. So believe in yourself.

—NORMAN VINCENT PEALE

Creating your own business cards gives you a sense of ownership over your writing career and encourages you to present yourself to others as a professional. Your business card covers the following basics.

YOUR NAME

Use one name for business purposes and the same name for publication purposes. Consider using your nickname as your professional name if you have a very common name. For example, Jenny Kales goes by Jenny instead of Jennifer.

YOUR E-MAIL ADDRESS

I suggest that you pay for your e-mail service so you don't have to worry about your account getting hacked or terminated without your consent. Think of your Internet and e-mail service provider as long-term relationships to avoid hassles that come with changing accounts often.

An e-mail address of "hotmama@hotmail.com" is not likely to make a professional impression. A much better choice would be: "[yourfirstandlastname]@areputableemail-provider.com." If your name is in use, play around with word order or add a middle initial and see if that configuration is taken.

YOUR MAILING ADDRESS

When you publicize your home address, you give everyone in the world access to your family. If you value your privacy and it's convenient to visit a post office box once a week, rent one. Doing so is inexpensive, and you can write off the business expense.

YOUR PHONE NUMBER

In order for folks to reach you, I suggest you share only your e-mail address publically. If it's crucial for potential clients to be able to reach you on short notice, go ahead and share your work phone number. If you think you might change your number soon or you have multiple numbers, choose the number that is least likely to change and most likely to actually reach you.

YOUR MISSION

Early on in your writing career, your mission statement is likely as simple as a sentence that describes the kind of writing you do. People who receive your business card will appreciate a clear reminder. Otherwise your card is just a generic piece of paper they can throw away. Come up with something that says either what you do or how you do it, and say it in a way that communicates the essence of your professional impact. Start standing out in the crowd right from the beginning. It's an important habit.

COLLECT EXAMPLES

You can't wait for inspiration. You have to go after it with a club.

—JACK LONDON

Even if you are mostly focused on writing and selling your work right now, someday you are going to want to build yourself a website, start blogging, or update your fans on your latest news.

At least, I hope this is the plan.

The best way to lay the groundwork for your self-promotion efforts is to start a collection of promotional samples from people whose efforts you admire.

When I need promotional inspiration, I flip through the examples I've compiled and come away with new inspirations for promoting myself.

When I pull out my file of this kind, I find all kinds of things I have noticed in both print and digital forms:

- Business cards
- Flyers
- Bookmarks
- Postcards
- Calendars
- Posters
- Checklists
- Schedules
- Coupons
- Gift certificates
- Book-discussion guides
- Reviews
- Catalogs
- Lists
- Press releases
- One-pagers
- Website designs
- Blog-post formats
- Class descriptions

The same idea that works for tickling your brain with writing forms and topics can also work with self-promotion formats. Start your own self-promotion inspiration file so you will have ample samples when you are ready to start promoting yourself.

Take your life in your own hands, and what happens? A terrible thing: no one to blame.

—ERICA JONG

When I think of great determination, I like to think of a friend of mine. This friend picked up a book assignment for a big-six publisher and cranked out a solid manuscript on a quick deadline. The publisher turned that manuscript into a book, published it, and unfortunately the sales of the book were less than vigorous.

The book went to book heaven, and my friend felt very discouraged indeed. She had put a lot of time, energy, and thought into the book. So she thought about it a little more and decided that she should really try to get more mileage out of the topic instead of just giving up on it.

She pitched a new book to a new publisher on the same topic with a different slant for a different audience. The publisher gave her a book deal and put some serious marketing juice behind the book.

And guess what happened? She's now collecting thousands of dollars a year in royalty checks. She was so happy that she wrote another book for the publisher, which has also sold through. Now both books will likely collect royalty checks for many more years to come.

My friend was seriously discouraged after her first book flopped. But she dug deeper until she hit upon her own great determination. Great determination comes from inside. Nobody can give it to you. When the going gets tough, you get to find out how resilient you are. You get to find out if you will bounce back or curl into a ball.

You could call great determination willpower but that's not quite it. Willpower is like a stubborn child stamping her foot when she doesn't get her way. Great determination is much more mature and patient. It comes from somewhere deeper—resolve, not ego.

Great determination is more like what the boxer uses to stand back up and keep fighting after he's been knocked out a couple of times. As a writer, your ego will likely get knocked around. And that's okay. It can take it. In the meantime, you get back up and carry on.

FALL:

BECOME RECOGNIZABLE

Maturity includes the recognition that no one is going to see anything in us that we don't see in ourselves. Stop waiting for a producer. Produce yourself.

—MARIANNE WILLIAMSON

The best time to start becoming visible to the general public as a writer varies from writer to writer. But generally speaking, once a writer has mastered publishing short and long forms regularly and with confidence, it's time to start thinking about ramping a specialty into an online platform. Like everything else, platform development is a process. The Internet is a deep woods any writer can become lost within. Not only is your platform going to take time and effort to establish, it's not going to necessarily change your career status right away. This section will help you build your platform slowly and learn to partner with others wisely while you continue to write and sell your work. The process of becoming visible is the equivalent of making an international name for yourself—make an art of it and you will succeed.

Social media can be extremely powerful, when used correctly, and a significant social media presence can be enough. But in addition to that, anything that draws attention to you and gets people acquainted with you can be part of platform building.

—RACHELLE GARDNER

So what the heck is a platform? Writers want to know.

I have a working definition that came into form after I published a book on the topic:

> A platform communicates your expertise to others. It includes your Web presence, any public speaking you do, the classes you teach, the media contacts you've established, the articles you've published, and any other means you currently have for making your name and your future books known to a viable readership.
>
> Basically, your platform is everything you do with your expertise. A platform-strong writer is a writer with influence. Once you establish a platform, it can work for you 24/7, reaching readers even as you sleep. Of course, this kind of reach takes time. If many others already recognize your expertise on a given topic or for a specific audience or both, you likely have an active platform.
>
> For writers, I find it helpful to define platform as a promise writers make to not only create something to sell (like a book or anything else), but also to promote it to the specific readers who will want to purchase it. This takes both time and effort, not to mention considerable focus.

Platform is not a one-time event; it's an ongoing part of your process as a creative professional. Think of your physical platform (website, blog, social media profiles) as the hardware of the dynamic you express in the world and think of your platform activities as the software (classes, presentations, articles) of your dynamic.

A lot of writers hire out their platform work so they can focus their efforts on writing and other priorities. I can respect that if you have so much writing work that it keeps you busy and paid full-time. But if you don't, you'll probably want to do things yourself, even while you partner with others. And a hands-on approach is a good idea because then you not only steer your own ship and stay abreast of all of the possibilities, you also stay in close touch with your audience. Your platform is not divorced from your creativity; it is part and parcel your professional portfolio. That's the last job you want to hire out.

85

SCALE YOUR SOUL

People say that what we're all seeking is a meaning for life. I don't think that's what we're really seeking. I think that what we're seeking is an experience of being alive, so that our life experiences on the purely physical plane will have resonances within our own innermost being and reality, so that we actually feel the rapture of being alive.

—JOSEPH CAMPBELL

What is it that makes great works of literature, compelling autobiographies, and timeless self-help books?

Soul, essence—it doesn't matter what you call it. When the core spirit of a person is expressed it can't help but connect us all with our deep humanity.

What's at the center of Oprah's empire? Soul. Translation: Every person has a soul and can tap into that power to live her best life. That's what her tagline promises.

What's at the center of Martha's empire? Soul. Translation: Home is where the heart is, I open my home to you, and let you come in. "Come in and see how I do things" is her offer.

What's at the center of Stephen King's writing? Soul. Translation: I can scare you so badly you will feel it in your bones. And he delivers pretty consistently, too. Right?

You get the idea. Look deeply at examples of phenomenal success, and you will witness the soul connection that the originator feels to her mission and the way that one soul can express a mission outward and touch so many.

When an individual expresses what he has to offer, he is expressing his soul. If you don't exercise your soul, nobody else will know what you are passionate about but you. And if you don't express your soul, you can't share it. Therefore, don't be angry if no one sees it or acknowledges it. You are the one hiding it. What's stopping you from sharing?

Granted, expressing soul takes time and practice. To start out, most people feel comfortable sharing themselves in a safe space. After that the expression of your soul has to scale, meaning you don't feel diminished by sharing yours with more people.

If you take a concept that is closely aligned with who and what you are and scale your soul's expression on a mass level, aligning it with what is meaningful to others, you will accomplish a glorious thing. You can share what moves you most with the whole world.

86
EVALUATE YOUR VISIBILITY

Believe wholeheartedly in your personal vision and resign to achieve it slowly, in baby steps.

—STEVE COHEN

Let's determine where you are at right now with the platform you've already established up to this point.

1. Are you visible and influential beyond your circle of family and friends?
2. Do the people who know about you automatically associate your name with a particular area of expertise or way of working with people?
3. Have you identified and cultivated a particular area of expertise or specialty?
4. Do you write for a very specific audience that is quantifiable and describable?
5. Are you informed about consumer and publishing trends?
6. Are you calmly passionate about your work and able to work at your platform consistently and cheerfully?
7. When you stumble upon a weakness or your own resistance, are you able to bounce back and keep going?
8. Do you partner wisely and well with others while maintaining your own independence?
9. Do you see yourself as the producer of your writing career and take 100 percent responsibility for your success?
10. Are you able to view yourself objectively and assess your ripeness for authorhood the way an agent or editor would?

> The day you say "that SOB stole my idea" is the day you need to face your own inability to execute.
>
> —JONATHAN FIELDS

What's the difference between a writer's platform and an author's platform?

What about a nonfiction writer's platform and a fiction writer's platform?

You can go deeper than this, of course. What is the difference between a science fiction writer's platform and a romance writer's platform?

Here's one I heard recently: What is the difference between a marketing platform vs. a nonmarketing platform?

You can see how so many questions about so many kinds of platforms become absurd at some point. Rarely do the same kinds of fruit look exactly the same, so why should platforms? Differences in a fruit's color, texture, and shape could never be predicted. So how could we map out the ideal platform for any type of author without taking that person's unique dynamic into account? We couldn't. And we shouldn't.

The point is that you are your platform, and your platform is you. Think of your platform dynamic the way that Michelangelo thought of finding a sculpture in a block of marble. Your platform dynamic is in you, underneath a whole bunch of everything else. Your job is to chip away, brush away, and clear away everything else until you discover the most essential expression of what you offer.

Statues don't change, but your platform dynamic is going to naturally evolve with time. It will morph and transform as your writing career grows tomorrow, next year, and in five years. Statues are static, but once you discover and release your platform dynamic, it's like a fire hose of energy that you can turn on or off, let out a gush or a trickle, a sprinkle or a spray, as you appropriately choose.

88

CONSIDER YOUR GOOD FORTUNE

Happiness is excitement that has found a settling down place. But there is always a little corner that keeps flapping around.

—E.L. KONIGSBURG

There is no question that we are fortunate as writers. Certainly in contrast with history, our challenges today would qualify as high-class problems (meaning we don't actually have any problems, we just think we have problems).

Here are seven reasons why there has never been a better time to be a writer:

1. There has never been more and easier access to information.
2. There has never been as much inexpensive continuing education available.
3. There has never been as much choice to publish what we wish to publish.
4. There have never been so many professional development organizations and so much access to publishing industry insiders.
5. There have never been more opportunities to connect with and learn from fellow writers and authors.
6. There have never been more ways to connect directly with readers.
7. There has never been a better time to view writing as part of holistic business model rather than a disempowered specialty all on its own.

We are experiencing an opportunity as writers like we have never seen before. And, naturally, with all of these opportunities come a ton of questions. Although we are living in a time of opportunity, we are also living in a time of complexity.

But generally speaking, for folks who take a long-term approach and pace themselves, your writing career can become whatever you make of it.

89

TRACK YOUR PROGRESS

The most terrifying thing is to accept oneself completely.

—CARL JUNG

The simplest and easiest way to track your platform progress is by using a one-pager. One-pagers have long been used by speakers as a quick, visual way to strut your stuff on paper.

Author and speaker Julie A. Fast shared her one-pager with me years ago. She was submitting it with her book pitches. I liked the idea that authors could use one-pagers and created a worksheet that would encourage my students to showcase their work in a similar formal way—once they had some work to showcase.

A bonus benefit of working on a one-pager is that you get a clearer look at your platform strengths and weaknesses. Consider listing the following:

PUBLICATION IN:
- national magazines
- daily newspapers
- magazines, journals, or newsletters
- a syndicated column (or self-syndicated, but active)
- someone else's book (with number of books sold, if impressive)

MEDIA EXPERTISE AS A:
- source in major publications, television, or radio
- regular expert on local or regional media
- host of your own popular media show

PUBLIC APPEARANCES FOR:
- large events or conferences
- national or regional speaking tours
- events you host regularly

INTERNET BUZZ IN:
- your high-traffic website(s) or blog(s)

- your newsletter with a large subscription base
- a high-traffic or high-circulation site, blog, or newsletter

PROFESSIONAL AFFILIATIONS:
- organization or association leadership positions
- memberships maintained

PROFESSIONAL ACTIVITIES:
- classes you currently teach
- prestigious (or numerous) clients you consult for, coach, or train

EDUCATION:
- prestigious colleges or universities attended
- pertinent to your career or topic

AWARDS AND CONTESTS:
- awards or recognition received
- major contests won

You won't likely have something to include in your one-pager from each category. But once you have everything down on paper, you can take a look at what you don't have and consider whether or not these are things to work on for the future.

190

ACCRUE PERSONAL POWER

Power is the faculty or capacity to act, the strength and potency to accomplish something. It is the vital energy to make choices and decisions. It also includes the capacity to overcome deeply embedded habits and to cultivate higher, more effective ones.

—STEPHEN R. COVEY

A certain amount of personal power naturally accumulates as we become older and wiser. This is where becoming a catalyst for creating something cool in the world comes in. You can make this happen, as a writer or anything else, when you tap into and expand your personal power.

At the core of personal power is integrity. People remember people with integrity. People with true integrity are impossible to forget. Integrity means you are true to yourself, you honor your personal power, and you honor the personal power in others.

Like the heroes and heroines in so many movies and myths, we need to recognize that we are on a personal power journey and we have our own potential. We can (and should) embrace the fact that we don't get to fully access our personal power until we learn how to handle the power we've already got. People who are on a personal power quest are patient. They don't want what they can't handle. They make the most of what they have right now and they feel satisfied.

Take the power you already have and wield it. Use it to volunteer, to teach, to speak, to start a project, to consult, to coach, to counsel, or to train (and, of course, to write). This is how your personal power grows, and this is how you become a stronger container for the additional personal power that will come through you, hopefully, in the future.

We can't talk about writing power without also talking about personal power. You can be the "best" writer in the room, but if you have not activated your personal power alongside your writing skills, you won't steer your ship as well as a person who is grounded in their personal power.

19

CALL PLEASURE YOUR BUSINESS

All the things I love is what my business is all about.

—MARTHA STEWART

I can always tell the passionate workers from those who are just trying to make a quick buck in the short run. The former give up pretty easily. The latter never do

I think the greatest factor in making these decisions comes down to passion. I am pretty sure that Martha and Oprah love what they do. But did they completely know what they were getting themselves into when they started? I doubt it. They had to learn to trust the process, or they would not be where they are today.

I believe these businesswomen love their callings. I believe they speak to the audiences they identify with most. There is no way that Martha Stewart could have gone to jail and made a comeback unless she genuinely loved her work.

And I think the fact that Oprah can take her production company and her audience with her when she chooses to leave a major TV network is indicative of how much passion she has. At the center of any career there has to be passion. You can't cultivate a multimillion-dollar multimedia network without the sunshine of passionate work.

Here's how the passionate person typically progresses from enthusiast to multi-millionaire:

- Identify your niche audiences.
- Narrow your niche along specific lines.
- Understand the needs of your niche inside and out.
- Identify your audience's problems and solve them.
- Amplify your role as the best person to do the job through storytelling.
- Find your connecting style and make a consistent impression on key people.
- Make sure you are consistently selected over the competition through consistent quality work.
- Communicate what you can deliver, how, and why your audience will be happy and satisfied afterwards.
- Align your solutions with your audience's needs and constantly communicate the impact of your work.
- Be the thought-leader who steers your tribe into a better future.

You can begin by being passionate about one thing and that one passion can grow into multiple passions—even multimedia-level passions—if you stay with it.

92
ALWAYS BE BUILDING

Be aware that author platform and credentials are of primary importance. It may take years to build the kind of platform necessary to interest an agent or publisher.

—RACHELLE GARDNER

Writers seem willing to acknowledge that nonfiction writers need platforms, but the debate on whether fiction writers, memoir writers, and children's writers need one rages on.

I can clear this up. Every writer who plans to publish or be published needs a platform. It doesn't matter what you write. As with most things, the sooner you get started, the better because platforms take time to establish, cultivate, and build. No exceptions.

Understand that platform applies to every kind of writer. Don't get platform confused with what you'd *like* it to mean. There is a lot of misinformation and quibbling about what platform is and isn't and whether or not writers need to work on building one and when. Blah, blah, blah, blah, blah … in all the time spent debating, a writer could have built her first platform.

To clarify, debating about whether or not you need a platform should not be confused with actually taking concrete steps toward building one. Get out of the debate club and get into the platform-building club. Take a no-whining oath and get to work building a productive platform that offers folks the value only you can offer.

Need examples? A handful of writer/author platform examples follow below. None of them are the superfast, slap-it-together-overnight kind. Just conduct an Internet search on each of these folks and you will see what I mean.

Remember, when you visit these sites, you won't see all the sweat these folks have invested into their writing careers over the years. Instead you will view *the results* of years of hard and steady work.

NONFICTION (HOW-TO)
- Ali Edwards
- Amanda Blake Soule
- Martha Stewart

FICTION
- Allison Winn Scotch
- Therese Walsh
- Sue Grafton

MEMOIR
- Melissa Hart
- Jeannette Walls
- Mary Karr

Don't envy someone else's success. Roll up your sleeves and do your own platform building. Carve out your own distinct niche in the literary world. I hope you are inspired to do it.

Creativity comes from trust. Trust your instincts. And never hope more than you work.

—RITA MAE BROWN

You are the creator of your career. And like a spider, you weave web after web after web. Often your webs are woven secretly in the dark, so they don't glisten with dew until the sun hits them. If you think this way, you can begin to understand the permanent and impermanent nature of your writing projects. How can you spin your latest writing projects into a blazing triumph so it won't fall to pieces from neglect?

Your writing career is yours as long as you keep weaving, as long as you keep standing by your work, waiting patiently for results, as long as you keep tearing down the old strands in favor of fresher, stronger strands.

Spiders spin silk and writers spin words. Spiders make webs and writers create all kinds of content. And when you expand the concept of spider wisdom to include what writers can do with their platforms, you get an even more appropriate analogy.

I like to think that spiders are happiest when they are spinning silk and weaving their webs, just as writers tend to be happiest spinning words and weaving them into a variety of pieces. But I think it is simply the nature of spiders to spin and the nature of writers to write.

I don't think the spider has an ego about what it creates; it just keeps going, as if its life depended on it (because, of course, it does). What would happen if you adopted the same attitude? Every chance you get, sneak up close to a spider and watch it. Watch it anchor each line and then dance itself around and around. Watch it dangle with gleeful industry and scurry into the darkest corner and curl into a tight ball. Watch it stand over its web and wait.

Think about how much power such a tiny creature can wield when it weaves together a web of fragile yet sticky thread to attract what it needs. Then throw all you've got back into whatever you are working on.

STAY STOCKED UP

The reward for work well done is the opportunity to do more.

—JONAS SALK

C. Hope Clark suggests stocking up on office supplies at the end of the year so you can claim your tax deductions. I like shopping for supplies during the back-to-school when there are more colors and designs to choose from. Here's a look at my must-haves to help you with a list of your own:

PRINTER INK. I buy these in sets but inevitably I need more black, so I buy a few double packs of black to fill in the gaps. Otherwise, I go through a combo pack about every other month.

PRINTER PAPER. I typically like to have regular paper and hole-punched paper on hand for editing purposes. I go through a couple of big boxes (ten reams) of printing paper a year.

THREE-RING BINDERS. I like the binders with the rings flat on one side, pockets inside (to hold clips until I file them), and the clear pocket on the front for a recent clipping.

MAGAZINE HOLDERS AND BOOKENDS. I don't need as many magazine holders as I used to because I'm trying not to hold onto things. For bookends, I just like the simple, metal kind. Somehow we never have enough.

CLIPS, PAPERCLIPS, AND RUBBER BANDS. I buy a big multicolor pack every few years.

PACKS OF PENS, HIGHLIGHTERS, AND MARKERS. I like G2s by Pilot for writing, including plenty of red ones. Fine and regular point Sharpies work well for book signing. I like to splurge on Prismacolor or calligraphy pens every once in a while for brainstorming.

SKETCHPADS, MEMO PADS, AND LEGAL PADS. I go through about four sketchpads each year. I like blank memo pads with fun covers and nonyellow legal pads.

STICKY NOTES. I prefer stickies that are whimsical and colorful.

FOLDING BOOK DISPLAY RACKS. These come in handy at book signings.

HANGING FOLDERS AND FILE FOLDERS. Colorful, of course, even though they cost more. I use these like crazy when I am writing a book and less often when I am not.

THINGS THAT MAKE OTHER THINGS STICK. Pushpins, adhesive tape, double-sided tape, magnets, staples—I like to have a couple staplers. One box of staples will last forever.

SOFTWARE. Microsoft Word. TurboTax. Quicken.

HOLIDAY CARDS. Pick these up on sale in January for the next holiday season.

BOOK-SIZED BUBBLE MAILER ENVELOPES AND POSTAGE.

I RARELY RUN OUT OF: Clear document holders, index cards, rubber bands, and pencils.

95
STRIVE TO SERVE

Sometimes in order for your dream to come true, it is you who need to take the initiative.

—HENRIETTE ANNE KLAUSNER

The most creative space in the world for you as a professional writer isn't some isolated room where it's just you alone with your imagination. The most creative place is wherever you can connect directly with your audience.

No matter if the place is actual or virtual; in person or online; in Portland, Oregon, or in New York City; I go to my audience regularly, so they will keep coming to me. And I firmly intend to keep those connections open and active going forward.

Do you want to know how I can tell when a writer hasn't taken the time to identify her specific audience? I can tell because the writer doesn't even try to connect with her audience. The writer creates and creates and creates, but doesn't connect what she creates to a specific audience who would appreciate her work most.

Therefore, nothing happens. No sales. No growing readership. No buzz. No ongoing connection between that writer and her audience. When a writer waits for the audience to find her, she will wait for a long time, when she could have sped things up all along by taking a more active role.

If you want to see your writing career take off, create an ongoing, engaged relationship with your audience. Soon you'll be delivering the most appropriate products and services directly to the kinds of people who will appreciate them most.

Here are ten questions to ask yourself when getting to know an audience you wish to serve:

1. The people in your audience are like you in which ways?
2. Are the people in your audience a subgroup of another larger audience?
3. Where do the people in your audience typically live?
4. Do the people in your audience work? If yes, where?
5. What ages are the people in your audience?
6. What do the people in your audience want?
7. What do the people in your audience need?
8. What frustrates your audience?
9. Are there subgroups within your audience?
10. When your product or service has a positive impact on your audience, what is the hoped for result?

96

DISTINGUISH BACK FROM FRONT

We freelancers are not in jobs where we have to be present all the time, like in retail. We can "disappear" and, using the power of technology, still be reachable if a client has an emergency (which they rarely do).

—LINDA FORMICHELLI

The back of the house is your private life. It's what you don't share with the public. You are allowed to choose what you share and don't share. You have to discriminate. Move what you don't want to share to the back and you will feel more comfortable about what you choose to share.

The front of the house is where you are visible and available. The front of the house is public. This is the "you" you show the world. It's not necessarily everything about you. Some writers show the world a very specific side and keep the rest of their life and creative process private.

I believe that any professional needs to have a front of the house and a back of the house in order for any focused work to get done. I don't believe that having all of your doors wide open 24/7 will accomplish anything better, faster, or more efficiently. Although I agree that it's important to have clear and frequent communication with your clients, readers, and prospects.

In my experience working with writers over the past ten years, most of the writing work is accomplished in the back of the house, whereas most of the networking and self-promotion is accomplished in the front of the house. I don't do my writing in the front of the house. I have to retreat to get my work done. But this doesn't mean I never come out and show my face. The key is to do it in short bursts of time that don't throw the rest of your productivity off course.

When you are "on," be on. And when you are "busy," be busy. Don't let social pressure determine how you work. Measure your productivity by the quality of your work, and trust what it teaches you.

If you are not accomplishing what you'd like to accomplish, determine the amount of time you spend in the front of the house and the amount of time you spend in the back of the house.

PUT YOUR WORK OUT THERE

After all, people buy people first. How are you leading with your person and following with your profession?

—SCOTT GINSBERG

The first platform you build will likely be more of a showcase than an interactive context. It's typically a showcase that introduces you and your creative power to the world.

If you are merely imitating others and following their "10-Step Formula" for overnight visibility, this strategy is going to get in the way of presenting yourself to the world as you are, as you want to become known.

Better to create something simple and straightforward the first time around that focuses not only on what you've accomplished but what you have to offer.

Here's what the first three writer websites usually look like:

1. THE MINIPORTFOLIO

If you already have published work and you want to share it easily with editors or agents, a miniportfolio is your best bet. The simplest of these sites can be easily posted using free blogging software like Wordpress.com. All you need is some copy that introduces yourself, an About page that describes your professional experience, a Clips page so editors can easily pull up samples of your work, and a Contact page. Make sure you select a template that isn't distracting, and put your best head shot on your About page.

2. THE EXPANDED PORTFOLIO

The nice thing about a miniportfolio site is that you can easily expand it for free as you continue to grow and earn. What other pages might you add? A summary of any personal or business writing services you offer. A Testimonials page with positive comments from professionals you've worked with. If you start blogging, you can link to a blog elsewhere (which I recommend, if you are new to blogging or unsure about your topic). And don't forget to add social media buttons if they represent you in a professional light.

3. THE PROFESSIONAL PRESENCE

At the point where you begin to have something to sell, like a first book, an ongoing class, or a series of workshops or presentations, it's probably time to upgrade to a professional-quality site. You can do this yourself or you can hire a Web designer to create a professional quality Web presence for you. Sometimes a professional upgrade doesn't include a lot of new or different information than the free site did, but a designer's touch can make a big difference on the impact it has.

Permission marketing is anticipated, personal, relevant.
Anticipated—people look forward to hearing from you.
Personal—the messages are directly related to the individual.
Relevant—the marketing is about something the prospect is interested in.

—SETH GODIN

In order to produce your own career, you are going to need to keep a lot of e-mail lists. Constant Contact or any other e-mail marketing program can help you do this in a permission-based way.

What will you need permission-based e-mail lists for? To send newsletters, announcements, teasers, news, freebies … all kinds of stuff that will grow your visibility.

Permission marketing has been the best way to connect with others online for many years now. Any person, organization, or business that does not understand permission marketing is ultimately doomed to failure because permission marketing is the key that makes the difference between being respectful in online communication and being a royal pain at every turn.

I can prove it to you. How do you feel when you receive spam in your in-box?

Annoyed, irritated, or even offended?

That's because spam is neither anticipated, personal, nor relevant. And I bet you would like to keep everything that comes into your in-box anticipated, personal, and relevant.

If you practice permission marketing, keeping and building your lists will become instinctive. Over time you will develop a swelling audience of individuals who are interested in your work. Occasionally, you will e-mail them en mass, and that's okay because you invited them to participate in a list for a specific reason, and they agreed to be on the list.

KEEP A LIST OF:
- Your frequent markets
- Your media list for press releases
- Your students
- Your writing friends/colleagues
- Any groups you target (like associations/schools)
- People you can speak/teach for
- Your newsletter subscribers
- More:
- More:

Today, you are You, that is truer than true. There is no one alive who is Youer than You.

—DR. SUESS

I talk a lot about self-filled service and not focusing too much on yourself; however, if you don't dip into your own uniqueness once in a while, you are going to start to miss yourself. And if you start to miss yourself, you might start blurting things out about yourself when it's not really relevant.

In all that you are, you will find some stories worth sharing, some insights that might have otherwise been overlooked, and some aspects of your good ol' self that are worth integrating into your writing career.

Answer these questions off the top of your head. I bet they will bring a smile to your face and a stirring to your soul.

1. What's your favorite color?
2. What's your favorite number?
3. What's your favorite smell?
4. What's your favorite food?
5. What's your favorite time of year?
6. What's your favorite day of the week?
7. What's your favorite animal?
8. What is your favorite breakfast?
9. What is your favorite lunch?
10. What is your favorite appetizer?
11. What is your favorite dinner?
12. What is your favorite dessert?
13. What is your favorite pizza?
14. What is your favorite ice cream flavor?
15. What is your favorite vegetable?
16. What is your favorite drink?
17. What's your favorite movie?
18. What's your favorite song?
19. What's your favorite activity?
20. What's your favorite chore?
21. What is your favorite type of exercise?
22. What's your favorite way to relax?
23. What's your favorite TV show?
24. Who is your favorite superhero?
25. What's your favorite way to communicate?
26. If you were a body of water, what would you be?
27. If you were a tool, what would you be?
28. If you were an appliance, what would you be?
29. If you were a city, which would you be?
30. If you were a country, which would you be?
31. If you had a past life, what was it?
32. If you have a future life, what will it be?
33. Who is your favorite actor?
34. Who is your favorite writer?
35. Who is your favorite singer?
36. What is your favorite restaurant?
37. What is your favorite date destination?
38. What is your favorite vacation destination?
39. What quality do you appreciate about yourself most?
40. What's your best feature?

It's one of the strangest attributes of this profession that when we writers get exhausted writing one thing, we relax by writing another.

—DAN SIMMONS

One of the reasons it's important to understand platform and to ramp yours up gradually over time while you strengthen your online marketing skills is because online platforms are complex.

Still, they can be broken down quite simply into the following components:

1. Home base: Blog/website
2. Niche communication tool: E-mail list/e-mail newsletter
3. Visibility builders: Social media profile activity
4. Niche water coolers: Social media hangouts
5. Community mixers: Guest visits at relevant online communities

If all you did was activate these five components, you would be amazed at what you could accomplish over time. These tools allow you to reach out to an international audience, not just a local or regional one.

I think the disappointment can come in with using these these tools if you rely solely on online tools. If you look at best-selling or mid-list authors, you will notice that they mix things up much more than this. They combine online activities with live activities. They are interested in connecting in person and online with their audiences.

I think the greatest power in the industry right now goes to the writers who connect directly with their best audiences. At the point where your name becomes known as much as your writing does, it's time to get out and interact with your fans face-to-face. A lot of folks will build up visibility based on a strong trust online. But trust means more than image; it means backing up what you do online with what you do in the world.

So if you are wondering if you should speak on a panel, offer a workshop, or start something locally, I think you should. (That is, if you can manage the time and energy investment.) Because personal interaction with the folks in your niche will pay off in the long run. You can lay the groundwork online, but be prepared to get out there and interact with real, live people or you are going to miss out on developing that all-important audience connection.

201

REPURPOSE YOUR MATERIAL

Re-slanting involves taking your initial story idea, spinning off other angles, and locating possible markets for it.

—KELLY JAMES-ENGER

Why not reuse what you've already written? And make more money with it! Think of the form your writing was in (whether it was an essay or a feature article) as a container. If you change the same content into a new container, poof! Your past work comes back to life anew.

Here's a list of ways you can reuse your words:

- Reuse a specific idea in much shorter or much longer form.
- Re-flex an area of expertise.
- Same gist, different form.
- Say what comes next on the same topic in the same form.
- Same message, new genre.
- Re-slant an article.
- Resell the same piece over and over again to new publications.
- Find a new story within the old story and expand it.
- Spin off more about a season or holiday you've covered often.
- Find humor in a serious piece, or vice versa.
- Reuse what you learned from a source.
- Write it as a sidebar, a quiz, or a game.

Can you be flexible with your material?

Can you see each piece as whole and complete in and of itself and then spin off another use of the same material?

Be flexible with what you create and your opportunities become unlimited.

The only thing all successful people have in common is that they're successful, so don't waste your time copying "the successful strategies" of others.

—SETH GODIN

I assume that you want more control over your career. I assume that you want to build a body of work in a specific area for a specific audience because doing so can pay off in larger and larger dividends over time.

Another good reason to grow and develop a body of work is because the Internet allows us to communicate directly with our audience, and writers who do this tend to have more influence and authority than writers who write on anything and everything.

Furthermore, the more you write about, the more difficult it is for other people to understand quickly who you are and what you are about. I want you to be unique and purposeful; I don't want you to be erratic and obtuse.

Go through the doorway of your own uniqueness to find not just the topic you wish to share but also the way you wish to share it. Don't mimic. Make your specialty unique to you. Be careful you don't follow in the footsteps of someone else's specialty instead of taking time to consider what makes the most sense for you.

The quantity of your specialty is composed of data and content, basically. But the quality of your specialty comes from that espresso we talked about. How the way you work with your material and with others transforms and elevates what you do into something unique.

Remember, there is no secret formula for success. So anyone who says they can give it to you is someone to avoid, not imitate. Steve Cohen, The Millionaire's Magician, says it best, "Magicians who e-mail me for advice in creating a show like *Chamber Magic* sometimes wonder if there's a secret formula they can follow to become successful. What they don't see is that I've dedicated my life to the show. My entire lifestyle revolves around the show. The show affects my availability to my family and prevents me from making outside commitments every single weekend. There's no easy secret I can offer to up-and-comers who think it'd be fun to have their own show."

*Many persons have the wrong idea of what constitutes real hap-
piness. It is not obtained through self-gratification but through
fidelity to a worthy purpose.*

—HELEN KELLER

We love a person who is one with a mission. And I'm not merely speaking to nonfiction writers. Novelists, memoirists, and children's book authors are no exception to
this rule.

Most authors find their mission by writing their way into it. Hence Janet Evanovich started as a romance writer, sweeping readers off their feet for Bantam Loveswept
,but ultimately decided that keeping readers hanging was more her thing. So now she
writes mysteries and plenty of them.

Behind everything you write, there is an ultimate thrust. Usually a bunch of short-
term successes build up and form a larger arc, and that becomes what compels you forward in your career. Even if the writer can't see the arc in the short run, whenever there
is forward momentum, the arc is happening.

Once you figure out which part of your job really makes you tick, your whole career
will likely experience a surge of wind underneath its wings. And to get to that sense of
liftoff, the question we all need to answer as writers is: What's my mission?

If you are a writer of horror, thriller, suspense, or mystery, perhaps your mission
has something to do with scaring the bejeezus out of your readers. That's a mission. It's
a plan that other people can appreciate and get behind.

If you are a romance writer, maybe your mission is helping your readers escape
from their dreary humdrum lives. If this is the case, you are entering a crowded marketplace, but who cares? If you tap into your strengths, niche, and best readers, you can
become successful.

Why not start by answering this question: What's my mission?

Once you have a pretty clear idea, it's time to ask others what they think. Simply
ask, "What do you think my mission is?"

If they can't answer, this tells you that you are not broadcasting a clear mission.
Ralph Waldo Emerson said, "That which we are, we shall teach, not voluntarily, but involuntarily."

What you are after is what you teach both voluntarily and involuntarily. Articulate
all of this into your mission.

LABOR WITH, NOT FOR

Friendship is essentially a partnership.

—ARISTOTLE

Never be confused about this: You work with others, not for others. This goes for publishers, agents, and everybody else in the business.

Partner wisely with others and create win-win relationships so you can advance farther, faster. When you work for others, you are an employee. You are dispensable, replaceable, and fireable. When you partner with others, you become a player, a partner, a professional who is sought out to work with, not for.

An exception might be when you are employed in a work-for-hire contract. Work-for-hire contracts take the most rights while offering the least incentive for doing so. Whereas the best and most potentially lucrative writing opportunities are those in which you maintain your independence and the majority of your rights.

How do you make sure your professional growth has integrity that is incorruptible? By keeping your goals clearly focused on the single next thing you need to accomplish in your writing career and taking care of that before you turn your focus outward.

You have a lot to think about in terms of getting your own career in order before you partner with others. The biggest mistake writers make in these highly distracting times is not paying enough attention to increasing their own professional power because they become caught up in somebody else's plan, agenda, or formula.

Good judgment is crucial to the success of any business. Always be prudent in business decisions and you will maintain your sanity. Once you know how to mind and grow your own business, you might be ready to partner with others who can mind and grow theirs. But don't try to live someone else's dream. Don't sacrifice your common sense for someone else's folly.

Embrace your own path. And remember that at the end of the day, success is not merely about how much you earn, it's about how much you prosper and help others to prosper, too. My best advice is wait until you know what you are about and what you are offering before you think about partnering with others.

CURATION BEFORE CREATIVITY

When I have carefully organized the information as a curator, and I take it all in and combine it with my own experience, intuition, and insight, then I am ready to create. At that point, the words seem to write themselves. The ideas flow. I'm in the groove.

—HEIDI SMITH LUEDTKE

Curation is a word that has gotten a lot of buzz lately and is therefore bound to be a serious cliché by the time this book comes out.

Therefore, let's cut to the chase. To curate basically means to be in charge of, for example, the accumulation of facts, data, or objects of art. The implication is that the curator is like a guardian or a caretaker of whatever she carefully pulls together.

You may already be a content curator for your tribe. According to Rohit Bhargava, "A Content Curator is someone who continually finds, groups, organizes, and shares the best and most relevant content on a specific issue online."

But don't confuse curating with creating. Curation can play an important role in creativity, but it's more like foreplay than the main event. It's the jumping-off place from which some really cool creativity can begin.

Curators are often purists. They may wish to keep their stream of whatever they are collecting pure from outside influences. And, of course, this often creates a temptation for those who have the opposite inclinations and would much rather mash up, remix, and disseminate whatever has been so carefully gathered and displayed.

As writers, we succeed by communicating our most insightful observations. Don't become so preoccupied with collecting that you neglect contemplation and the full expression of your thoughts.

Preoccupation with what is "out there" is not curation; it's distraction. We're much more interested in the observations that come to bear from a well-lived life than we are of the preoccupations of a one-note mind.

Curators rehash. Creatives say things that are fresh and brave and true. Curation is one thing. Creativity is another. Let's keep them straight. We don't want a curation nation. We want a creation nation.

You must validate your existence. You can be remembered as the meanest, cruelest, most useless hunk of humanity ever to insult flesh. Which will give you a wee but vile nick of immortality. Or you can be remembered as a giving, sharing, positive person who made a difference.

—GORDON BURGETT

Any topic you write on that receives an energetic response can be turned into a niche, of sorts. If you develop the habit of noticing what people like and want, you can channel your efforts of creating more of that type of writing. If you continue to receive green lights that your type of writing is needed and wanted, why not continue to grow a body of knowledge and resources on those topics?

Why not create "silos" of your niche topics by letting what you write pile up? This will help you identify potential markets you can align your writing with as you go forward. For example, one of my students writes about storms, sustainable living, and health. By thinking of her content as existing in silos, she can better understand which of her topics is getting the most play. Right now, the storm articles are winning.

Don't apologize for having specific interests in certain audiences or for being a member of certain tribes, because these choices simply reflect the truth about who you are and what interests you. Don't try to write for everyone. Write for whomever you want to write for, so long as they are a viable market. Write for the audiences you feel most comfortable writing for and about.

So even though you often start out with just one or two topics that you develop into niches, you can see that these focuses and interests grow and evolve over time, and this is just the way it should be.

Commit to writing for a time on a certain topic, for a specific audience, with your unique slant or take on the topic. You are never going to run out of publication opportunities and you are never going to run out of material. Watch your clips pile up!

PARTNER CONSCIENTIOUSLY

Is the system going to flatten you out and deny you your humanity, or are you going to be able to make use of the system to the attainment of human purposes?

—JOSEPH CAMPBELL

You've worked long and hard to get to this point in your writing career. Should you now go ahead and partner with anyone and everyone?

I think not.

Just as you would not sleep with everyone you met, nor marry them, nor share your gross annual earnings with them, nor let them care for your children or pets, don't partner with people just because they happen to be standing right in front of you. For goodness' sake, don't partner with them because they are filling your in-box with propositions. In this day and age, anyone can do that.

Remember that every person you choose to partner with is a reflection of your integrity. Some authors will team up with other authors in the short term because they share the same topic or type of audience without much exploration of shared values or objectives.

Always think about your partnerships as formal and informal, small and large, as either benefiting you in the long run or harming you in the long run. Beware of going for short-term gains that will bring you long-term losses.

Your ultimate business goal is to act like a conscientious, poised professional who only enters into carefully considered win-win partnerships with others, without letting those partnerships disrupt or interfere with your own professional growth.

If you partner with people who don't have your audience's best interests in mind, you compromise all of the hard work and integrity you've invested so far. Even worse, you gamble with the trust that you have worked so hard to establish.

Expect to work with the best. Don't settle. Stand up for yourself. Avoid anyone who seems desperate or sneaky. Don't assume that because a long-standing partner was trustworthy you don't need to conduct due diligence. Examine every contract carefully. Cross out anything you can't live with before signing and returning.

The people you want to partner with are steady, grounded, serious businesspeople. They can be playful and fun, but they understand that good business is about making constructive things happen and leaving a respectable legacy, not just about increasing profits in the short run.

In the digital era, writers sell stories, while creators build story-worlds.

—GUY LECHARLES GONZALEZ

Content may have been king in our brave new techno-world, briefly. But we've entered the age when context is queen.

A context is like a womb. It's the place that houses the creation, in this case, a baby. A book is a context. A movie is a context. A curriculum is a context. A blog is a context, too.

But the baby is not a context. The baby is just passing through, so to speak. Therefore, the baby is the content. Once the baby is fully formed, it will outgrow its need for the womb and head on into the world where it will do its thing.

I'm not saying that all contexts are for birthing, or creating either. Therefore, if you just crank out content, say in an online format, readers might come for a while (as in "if you build it, they will come"), but they will eventually move on in search of a cozy context where they feel safe and happy, and where, perhaps, they are not even all that concerned about content.

What they are more concerned about, perhaps, is the conversation that engages them and helps them grow, a learning experience, or a storyworld, because these are things in which they can participate.

What people really want is to grow. They are naturally attracted to contexts where their growth is invited and encouraged. When I create contexts, they are temporary. They are temporary because I don't have a staff. I can't afford a staff. And it takes a staff to build and maintain a complex context.

But Oprah, for example, has a staff. And if I were going to speculate, I would be willing to bet you ten to one that she intends to use her staff to build a context that takes her former network television platform and turns it into a dynamic learning context where fans can work at living their best life. Because Oprah is smart enough to know that her platform dynamic is something she takes with her wherever she wants to go.

We have entered the age of context big time. And it's going to transform the idea that content is king into content is the court jester. And the jester is going to be dancing for the new queen. And that queen is context.

Live out of your imagination, not your history.

—STEPHEN R. COVEY

What are the twelve biggest pitfalls for writers building their platforms?

1. They don't spend time clarifying who they are to others. Who are you to others?
2. They don't zoom in specifically on what they offer. What do you specifically offer?
3. They confuse socializing with platform development. How purposeful are you in your platform building?
4. They think about themselves too much and their audience not enough. What can you do for your audience today?
5. They don't precisely articulate all they offer so others immediately understand. What exactly do you offer?
6. They don't create a plan before they jump online. What's the plan for this month, six months, one year?
7. They undervalue the platform they already have. How can you spiff up what you've already got?
8. They are overconfident and think they have a solid platform when they have only made a beginning. How honest are you being with yourself about what you have accomplished and where you need to go next?
9. They burn out from trying to figure out platform as they progress without an ultimate plan. What's your ultimate destination? Where will you be in ten years, twenty, thirty?
10. They imitate "insider secrets" instead of trusting their own instincts. What do you know about what works for you?
11. They blog like crazy for six months and then look at their bank accounts and abandon the process as going nowhere. Do you understand that blogging is a communications tool, not a get-rich-quick machine?
12. They always want to be farther ahead rather than embracing where they actually are. How do you feel about where you are today? Make peace with that before you proceed.

*The very essence of leadership is that you have to have a vision.
You can't blow an uncertain trumpet.*

—THEODORE HESBURGH

Writing is a form of leadership. And leadership, these days, is all about social artistry. Social artistry is a concept I learned from human potential leader and author Dr. Jean Houston. What it means is that you are not just a writer creating a product and then slinging it out to the world, you are a creative soul inspiring a movement (or, if not a movement, you have at least one lofty goal to share).

An important part of social artistry comes into play when you align what you want with what your audience or readers want—when your best interests are their best interests. When you keep others' best interests in mind because their best interests are your best interests, you are in alignment, and that's when the magic happens.

When you are ready to start ramping up your platform, you probably won't feel like much of a social artist. You will probably feel overwhelmed with all there is to do and underwhelmed with all you have accomplished. You will feel like you are putting yourself out there and it is amounting to nothing.

But if you remain calmly focused on serving your tribe over time, you will be amazed at how opportunities for social artistry crop up. And if you become sensitive to the needs of your particular tribe and come up with ways to address your tribe's needs, they will likely reward you with their loyalty.

I think the best way to think of social artistry is to imagine that you are in a huge arena with all of your tribe. Imagine there is big stage right in the middle of the arena and you are leading the entire group in creating something meaningful.

When you get up on that stage, what will you do? What will you say? What's your message? How will you inspire or inform or entertain everyone?

When you start imagining that you are the one making the plan, holding the mic, calling up folks to contribute, that's when you activate your power as a social artist. So, go ahead, stand in the center of the stage with something compelling to say and say it.

Writers basically have two choices: They can build enough of a platform to entice an acquisition, or build one that's bigger than just books and enables their long-term independence.

—GUY LECHARLES GONZALEZ

Most writers I work with don't want to write about anything; They would rather write about something. Specifically, they wish to write about topics that are meaningful to them. They want to write for people they care about, audiences of a particular stripe.

One thing that helps writers sell more of their work is deciding what kind of writer they are, based on the work that is getting published or causing a stir, and making a bigger commitment to this particular topic and/or audience.

A lot of women who become mothers start writing about parenting because it's a road in life that they are going to be on for many years once the first child is born. Understandable, right?

But, of course, parenting is not the only road in the writing biz. There is an audience for just about any topic you can think of, and the Internet allows us to gather all kinds of people together into tribes, regardless of the interest focus. Think about and draw from the roads you are going to be on for a while.

For example, perhaps you are interested in spiritual growth, extreme sports, recovery, gaming, fantasy writing, or collecting. There is no reason you can't add these topics to your specialty topics.

Perhaps you hang out with spiritual seekers, athletes, workshop goers, gamers, writers, or collectors. Why not write about them, or for them?

What I'm saying is that we have lists of types of markets available to us every year in *Writer's Market*. But how often do we take the time to think about our relationship as writers to those topics and audiences? Probably not often enough.

Fortunately, it's a lot easier to succeed as a writer when you know what you want to write about, who you want to write for, and what type of piece you want to write. Editors and publishers certainly think this way, so it's a great idea for writers to develop the skill, as well.

212

COIN YOUR SUCCESS

Time is the coin of your life. It is the only coin you have, and you can determine how it will be spent. Be careful lest you let other people spend it for you.

—CARL SANDBURG

At some point in the writing biz, you've been around the block enough times to know what your style of success looks like. I'm not saying that your style of success won't evolve and grow because, naturally, it will.

But I am saying that you will eventually start to get a feeling in your bones of what you truly stand for, if you haven't figured it out already. And once you start to have this self-awareness, you'll discover that your work is coinable. And that you can mint your writing efforts into profit and more profit because everything you do, once it catches on, has your indelible stamp on it.

Once you have stumbled on what readers most appreciate about your writing, you can fulfill that need, that is, coin your creative efforts for readers.

It's a good feeling when awareness of your worth as a professional writer settles in. But it's also exciting when you realize that within the context of writing you have particular strengths that can be put to work for you and can pay off for you now and later.

Once a writer experiences this feeling of his own worth as a professional writer, his writing career takes root, settles in, and gets ready to expand more widely because that sense of security in himself extends into the world.

When you get your first strong sense of what you are all about, it's a fantastic feeling. It's nothing anyone else can take away from you. Once you start coining your success, you are on your way to ownership.

So, coin away. What are the most valuable parts of the work you have already done? How can you do more work like the most valuable work you've already done? Don't imitate yourself but take what you do tomorrow to a deeper, richer level by paying more attention to the best of what you've done.

213
MULTIWEAVE CONNECTIONS

*Making connections, creating and continuing meaningful inter-
actions with other people, whether in person or in the digital do-
main, is the only reason we're here. Remember that, set the tone,
and build legacy.*

—GARY VAYNERCHUK

Connecting means forging relationships with whomever you happen to bump into,
when the mutual interest to do so is there. Trusting connections and the way you prefer
to connect is a central thrust of what I call multiweaving connections.

Multiweaving builds on the idea that connecting is a more intuitive way to navigate a world crowded with people than old-fashioned networking.

What's fun about connecting is that you never know whom you will meet or what
you will talk about or where it all will lead. The idea is to follow your gut rather than
follow your logical mind.

What would happen if you used your instincts rather than your head to govern all
of your connections, including those relationships you accumulate over time? What
if you followed your instincts, your intuition, your gut, and your curiosity, and allowed these things to lead you to new people more efficiently than left-brain networking strategies?

How might your tapestry of connections be woven more tightly and brightly if all
of the people you connect with and stay connected with are people with whom you have
made personal connections?

Multiweaving won't zap all of your creative energy and time because a big, hectic
world full of busy, distracted people can be made more meaningful when you connect
with and stay connected to the people it feels right to stay connected to. When you connect people with each other, keep in mind that everyone is going to connect or not connect according to their instincts. We each connect as we like.

You might enjoy meeting people in person better than connecting with them online. You never know. Pay attention to your own likes, needs, and wishes, and don't let
anyone tell you you're not networking properly. The person standing right in front of
you may prove to be just as instrumental in your career in the long run as the industry
gatekeeper you never hear from.

Writing a book is not as tough as it is to haul thirty-five people around the country and sweat like a horse five nights a week.

—BETTE MIDLER

The most powerful platform you can build comes from establishing four levels of visibility: local, regional, national, and international.

THINK LOCAL: I live in a town of less than twenty thousand people, and I am certainly not the most internationally known writer in town, but I am probably one of the most well-known locally thanks to the Northwest Author Series I've been hosting here for the past several years. How hard would it be to do some regular good around your town? Think of all the things you love to do with all the folks you love to do them with, and what do you come up with? Create something cool, and send out some regular press releases about it. Over time, you will become known for it.

REGIONAL ACCLAIM: There are several simple ways to become more regionally known. You could write regularly for regional publications. You could volunteer in a visible position within a regional organization or at an annual conference as a way of increasing your visibility. You could do a regional circuit of appearances via an already established organization or association. In Oregon, I've given workshops at all five branches of Willamette Writers, a statewide writer's association.

NATIONALLY RENOWNED: Hop on the social network and connect with your tribe all over the country. You could publish an e-book that has national appeal and distribute it via the Internet. Or you could get a traditional book deal, which would result in your book being circulated to hundreds of bookstores and libraries all over the country. Your Author Central account at Amazon will give you access to your Bookscan sales by geographic location.

INTERNATIONAL PRESENCE: Social networking, e-publishing, and getting traditionally published can also help you become internationally known. But one of the best ways to become internationally known is to blog regularly for a targeted audience and then study your website analytics (using a service like Google Analytics), which tracks how many readers you have in other countries.

Technology is a word that describes something that doesn't work yet.

—DOUGLAS ADAMS

The problem with trying to stay right on top of new technology, for writers, is that technology is always evolving and there's more and more of it every day. So to commit to staying current is practically a second job. So just say no, or at least not now, to the allure of a steady stream of new toys. Like fine wine, technology improves with age. In fact, it improves a lot faster than wine.

I never buy the newest Mac. I don't have time to stand in lines to be first. I'd rather give whatever is coming out tomorrow six months to a year to mature.

I waited before I bought my iPod. I waited before I got my iPhone. I'm still waiting for my iPad. I can afford to wait because I could never exhaust all of the technology that is already available to me via the tools I already own and use. It would be silly and wasteful to toss aside what I already have just to be the first one to own a new gadget.

Wait for the technology to be what you need it to be, to do what you need it to do. And then use it as you need, preferably after all the bugs are out. You'll go farther faster this way. And, as an added bonus, your technology will be cheaper and work better.

Sometimes being first comes with a high cost. For one thing, pioneers typically have to put most of their ideas into pioneering instead of creating and serving. If you want to put the lion's share of your energy into creating and serving, don't feel like you have to be first. Just be open to new tools, eventually, when you actually need them.

Gadgets that come in handy for business:

Smartphones for taking photos, recording ideas, checking e-mail, texting, talking, and surfing on the go.

E-readers for reading and sharing books and magazines at home or on the go.

Desktop or laptop computer for running your entire business.

I never perfected an invention that I did not think about in terms of the service it might give others ... I find out what the world needs, then I proceed to invent.

—THOMAS EDISON

People want solutions. And readers are no different.

Writing success boils down to this: Do more of what's working, but occasionally stand back to assess your approach—you need to know what's going well and what's not going well. With these two strategies, any writer can go from not growing to continually growing.

How do you know what's working? Working means successfully serving others. You can't have writing success without serving someone.

What problem could you help the members of your audience solve? If you are one of the few people on the planet with the skills and insights to serve your audience on a macro and micro level, you will never run out of meaningful work.

Look for the sticking points. Where do your readers get stuck? Anything you can do to address those challenges? Put on your problem-solver hat and create a long list of ideas. Then narrow those ideas to only the best ideas for you to write about. Then take the best idea of them all and ask yourself how would you tackle it.

Don't try to solve too many problems at once. Tackle a problem that is complicated enough that you can't solve it in one sentence, or even a page of writing. If a problem is too easily solved, chances are good that nobody needs the help of a professional to do it.

What problems can you solve? First name the problems, then the solutions. Then get writing about each solution.

Problems: _____
_____
_____

Solutions: _____
_____
_____

SAFEGUARD YOUR ROLODEX

A creator, such as an artist, musician, photographer, craftsperson, performer, animator, designer, videomaker, or author—in other words, anyone producing works of art—needs to acquire only 1,000 True Fans to make a living.

—KEVIN KELLY

Once upon a time, a Rolodex was a cute little holder of tiny cards with tabs to help you flip through all your contacts quickly. You could have a bunch of cards in a single row or, if you were really popular, you had a whole plastic carousel to twirl around.

Today, the Rolodex is much more scattered and much more multifaceted. We have our personal address book: presumably, full of our family and real friends. We have our friends, fans, and followers in social media. We also have our business e-mail contacts, possibly in lists or databases, and hopefully segregated into specific kinds of groups.

So, the idea of Rolodex now defies the word "list." It should be called "lists," and perhaps this is a good way to think of it for business, because in business it is critical to segment your lists. You do not want to send inappropriate material to anyone on any of your lists. And naturally you decide what various contacts mean to you and how to categorize them.

Juggling personal and professional relationships is complicated by becoming publicly known. You want to get known so you will become more visible, but once you become known you discover that being known adds new, unanticipated layers of social complexity that you may not have considered when you were basically only known to your family and friends.

I have been paying close attention to the folks whose work I respect most, and one thing I've noticed is that they do not seem to have an open-door policy on their Rolodexes. Remember this the next time somebody you hardly know tries to tell you what you can do with your Rolodex for them.

Share what you want, when you want, the way you want—and this goes for your contacts just like anything else. And if you don't want to share, don't. People are often suggesting what I can do for them with my Rolodex. I reserve my personal and business referrals only to those people, products, and places I am genuinely enthusiastic about.

In permission marketing, the most important aspect of your connections becomes the word *appropriate*. I think this word is the key to knowing when, how, and whether or not to share your contacts.

FOLLOW GREEN LIGHTS

Before you agree to do anything that might add even the smallest amount of stress to your life, ask yourself: What is my truest intention? Give yourself time to let a yes resound within you. When it's right, I guarantee that your entire body will feel it.

—OPRAH WINFREY

Because writers face so many challenges and questions in our day-to-day professional efforts, I have come up with a shorthand method of navigation that I call "The Universal Yes."

The Universal Yes is that feeling, for example, when you have just the right idea for the right publication, and you just know deep down in your gut that you are going to get the assignment, if you handle it well.

If you are uncomfortable with these particular words to describe this feeling, you can come up with your own words. The point isn't what we call that sure feeling, it's that we recognize it when it occurs. Or, if we don't have it, that we keep working toward it.

Recall all the times you just knew that you had a perfect idea for the right publication and your instincts turned out to be right on the money. Conversely, think of all the times you have seen your ideas printed underneath other people's bylines.

Okay, you missed matching your idea to the proper market, but still, you are that much closer to The Universal Yes because you had the right idea.

Hold onto that feeling, because you're going to use it again and again as a writer.

LESSONS:

Do I feel The Universal Yes about whatever I am working on? Or am I lukewarm or overly optimistic about my chances?

Do I feel like I have a slim chance, but I proceed anyway? STOP. You are targeting the wrong publication. When you find the right one, you will feel a sensation of Yes.

Do I feel the Yes, though I'm not communicating all I know when I reach out for gigs? Is it time for a rewrite and/or to share what I'm trying to say with a supportive listener so I can better get it down on the page?

Do I feel calmly confident about what I'm writing? Am I able to articulate clearly and logically why I am the best writer for the job?

If you can answer all of these questions in the affirmative, you probably feel The Universal Yes.

We are all apprentices in a craft where no one ever becomes a master.

—ERNEST HEMINGWAY

You are going to win some and lose some, no way around it.

Here are the things that make you feel as if you've won:

- Acceptances for publication
- Assignments
- Warm responses from readers
- Acknowledgments and awards
- Invitations to attend or appear
- Interviews or features
- Positive Amazon reviews
- Thank-you letters

Here are some things you will sometimes lose:

- Gigs
- Editors
- Agents
- Friends
- Assignments

When you are passionate about what you do, it's easy to get emotional and it's easy to slip into ego. Writers need to learn to see the good news as a doorway and the bad news as a closed door.

When a door closes, don't spend too much time beating yourself up about it. Maybe it's for the best if you don't go through it. Learn to ignore the closed doors so you can proceed through the open doors. If you dwell on closed doors, you are likely to miss the doors that are swinging open all around you in other directions.

The bottom line is this: Don't give up unless you feel like you are on the wrong path. Deciding to pursue a new career path because you really want to isn't a bad reason to give up writing. But giving up because it's too hard or because you received some rejection is silly. Every successful writer knows that writing careers are not easy and always involve tolerance of rejection.

And as soon as you try to see every negative situation as a learning opportunity, you can start looking for the next open door.

Go up on the roof at night
In this city of the soul.
Let everyone climb on their roofs
And sing their notes!
Sing loud!

—RUMI

When I encourage writers to build their platforms, I am not merely encouraging them to promote themselves. I am encouraging them to become self-supporting by flexing their value in the short run and the long run.

The reason I don't want writers to wait until they write a book to start building a platform is because the money earned from a traditional book deal is not usually enough to provide a full-time income. So writers need to learn not only how to create a platform to market themselves and their services, but they also need to create a platform as they become profitable so they can become more profitable.

A full-time income is something most people require to be able to live comfortably, pay their bills, save for a rainy day, and still have a little left over to enjoy the pleasures of life. Writers also need to earn in order to have some money to invest in growing and sustaining their platforms. Therefore, it's not realistic to encourage writers who are busy developing their writing craft and sales skills to pour excess amounts of time and money into platform development and online networking.

Too much platform emphasis and networking before you become profitable is not only putting the cart before the horse, it's distracting writers from what is most important: becoming the writer you are meant to be.

Because we are social creatures, we can't avoid the influence of the group mind. If your process of becoming a writer happens largely online, writing a blog or contributing to community-supported sites, you may not become the writer you are meant to be; you might instead become the writer outside influences want you to be.

This is why it's so important to protect yourself from the sway of outside influences. They are a lot less concerned with the development of your creative instincts than they are interested in recruiting you to their causes.

221
PROTECT YOUR PRIVACY

Authorship is exhibitionism, and readers a species of voyeur.

—CARRIE LATET

Becoming a published writer means it's time to start making some decisions about your limits, your privacy, and your family values. Certain writers, like memoirists and essayists, are typically more open about sharing personal details from their lives because it comes with the territory. But for writers of other genres, your life doesn't have to be an open book. What you share and how much you share is up to you.

Everyone is living out loud these days. But you don't have to. Remember that you get to decide what to share and what not to share. Bloggers tend to post personal and family photos in their blogs. They often include members of extended family. As a writer, you can choose to keep your blog and social media content more focused on what readers want than on sharing personal details.

The concept of transparency still has a long way to go. Some equate the concept with oversharing about everything and anything. But for many audiences, TMI is still TMI (too much information). Calling it "transparency" doesn't justify oversharing.

If you don't maintain a sense of privacy and control over your life, you might start to feel victimized by your own success. Everyone needs a sense of containment: a sense of mine, yours, and ours. A place or places where you can draw the curtains, put on your sweats and a baseball cap, and exist without feeling scrutinized or on display. Don't compromise this, or you might compromise your peace of mind with it.

It's crucial for writers to take responsibility for creating their own personal privacy thresholds. For example, when my family and I moved recently, I decided it was time to get rid of the landline and keep my street address private except with close friends and family.

My writing career makes me visible, but my mental health requires respite from the world. I owe it to myself, to my family, and to my career to provide for my personal needs even as I serve the needs of the writing community.

Since I work with a lot of moms, I am especially in tune with a mother's desire to protect her children and family from the world. It's a good instinct. An important one. I predict discretion is an ability all writers who work any kind of spotlight will increasingly value in the coming years.

Nobody wants to live under a microscope. All Americans have a constitutional right to privacy. And therefore you get to pick and choose what to share from your life and what to keep private. Use your privacy to preserve and protect your creative process.

Follow your instincts. That's where true wisdom manifests itself.
—OPRAH WINFREY

Did you ever see the movie *City Slickers*? Remember the ominous mentor Curly and how he holds up his index finger to demonstrate the necessity of focusing on "one thing"?

This idea of "one thing" is a good example of purity of intention.

When you focus your writing career on one thing, your productivity will skyrocket, your work will flow with ease of effort, and your mood will be light and loose.

And when you are scattered and going in too many directions, your productivity will wane, your health may suffer, and your work will be affected by the overload you have in your life.

Purity of intention is not a reflection of how many projects you pursue. How many projects you pursue is best dictated by how much you can carry, what's practical and prosperous for you, and what your current schedule can bear.

When you allow your purity of intention to dictate how, where, and with whom you spend your time and energy, everything is better, easier, happier, and more fruitful.

Set clear intentions at the beginning of the year so they bear fruit before the year is out. Typically, when you are clear and focused, your intentions bear fruit even sooner.

You can't focus on your intentions when you are focusing on someone else's. Stay clear about what you need to do, not what others need you to do. Pure intentions offer writers a big payoff in terms of clarity. Clarity leads to a certain amount of freedom.

Because intention is everything, it's hard to have clarity if you don't have purity first. And it's impossible to have freedom without both purity and clarity. So keep things as pure as you possibly can. Just remember, as long as you focus on "one thing," you will have an easier time making the next best career-growing choice.

You won't be of much value to others if you don't learn to value yourself and your efforts.

—TWYLA THARP

I was presenting at a writers conference, chatting with another author in the green room, when a writer burst through the door. She ran to the refreshments table, grabbed a fistful of napkins, and then ran sobbing out of the room.

She had obviously received some bad news about a book concept she was pitching. I don't know any of the details, but I know a writer who has put too much of an emotional investment into a book project when I see one.

In my experience working with writers on book-pitching preparation, I have found that most writers grossly underestimate how much professional preparation is required of a book and how much is required of an author writing a book and promoting it. Therefore, they underestimate what is required of authorhood before, during, and after it happens.

So did I. I didn't know any better. I had no prior experience with book writing.

Not only does this naïveté lead to disappointment, it also leads to frustration and aborted dreams.

For some writers, sadly, I think book writing is an act of desperation. They either assume they are going to earn an unrealistic amount of money, or assume they will become famous no matter what their book topic. Still others think that writing a book is going to make them happy.

Writing is not going to make you happy, necessarily. But it might make you a little bit happier in the short run because there are short-term payoffs in making a large investment of creativity in a project. But those are typically only payoffs you can benefit from if you can leverage them at the same time as writing a book.

If you can view the book-writing process as an educational experience, you don't put all of your expectations in one basket, and you can steer yourself through it based on your common sense and resiliency, you will have a chance as an author.

No agent or publisher can make you feel better about yourself. And anyone who thinks that they can transport you from hardly writing to internationally known overnight is always going to be disappointed. Success is the writer's job from start to finish. Agents and publishers are only looking for writers with their own momentum.

The man who writes about himself and his own time is the only man who writes about all people and all time.

—GEORGE BERNARD SHAW

One way that writers decide which direction to steer their writing "ship" is by paying attention to trends. Not that you always have to pay strict attention to trends. In fact, sometimes bucking the trends can make for a juicy writing angle. But paying some attention to trends will likely do your writing career more good than harm.

While some writers look down on those who follow and enjoy trend spotting, being tuned in to the zeitgeist gives writers an edge in a competitive marketplace. And I'm not referring to nonfiction writers only.

Writing sells when it taps into the national, global, local, or regional zeitgeist. What is the zeitgeist? The zeitgeist is whatever everyone is buzzing about. And you guessed it, different interest groups are buzzing about different things all the time.

If one of my niche audiences is moms, I can explore what moms are buzzing about in order to have a more informed perspective about my audience *before* I start writing. If you are already informed about what your specific niche audience is buzzing about right now, excellent. Make a quick list off the top of your head.

If you are lacking ideas, hop on the Internet, scan some headlines, think about movies that are out, TV shows, and what's hot on talk radio. What's the buzz? Don't spend too much time indulging in all of this media, however. Five or ten minutes is enough. You want your ideas to be fresh and connected to what's happening now and then put them in the back of your mind as you go about the rest of your day. Then trust that insights will pop up in a few days.

Of course, being in touch with trends alone does not a published writer make. However, writers who pay attention to the trends that are coming can often launch their projects (and relaunch their old projects) with the wave and see a boost in sales as a result.

For example, before you turn up your nose at any novelists who may have tagged along for the ride with Stephenie Meyer or J.K. Rowling, just remember, if those trend-followers were writing and making sales, they were writing and making sales, which sure beats being blocked and poor. And if those who tagged along were writing in the vein that they wanted to be writing in anyway, those trends were boons to their creative growth.

The problem with cynicism about writing for the times is it cuts you off from the times. John Naisbitt, the author of the Megatrends books, says, "Trends, like horses, are easier to ride in the direction they are going."

It's nice to sign a letter, "sincerely yours," but far more powerful, I think, to sign it, "with respect." It says something compelling about the recipient, something earned.

—SETH GODIN

When you approach anyone who has more professional experience than you do, be sure you always approach respectfully and humbly.

The Internet has revolutionized access. Access to people. Access to information. But access is just an entry point. It isn't everything. In fact, it's hardly anything. It's what you do with your access, how wisely and well you tap into your access, that truly matters.

If you are online friends with someone you admire, this is not nearly the same thing as actually being friends with them. We all know this, but it's easy to forget when we are drunk on accessibility. So here are a few suggestions for approaching someone you respect:

- Be a genuine fan.
- Let your respect flag fly.
- Introduce yourself properly.
- Articulate your appreciation.
- Be sincere.
- Don't ask for anything.
- Be present and genuine.
- Don't be presumptuous.
- Don't critique.
- Don't offer your ideas.
- Don't grovel, hound, or stalk.
- Support her cause but don't fawn.
- Strike up a genuine conversation.
- Don't ask for favors.
- Be gracious and sincere.

If you are contacting a person with the intention of asking for something:

- Craft a quick, complete request that won't take up too much time.
- Make him a win-win-win offer.
- Consider how it's worth her time before you ask.
- Don't ask for too much.
- Don't expect a response.
- Don't take it personally if she says, "No thank you."

Remember, when you approach someone who has thousands of fans, she is not experiencing you as an individual but as part of a crowd. Treat her the way you would like to be treated, and you will stand out.

PERK UP YOUR PROMOS

*Too often, we're in such a hurry to show off what we'd like to build
we forget to sell the notion of what we built it for.*

—SETH GODIN

You have a lot of writing to do. And I mean in addition to all the writing you already do. You need to write the copy that encapsulates who you are and what you do. And then you'll need to update it regularly. Here's a quick list of the important copy that is key for your platform:

- Bios (short and long)
- Your professional history/a profile of your career
- Customer stories/testimonials
- FAQs
- Names/titles
- Taglines/slogans
- Mission/vision/values statements
- Questionnaires/surveys
- Award nomination requests
- Free content
- Catalog of what you offer
- Business examples/you in action/your impact
- Annual giving report
- Advance information/announcements
- Web page copy
- Fund raising
- Case studies of project/student growth/project profiles of past books/articles

GIVE CONSCIOUSLY

When we have filled-up people, they will go and share more love with the world ... it's absolutely the opposite of selfish.

—SARK

When you connect your abundance with what other people need, you discover how it feels to be genuinely generous. You become the gift, and your writing flows through you.

What writers can cheerfully give:

- Advice
- Assistance
- A percent of money earned or accrued
- Books
- Clothing
- Food or goods
- Volunteer time
- Consults or critiques
- Interviews, publicity, or endorsements

But writing is not the only way to give. Why not give from a sense of overflowing and a feeling of abundance wherever that exists in your life? In other words, don't give away what sustains you, or from a place that you don't want to give from.

There are so many ways we can give from our place of overflowing. Turn generosity into a practice, like purging your bookshelves and passing along those books you no longer want or need to good causes. Or, you might sort through your clothing and donate the outgrown clothes to charity. You will feel better when you consciously give.

Ask yourself this: Has anyone been generous with you? The reason I give scholarships to students in my classes is because others have been generous in this way to me. How could I justify not being generous, within reason, to others on an ongoing basis?

Maybe giving could be a monthly thing, like discovering something you have in abundance each month and finding a way to pass it on.

Of course, you need to pay your bills, and they cost so many dollars per month. So you can't give all that money away. I urge you to be practical. Give from what you can give. Don't give what you can't afford because that won't help you be generous on a continuing basis. If you give too much, stop giving for a while and let your well of generosity fill back up. You are allowed to have needs.

But you won't lose power if you give from your overflow. In fact, you will always gain power, and feel good, if you are giving in the spirit of generosity, and if you give consciously and consistently.

Just over eight hundred people were gathered around the cooking stage, all eager to learn about my five-minute flavor cooking. The demonstration had to be done right then and there, in front of everyone.

—ROCCO DISPIRITO

Once you have a specialty topic and you know who your audience is, there are many ways to grow your audience as you grow your own expertise.

I'm not talking about how to grow your reach once you are already an expert. I'm talking about how to grow your expertise as you begin to become known.

A lot of writers want to just slap up their shingle and declare themselves experts, but people are more easily persuaded to listen when you demonstrate your expertise rather than simply stating you are an expert.

They are also more likely to listen if you have stamps of approval from others who have experienced your expertise.

DEMO 1: WRITE ARTICLES, ESSAYS, OR OP-EDS ON THE TOPIC
Skills you'll need: organizing ideas, drafting forms, polishing and submitting

DEMO 2: SPEAK, TEACH, OR TRAIN ON THE TOPIC
Skills you'll need: pitching your services, planning and writing curriculum and materials, managing learning experiences

DEMO 3: WRITE FEATURE-LENGTH PIECES ON THE TOPIC
Skills you'll need: pitching the idea, interview and research skills, drafting and polishing skills, meeting deadlines

DEMO 4: LEARN AND SHARE THE BEST OF WHAT YOU LEARN
Compile a stream of regular reading material via the blogs of the primary experts on your topic. Share the best of what you read on social media.

DEMO 5: BLOG ABOUT WHAT YOU LEARN
Respond to what you read and learn as you go along in your own blog. Become a commentator on a specific topic.

DEMO 6: GUEST BLOG ABOUT WHAT YOU LEARN
Offer to share what you know on other people's blogs.

How vain it is to sit down to write when you have not stood up to live.
—HENRY DAVID THOREAU

Win, win, win is not the same as happy, sad, miserable. My eight-year-old pointed this out to me when I tried to explain the concept of win, win, win to her. In the process, I realized that win-win-win is not the same as win, win, win. Editors will appreciate the difference that a little bit of punctuation can make.

Win-win-win implies that everyone is going to win all at the same time. Woo-hoo! We are all winning. Right now. Instantaneously.

Whereas win, win, win implies that everyone is going to win eventually, once time factors in.

In order for win, win, win to work, a certain amount of trust needs to have been established. If you don't trust a person, and winning is going to take time, you are not going to let that person help you win. You are not going to be willing to invest the time and energy in the interaction to allow the mutual success to unfold.

But win-win-win means that everyone benefits altogether and at the same time.

Most things in life occur in the win, win, win cycle. But a lot of people are starting to want and to demand win-win-win. We want win-win-win and we want it now!

But maybe what we actually need is a transitional plan. If we can roll with win, win, win for a while, maybe we'll be in a better position for win-win-win to occur. That is, if we ever get to the point on this plane where we can instantaneously create good for everyone all at the same time in the snap of our fingers.

I am saying that good for all, otherwise known as progressive change, still seems to be happening in increments. But maybe people are starting to demand it sooner because they sense that with a little creativity maybe it should not have to take this long. Maybe folks with more power are dragging their feet about sharing. Maybe we really can raise all boats. But we need to do it wisely and think through the impact of our role.

So work on win, win, win, for now. If you do, I think you will be ready for win-win-win, when and if the opportunities arrive.

ADDRESS YOUR ANGER

The next time you get bad news, resolve to use that pain to drive your work. Show fate that when it pushes you, you push right back. By writing. By querying. By marketing.

—J.A. KONRATH

On the topic of anger, I have picked up some wisdom from others and my own experience, for instance:

Your anger can be turned into fuel for your writing career. But be careful. Make sure you are not motivated by anger in your actions, or you may risk acting out rather than acting thoughtfully.

The first stage of turning your anger into determination to succeed is to feel it. Painful as that anger may be, you don't want to carry it around, or, heaven forbid, have it turn back on you.

Process your feelings before moving forward. Punch some pillows, scream into a pillow, or tell the truth about how angry you are to someone you trust before you move forward.

Processing your feelings might take a while—it takes as long as it takes. But don't skip it, or you will likely feel terrible later. If you deny or ignore or avoid your anger, you won't shift that anger into energy.

You have to let the anger roar out in order to reopen up a creative channel. If you keep your anger pent up or if you don't express it because you feel like it's not nice to do so, your anger is going to leak out, and it's probably going to come out sideways or in unexpected bursts.

Furthermore, if you proceed while you are still angry, some of your anger is going to become apparent. It's going to interfere with sending out a clear signal.

Take these steps next time you are angry: Pinpoint what you are angry about, articulate what you are angry about, express what you are angry about, release what you are angry about, and let go of what you are angry about.

The ultimate goal is to get to the place of accepting how you feel, and only time will tell how long it will take to get there. Hold the intention to accept your anger no matter what it's going to take and you will get to serenity eventually.

The longer you're online, the deeper and more effective you'll be. The more impressions you'll make over time, the more people will head to your hub.

—JANE FRIEDMAN

Cultivating a rich, dynamic website comes first. Everything else follows. A mistake platform builders make in the early stages is posting the best of their work all over kingdom come. You don't want your best work everywhere but home. You want a wealth of content to pull attention to your website like a homing signal. The richer and deeper your content the better. You can spread yourself around later.

Here's a roundup of helpful tools for setting up an alluring home base:

1. Firefox is a browser that is easy to download and update, and is fun to use. You can even customize the look of the header to suit your personal style. You may as well entertain yourself with the way your web browser looks, since you will be looking at it every day. Other browsers to consider include Explorer and Safari.

2. Purchase URLs for the name you plan to use in the long run. Also purchase URLs for any books or e-books you have written and any signature taglines you use. You can purchase extra URLs and forward them to your primary URL (usually your name). Purchase your primary URL for five to ten years at a time. I use GoDaddy.com because it's the biggest and therefore the cheapest. Conduct some polls online and get your concerns addressed before you commit to any provider.

3. Wordpress.org is considered one of the easiest and cheapest ways to own, build, and manage your website (not to be confused with Wordpress.com, which is fine for a practice blog but may not be monetized). With minimal tech knowledge and hosting from your URL provider, a writer with modest technological know-how can create, launch, and manage a site at Wordpress.org. Or you can hire out the setup or final bells and whistles.

4. I use a custom theme, Thesis, for my blog but Wordpress.org offers plenty of free themes. A custom theme is a template designed specifically to enhance the use and findability of a blog. Like many other blog themes, Thesis allows me to become an affiliate, if I like. There are plenty of blog themes you can use for free, purchase inexpensively, or affiliate with (or not), according to your interests.

JUST SAY NO

Saying no can be the ultimate self-care.

—CLAUDIA BLACK

There is one word that is the most powerful word in the world. Do you know what it is?

It's not the one you would guess first. It's the second.

Did you guess the word *no*?

But when you use it, say it more nicely than that.

Say, "Oh, man, I'd love to. But I can't. Thanks so much for asking."

And then take all the time you save yourself by being able to say no and use it to get your writing done.

But don't explain why, because when you explain, you disrespect yourself. You are allowed to say no, so say it when you feel like saying no is the right thing to say.

Despite what popular online culture is telling us right now, you have to have limits if you want to carve out a creative life for yourself.

Don't do what everyone else is doing. Do only what you want to do and what makes good sense for growing your business.

If you are not sure what to say yes to and what to say no to, complete these sentences off the top of your head:

1. I am no longer willing to …

2. Something that bothers me is when …

3. I lose my rhythm when …

4. These kinds of supposed opportunities suck all of my energy …

5. Things I won't trade for the promise of "good exposure"…

6. Another important question:

7. Another important question:

8. Another important question:

Unlike people in most fields, journalists are constantly building brand-equity through their work. So all talented jounalists have to do is take advantage of the technological and cultural shifts that are sinking their media platforms like leaky ships, go into business for themselves, and crush it.

—GARY VAYNERCHUK

Use this combination of tools to be the most networked professional in your niche.

1. **PUBLISH WIDELY.** Your blog has an RSS feed, which sends your content or summaries of your content to readers. FeedBurner is a feed enhancer that allows you to reach more readers, more easily, in more ways. For example, get a FeedBurner account and use FeedBurner tools on your site so your blog posts can be delivered directly to your readers' e-mail in-boxes. Readers will appreciate the convenience.

2. **SHARE BETTER.** The ShareThis tool takes your blog posts and shares them on social networking sites. I added the ShareThis button to my Internet browser so I can quickly share anything I pull up on my browser with my friends, followers, and other connections. You can also add ShareThis buttons to the bottom of each of your blog posts to make them easier for readers to share with their networks.

3. **STREAMLINE YOUR REGULAR READS.** No, you don't need to relinquish sleep to keep up with the blogging Joneses, but you want to skim the posts you carefully curate and organize in your blog reader roughly once a week. You can't be a thought leader if you don't read and respond to the most current conversations on your topic. I use Google Reader to help me keep up. Even just barely keeping up with a handful of quality blogs will give you plenty of food for thought.

4. **HANG WITH YOUR PALS.** The folks on Facebook aren't working hard to network; they are just hanging out at the virtual water cooler with their pals. Facebook is a great way to connect with fellow authors, readers, and fans in an informal setting. I don't think it is as important to have a fan page as it is to just pop in on Facebook regularly. Feel free to friend me next time you are there.

5. **BE TWITTY.** Once you get the hang of it, Twitter is pretty fun. Twitter is kind of like windsurfing. It looks easy, but seems impossible when you first start doing it. However, if you stick around long enough, you'll eventually get the hang of it. Feel free to "follow" me.

6. **PROMOTE EVERYTHING YOU OFFER.** I've been using Constant Contact to send quality e-zines, announcements, and offerings to my growing e-mail lists for years. Its span of services expands all the time and includes services like event management, polling, and e-mail marketing training.

We all operate in two contrasting modes, which might be called open and closed. The open mode is more relaxed, more receptive, more exploratory, more democratic, more playful, and more humorous. The closed mode is the tighter, more rigid, more hierarchical, more tunnel-visioned. Most people, unfortunately, spend most of their time in the closed mode.

—JOHN CLEESE

The Eagles wrote a whole song about taking it easy but the bottom line is if you're tense and worked up about what you are doing, it's difficult to write anything well.

If you take a relaxed, focused approach to your writing, you will be able to engage and make better progress faster.

I can sometimes get more done in one focused hour than I do for the rest of the day. If I can just sit down, open up a new document, and start nudging the cursor across the page in little flurries of tapping fingers, it's going to be a good day.

But let's talk about stress for a minute. We all know how it feels, right? It's an escalating tension that you can't release.

Well, actually, if you are writer, you can release it. You can release it onto the page. If you are feeling worked up about something, try this: Grab some paper or open a new document and just let your thoughts rip. Write as long as you want. Or set a timer for twenty minutes and write that long. Don't try to say anything profound. On the contrary, say anything. Let it rip. Let it riff. Let it roar.

When you are done, you will feel so much better that focusing on whatever writing project you have on hand will be easy.

Take the permission you gain from writing for release and open up the truth-gates within whatever project you are working on. Let it rip. Let it riff. Let it roar. Just get it done.

Take it easy. And if you can't take it easy, take it out on the page—and then take it easy.

The soul should always stand ajar. Ready to welcome the ecstatic experience.

—EMILY DICKINSON

You can be alone and spend time alone without feeling lonely or desperate—as a matter of fact, you can feel happy or even joyful. Most writers experience a certain level of ecstasy in the process of writing while all alone in a quiet room.

Experiencing ecstasy sounds glamorous but it isn't because you experience it even writing in your pajamas or in the middle of the night when you have insomnia or scribbling something down while the baby is taking a nap.

You won't always get the long stretches of time and the luxury to get lost in your work, although it's great when you can because they can lead to longer periods of ecstasy. Just squeeze in whatever you can get, however you can get it.

This kind of creative expansiveness is a daily happening for writers. You can cut the lawn and then sit down to write and, there it is, another wave of ecstasy. You can have an epiphany in the shower.

If you are going to work on long pieces of scholarship, journalism, or any genre work, I bet you won't experience aloneness as isolating. I bet you'll be able to mount the horse of your self-expression and take it for long galloping rides until you remember the feeling of wholeness and purposefulness that comes with writing. It's like bliss, right?

Writing has an "everyday infinite" nature. I suppose that's why I enjoy it so much. I suppose that's why so many writers have stuck with it for so many centuries with scant financial gain.

So we need to grab those little moments and immerse ourselves in them as much as we possibly can ... before it's time to change out of our pajamas, before we feel sleepy again and are ready to climb back in bed, and before that baby rises from her nap.

Enjoy whatever amount of writing ecstasy you can get, whenever you can get it.

You can choose to self-publish from the outset and retain control. And if you decide to go with a traditional publisher, you can choose to back out if the contract language doesn't suit you, or if the publisher isn't putting forth a good-faith collaborative effort and is instead disrespecting you.

—RACHELLE GARDNER

Let's look at what you can and can't control in the professional writing arena.
What can you control? Everything that has to do with you.

- The quality of your ideas
- Your timing
- Your preparation
- How much research you conduct
- How much heart and soul you put into your work
- Your willingness to get the job done
- Your outreach and alliance development
- How well you follow through

What can't you control?

- How your idea is received
- Whether or not it's a fit
- Whether or not you get any feedback
- Other people

There is no point in trying to control others. The best you can do is control your own actions and hope that folks follow through on their commitments.

And when your work is as impeccable as it can be, it will sell. Until then, keep working!

PERSONABLE NOT EGOMANIACAL

Watch me for two seconds and you know exactly who I am and what I stand for. Authenticity is key.

—GARY VAYNERCHUK

I wrote about why it's important not to base your body of work on your personality in *Get Known Before the Book Deal,* and I took some flack for it.

I suspect that writers thought I was suggesting they hide their best qualities under a bushel basket, which could not have been further from what I was suggesting.

What I was trying to say was this: Don't make it all about you and your personality, or you are going to come across as an egomaniac.

Most writers are successful because they focus on self-infused service, not the me-me-me show. Your personality may help you get gigs, but I would not advise relying on it too much. Writers are more often sought after for reliability, solid writing skills, and their good track record for making a deadline (or at least coming close).

And yet, how many times will an unproven writer suspect that the reason she got the gig was her personality, not her talent or professionalism, and she ends up feeling like a fraud?

On the contrary, if you are not a schmoozer, that's okay. Just focus on being professional instead. Swim the waters for a little while first, get some professional experience under your belt, then let your personality shine through in an appropriate way according to the situation.

In this gig economy, professional means reliable, skillful, and service oriented. Not someone who blows others out of the water with personality. Try personable first, then gradually share more of yourself if you're invited to do so. An editor can always friend you on Facebook if she wants to get to know you better. But if a person only wants to keep things on LinkedIn, take it as a sign that this is going to be purely professional exchange.

Another problem with relying excessively on personality is that some folks will appreciate your personality while others may not. So by relying overly on personality rather than professionalism, you might be making connections half the time and turning people off the other half. You can do better putting professionalism first and simply being personable.

Not every song is a hit, and not every ballplayer makes it to the Hall of Fame. Likewise, an online campaign won't make a bad book successful.

—STEVE WEBER

I know what you want when it comes to understanding platform development. You want a quick, comprehensive overview of everything you need to know in terms of the basics. From there, you plan to hop online and check out what latest author gimmicks are popular. Great! Here are three books you can read in the span of one week:

CRUSH IT! BY GARY VAYNERCHUK (Harper Studio)
Here you'll find the kind of pep talks Gary Vaynerchuk is known for from five years of producing his own online video series, *Wine Library TV*. If you need hope, inspiration, and a kick in the pants, Gary is your guy. A very quick read.

GET KNOWN BEFORE THE BOOK DEAL BY CHRISTINA KATZ (Writer's Digest Books)
It's difficult to speak objectively about your own book, so I've borrowed a few lines from Amazon reviews and paraphrased them: *This book is full of exercises that will help you understand the complicated concept of platform development, get you brainstorming, and build your self-promotion confidence by actually working on and building your platform.*

PUBLICIZE YOUR BOOK BY JACQUELINE DEVAL (Perigee Trade)
Traditional publication still matters, and any author can learn important etiquette tips and glean adoptable advice with a read-through of this comprehensive analysis of the traditional publishing book publicity process.

Begin doing what you want to do now. We are not living in eternity.
We have only this moment, sparkling like a star in our hand—and
melting like a snowflake.

—FRANCIS BACON SR.

Never imitate yourself. If you do, you will surely bore yourself and your readers.

You never want your work to become dull and flat. You certainly don't want to repeat the same old things you've said over and over. For a creative person, repetition is the fast track to a dead end.

Instead, let surprises well up inside of you, let them stir and swirl in your mind. Let them make you giddy, kind of the way you feel when you look out the window and see the first snow of the season.

Snow is such an ordinary thing. But, even so, the first time you see it each year, you get that little chill down your neck. *Look. Snow!*

And something inside of us stands up and says "hurrah!", even though it's not new. It's just snow. Just like the snow we have every year, only newer.

I think this summarizes well what readers want from writers over time. We want the same old you, only newer.

So don't settle for second acts. Don't give us the same old same old. Dazzle and impress yourself with your fresh ideas so you can dazzle and impress us with them.

After you've had a major creative push, it's okay if you don't feel inspired for a little while. You probably just need to restock the well, and you'll be teeming with ideas in no time.

When the perfect interior conditions meet the perfect exterior conditions and your level of inspiration is just right, ta-da! Your fresh ideas will fall gently from your mind and build up on the page.

Now, I know you are not a creative snow globe. You can't re-create perfect conditions day after day. Nobody can. But if you pay close enough attention to the circumstances, you might be able to attune your internal thermostat. If you can get yourself in the right frame of mind, and add the right amount of inspiration, you might just figure out how to make a tiny flurry. And once you are practiced at this, working yourself into a creative blizzard can't be far behind.

These days our water coolers are increasingly virtual—there are many different ones, and the people who gather around them are self-selected. We are turning from a mass market into a niche nation, defined now not by geography but by our interests.

—CHRIS ANDERSON

In any workplace that has a break room or a snack bar or a local bar or coffee shop where folks go to hang out, the purpose of the water cooler is to take a break from work, blow off steam, vent about what's not going your way, and refresh yourself before returning to more work.

Social networks are like giant international water coolers. They are the places where people hang out, take a break, blow off steam, vent, and find refreshment. Social networks are also places to chat, to share news or resources, and to decompress.

And woe to the folks who think of social networks as opportunities to fire up their mass-marketing machines. Who struts into a virtual break room with a soapbox and a megaphone and shouts in people's faces at close range? Only a person who wants to wear out the good graces of others quickly.

For writers, social networks present opportunity that must be carefully balanced with common sense. These work/play wonderlands offer the opportunity to multitask, if we know how. We can poll our networks, create hubs of students, and participate in a virtual roundtable the likes of which were not available to the members of the original Algonquin Round Table.

We can use social networking as a way to be in touch with those people we want to be connected to without taking on pressure to perform tasks or accommodate behavior we do not explicitly intend or invite.

Keep your social networking behavior professional and consistent, as you would all of your writing career behavior, even if you occasionally mention an offer or a plug.

Don't let the pressure to sell turn you into an online marketing machine for yourself or others. Use the Internet more gently than that. Use it as a tool to connect with others, to create intentional contexts where folks can gather, and to create a context of international quality that serves the common good.

Be clear about who makes up the community at large and who makes up your marketplace, because confusing the two can be deadly.

—CHRIS BROGAN

Nobody is going to suggest you move to a mountaintop and sequester yourself from the world in order to write. However, with the social media booming full blast, your blogger friends (or your teenage children) might criticize you if you don't start living out loud 24/7.

But before you jump on the bandwagon, consider your intentions for going online and base your choices for how you will spend your time online on your wants and needs, not the wants and needs of others.

For example, maybe you'd like to get online to find your tribe—a group of like-minded others. Maybe you'd like to share something you know or something you've created. Or maybe you are ramping up to share something in the future that you are working on now.

Base your actions on your objectives and also on the sense of satisfaction you hope to gain from connecting with others daily. Go ahead and jump online—start hanging with the cool kids—but if your intentions are professional do offline preparation first.

Get mentally prepared before you hop online and save yourself a huge learning curve.

Before you create your plan for online community building, I suggest you read:

- *Tribes* by Seth Godin
- *Crush It!* by Gary Vaynerchuk
- *Trust Agents* by Chris Brogan and Julien Smith

NETWORK WHEN APPROPRIATE

It isn't just what you know, and it isn't just who you know. It's also who you know, who knows you, and what you do for a living.

—BOB BURG

If you have nothing in particular to say, nothing to bring to the table right now, and are not on any particular kind of mission, maybe you don't need to spend a lot of time social networking. Maybe your time and creativity would be better spent in other ways.

Let's examine three reasons to start social networking in earnest:

1. You have something important to say and share.
2. You have some thing or some things to bring into the conversation (classes, books, etc.).
3. You are on a mission and you are there to spread the word about it.

Here are a few questions to test whether or not you are ready to go social:

- Are you a thought leader on a particular topic? If yes, what is the topic?
- Are you interested in connecting with a particular audience? If yes, which audience?
- Are you on a mission about something? Do you really want and need to get the word out?
- Do you have a product (a book is a product) or a class or anything at all to promote?
- Do you either have something important to say or wish to join in conversations on a specific topic?

By answering these questions, you should be able to determine for yourself whether or not this is a good time for you to jump into social networking.

Some good reasons not to jump into social networking include:

- You are engaged in a deeply creative process and being on social media could knock you out of your process.
- You are doing pretty well already with your writing, and you don't see how social networking can advance your work at this time.
- You are already so busy that you can barely fit the people who are already in your life into your day (social networking will bring more people into your life). Get your regular life in order before you hop online.

We do tend to use our in-boxes as electronic to-do lists. We get behind on our e-mail correspondence and then we catch up. We thrive—or, at least we think we do—on a modicum of disorder.

—DAVID SHIPLEY & WILL SHWALBE

Say it with me: "I am the master of my in-box."

One of the most important skills you will need to learn as a writer is how to manage a very busy in-box. At any time, you are likely communicating with people with whom you have and maintain a complex network of relationships.

For example, you may communicate with new-to-you editors, editors you work with on an ongoing basis, and editors you are working with at the moment. If you are a teacher, for example, you also communicate with former students, current students, and potential students.

You may receive e-mails inviting you to speak, asking you for advice, hoping that you will plug some company's latest offer. And, of course, you will receive inappropriate requests too absurd to mention (which are basically spam).

I receive personal e-mails, as well, from my daughter's school, my writer mama friends, my daughter's friend's parents, family members, and e-mail lists I opt into.

In order to keep everything neat and orderly in my in-box on an ongoing basis, I use e-mail rules, which I set to automatically forward mail into specific folders right in my e-mail.

When editors e-mail me, if they are known to me, their correspondence goes into my "Editors" e-mail folder. When current students e-mail me, their e-mail goes into the file with the rest of their classmates' e-mails. Subscriptions to newsletters and catalogs go automatically into a "Subscriptions" folder. Letters from friends, family, and my daughter's school enter into my regular in-box along with unsolicited e-mails.

Because my in-box is orderly, I don't suffer from e-mail overload. All the anticipated e-mail goes into a folder. I can tell the prioritized correspondence from the junk, and if I was added to a list without being consulted, I notice and can unsubscribe quickly.

It's your turn to conquer your in-box once and for all. Arrange the flow of correspondence the way that works best for you and your daily rhythms. In about an hour, you can become the master of your in-box.

I've learned that people will forget what you said, people will forget what you did, but people will never forget how you made them feel.

—MAYA ANGELOU

I was working with one of my students in my platform class, and I could tell that her enthusiasm for her own work was flagging. She'd finished her first novel. She'd read my platform book. She'd launched her platform. She'd gone from unknown to somewhat known … and then she hit a wall. So I gave her an assignment. Go to the website of an empowered author and analyze everything there that is working. She came up with some great observations, which I've paraphrased here:

- She felt he shares "wisdom" with his audience, meaning he doesn't just rehash other people's ideas.
- She got the feeling he would do the work even if he didn't have published books to sell just because he loved what he was doing.
- She noticed that he built momentum and word of mouth by including other experts, such as folks who had been involved in his book research.
- She noticed that his blog is rich with content, more like four blogs within one blog.
- The said the author is passionate about asking questions about his focal topic and then answering them for the reader in a way that helps the reader accomplish his goals.
- The ultimate accomplishment of the blog, she said, was that she felt energized when she read it.

The author's passion for his topic opened her up. She went to his website stuck, blocked, and frustrated, and what she found and read there lifted her up and got her psyched and ready to revamp her own platform.

When we get to the point where our mere Web presence can unblock others, we will have arrived as writers. Aim for it in your own platform development.

There is nothing enlightened about shrinking so that other people won't feel insecure around you. We are all meant to shine, as children do.

—MARIANNE WILLIAMSON

People on social media will listen to you on an ongoing basis because you will have earned or learned qualities that make you worth listening to. Therefore, assuming you are not a royal, a celebrity, or the offspring of a celebrity, we are likely paying attention to you because you are:

AN AUTHORITY: You have a depth of expertise and you know how to wield it. We respect that.

A REFERRAL: Someone has pointed us toward you and we trust her judgment.

A CREDIBLE RESOURCE: Many people agree that you deliver; we want to know what or how.

AN EXPERIENCED EXPERT: You have a long track record, so we are curious about what you know.

A SPITFIRE: You have chutzpah. You dare to say and do things nobody else is saying or doing. We admire you for it.

A PIONEER: You are the first to champion a mission people recognize as crucial to the future. We can respect that.

AN INFLUENCER: You have a lot of influence. This mesmerizes us.

A BESTSELLER: You are on the list and we want to know how you got there.

A HEADLINER: You are in all the news, which means you are either genuinely buzz worthy or part of a very clever and sophisticated publicity campaign. Either works.

AN OMNIPRESENT PERSON: We hear your name everywhere.

A FAMILIAR FACE: You have been around for so long that we feel like we know you.

A RISING STAR: If we think you are a rising star in an area that interests us, we might bet on you for the satisfaction of betting on the right horse.

A CONNECTOR: You like connecting with others and you like connecting people you know with each other. You may consider yourself a matchmaker of sorts.

*I call them energy-sucking vampires—they don't contribute any-
thing positive to the world, but they enjoy lashing out and attempting to suck the life away from other people.*

—CHRIS GUILLEBEAU

Along your merry writing way, you will encounter all sorts of people who may be interested in working with you. And yet, when you partner with others you are investing a
significant amount of time and energy. So the last people in the world you want to partner with are folks who will drain your energy.

You don't need fans with oversized needs. You need fans who are interested in what
you offer. So make an effort to prioritize the kinds of people you want around:

- The people you serve
- Your genuine fans
- Journalists or prominent bloggers
- Professional colleagues or partners

Here are requests you might put in a separate folder in your e-mail program called
"Save for Later":

- Anyone looking for something called "help"
- Anyone who is contacting you from jail
- Anyone who requests frequent "help"
- Anyone who does not respect your time
- Anyone who takes you for granted
- Anyone who mistreats you

How will you be able to tell if a person is an energy vampire? These folks are usually creatively blocked. Here are a few signals that you are about to get hit up:

- They describe themselves as a person who experiences incredible luck, continual serendipitous good things, or as leading some sort of charmed existence,
  as opposed to a person who succeeds based upon her own efforts.
- They have a strong sense of urgency. What you can offer them today is never
  going to be enough. They need more and they need it on an ongoing basis.
- They want to leverage your established name to further their unknown name.
  Beware of hangers-on. Ask for formal terms in time requests so you can make
  the best use of your time.
- Beware of excessive flattery followed swiftly by what you can to do for them.
  Trust your instincts as to whether an offer is win-win-win or the other person
  wins while you get drained.

Play widens the halls. Work will always be with us, and many works are worthy. But the worthiest works of all often reflect an artful creativity that looks more like play than work.

—JAMES A. OGILVY

More reasons we may pay attention to you on social media. Because you are:

A FAN EVANGELIST MACHINE: You have a lot of people pulling, rooting for, or cheering you on. We want to participate, too.

A BIG GIVER: You have a lot of payback coming. This means you have done a lot of good for free or cheap in the past, and we owe you, too.

A CHALLENGER: Some folks are seeking something to push against or someone who can push them to the next level. Coaches and taskmasters fall into this category.

AN ORCHESTRATOR: You solicit participation. There is a benefit for participation.

A TEACHER: The more rich content and examples you provide, the more others learn. You raise all boats.

A REFUGE PROVIDER: You provide a safe space that will make folks feel better or heal.

A CONTEXT CREATOR: You create an interactive "place" that allows us to come and discover something we are looking for.

AN ENTERTAINER: We are more than happy to let you entertain.

A COMPETITOR: We keep up with you so we can learn from you without actually interacting with you directly.

A CONSISTENT CAREER: We feel like you care about something or somebody (or everything and everybody). This pulls us in.

A CURIOUSLY UNFAMILIAR PERSON: We are not sure who you are exactly, but you are always around, so you become part of the crowd. We might even check you out.

You can become the talk of the globe when you consistently express who and what you are on social media.

248
STAY CURRENT

The real beauty of Twitter and Facebook (and all the other social networking sites) is that they offer a massive opportunity for every entrepreneur and business to keep constant tabs on what their customers are thinking about them. This kind of interaction with the consumer should be happening in every business every single day.

—GARY VAYNERCHUK

As you become increasingly known, you will be meeting more and more people until the number of folks you know in total no longer scales with the amount of time you have for connecting online. If you had to keep up with all of these people all the time, you would never be able to finish the work you need to accomplish today. You need to use tools to streamline your attention.

Do yourself a favor by using the following online tools to help you keep tabs on everyone at your own convenience. Here are three key resources to help you follow the streams of your various peeps:

MAINTAIN A BLOG READER

I use Google Reader to collect all the blog posts I read into one ongoing batch. By setting up my blog reader wisely, and dividing the blogs into folders, I can quickly catch up on the latest blog posts from my favorite bloggers in a much shorter time than if I tried to keep up in real time.

TWITTER SOFTWARE

When you are just getting started with Twitter, I would not worry about sorting folks into groups. But once your followers numbers over a thousand and every thousand thereafter, it's probably time to create lists based on categories that make sense to how you want to spend you attention. You can then feed those lists into Twitter software that allows you to view up to five columns of tweets at the same time.

DOUBLE-CHECK FACEBOOK SETTINGS

The biggest challenge with Facebook in terms of keeping up with the conversations that take place there is monitoring your settings. Facebook has a habit of regularly upgrading their features without necessarily letting you know. So just make sure, for example, that you are seeing the latest status updates from everyone, and not only seeing the same folks over and over, which is the default setting if you don't stay on top of your settings.

How will you know it's time to start sorting, organizing, and updating your streams of friends and followers? The moment that keeping track of everyone starts to feel unmanageable or unproductive, it's time to start sorting. If you consider your options quarterly, that's a good way to get the most from well-organized connections.

Even the dullest introvert has pizzazz when talking about something he is passionate about, and when he's using the right medium to talk about it.

—GARY VAYNERCHUK

Once you have all of your platform ducks ready to quack, think about what you are broadcasting about yourself when you get on social media. Don't put your straight-up business self out there when everyone else is operating in business casual mode.

Connect your social media hangouts to your home base site like satellites. Go ahead and link to your site. RSS feed your blog to post automatically and anything you need to do to interlink your social media presence so it will lead people back to your home base hub.

Take a minute to stand back and take a look at your entire platform as it already exists. What is interesting not just about your business but also about you? Mention your mission, casually, in your social media profiles.

Stand back and look at the bio you use for most things. Is it the same bio you want to use on social media, or would it make more sense to go with something less formal and more personal?

Here are a few example bios on Twitter:

> Jane Friedman: @JaneFriedman Follow Jane for links on publishing + new media + life. Writing/media professor. Former Writer's Digest publisher. Literary adventurer + bourbon devotee.

> Allison Winn Scotch: @ASWinn Novelist, NY Times bestseller (yeah, I had to get that in), celeb profiler, diaper changer, dog walker, ass-kicker, pop culture junkie, superwoman.

> Meryl K. Evans: @MerylKEvans Content maven aka writer, editor, and bookwormette who plays with words and games in between volunteering and refereeing the kids.

Because social media channels change so rapidly, I won't try to list them all here, but consider participating fully in all those that make the most sense for you and your mission.

It takes courage to grow up and become who you really are.

—E.E. CUMMINGS

What would the witty members of the Algonquin Round Table have thought of the Internet? How would the founding of *The New Yorker* been affected if it *was* in fact available to the "old lady in Dubuque," for whom Harold Ross famously proclaimed it was specifically not intended. Maybe the vicious circle of brilliant practical jokers would have hung together longer if they could have hopped online to video-phone each other or sent a witty text message.

Or maybe not. The story goes that they ran out of things to say to each other. But those infamous lines they did deliver might have been blogged about by some of the less official members and immortalized by the Internet. Perhaps a writers conference could have been set up around the Round Table crowd like BlogHer has done for a select group of women bloggers. Maybe their many fans could have acted as citizen journalists broadcasting their verbal sparring so the whole wide world could hang on to every sarcastic remark.

Perhaps devoted fans would have encouraged Dorothy Parker to seek help for her now-famous drinking problem. Who knows?

Or perhaps exclusive ongoing insight into what the Algonquin Round Table members were really like would have harmed their reputations, rather than making them "famous for being famous." After all, contemporary futurist Faith Popcorn has said we live in time when "it's survival of the media friendliest." And since the members of the Algonquin gang all tended to work with each other and were, in fact, members of the media, it wouldn't have been too hard to manage their online reputations, collectively and individually, were they still with us today.

While it's certainly fun to speculate, no one can say for sure how the past might have been changed by our modern-day innovations and, really, no one can say for sure how the future will be changed. However, change certainly seems to be afoot.

We don't get to decide how others will view us as professional communicators but we do get to decide what to say and how to say it. Choose wisely. And be leery of membership in any group or groups that encourage or provoke your dark side. The world is watching and the Internet is taking notes.

You don't need public speaking lessons; you need to learn how to cut your soul open.

—SCOTT GINSBERG

How wonderful to work long and hard on your career until the point where invitations start rolling in. Usually invitations start to come from an accumulation of hard work. You have an established track record. You are likely a known expert in your field. You have established enough authority to be in demand. Now it's time to get invitation ready.

- Create a page on your site where you list all the topics in which you have professional expertise to share.

- If you have a signature style to your presentations or workshops, describe it. Describe the effect your style will have on audiences and what makes your presentations unique.

- Let people know whom you have already worked with. List them all or just hit the highlights.

- Gather a few testimonials from folks who have heard you speak. Make sure they are actual audience members who have heard you and gotten in touch with you; do not solicit friends of yours to rave about you.

- Be helpful. Remember, nobody has to invite you to their event. So always be serviceable without being servile. Discuss needs, offer to customize your program, work within people's parameters, and offers will come.

- Show yourself in action. Pepper your site with pictures of you speaking and connecting with fans.

- Be sure you have a call to action with your offerings, like "Book [your name]" or "Contact [your name]" or even simply "Let's Talk."

Don't try to figure out what other people want to hear from you; figure out what you have to say. It's the one and only thing you have to offer.

—BARBARA KINGSOLVER

Writers are all working harder than ever and juggling more to-dos in order to stay relevant as well as visible. But I would go so far as to say that even harried as we are, we are still somewhat spoiled and we don't even realize it. Can you imagine William Shakespeare whining because the Queen didn't respond right away to his latest play?

I bet you can't because he was too busy writing 38 plays, 154 sonnets, and 2 long narrative poems. He was focused on creating a body of work. And look at how his body of work has served the greater good over time.

Shakespeare was a great example of what I call an empowered writer. He wore many hats: He was a playwright, an actor, and a businessman who invested in theaters. He was totally committed to and in immediate contact with his audiences as much as possible. He understood that while the Queen's stamp of royal approval was important, his words were for the people of London. And because he did such a good job writing for them, we benefit from his amazing craftsmanship five centuries later.

I think contemporary marketing expert Seth Godin would have approved of the Bard's direct connection with his audience. Shakespeare definitely understood viral marketing and maintained a razorlike focus on the impact his words would have on theater goers. And then they'd tell a friend, and they'd tell a friend, and ... you get the idea.

So next time you don't get any strokes from your editor or your agent, remember that you work without the continual threat of the gallows or the rack. Instead of focusing on how challenging things are or how much there is to juggle, determine to learn more about what your readers think of your work and forget about what everyone else thinks. The allegiance of your fans is worth its weight in gold.

They say that Shakespeare made a comfortable living by paying close attention to his audience. I think we should all follow suit.

253
SOCIALIZE LIKE THIS

What you are speaks so loudly I cannot hear what you say.
—RALPH WALDO EMERSON

There is a lot of mumbo jumbo out there about social networking right now that is going to hurt your writing career, if you swallow the party line. Here is a partial list of some of the baloney you will hear:

- Join the conversation.
- Hang out before you share.
- Listen more than you talk.

Okay. So I don't know about you, but I'd rather spend quality time with my real-life close family and friends hanging out and having authentic conversations than skulking around on social networks, politely waiting for the perfect opportunity to speak. This is really not the best way to cultivate what you have to offer.

On the other hand, I have seen far too many writers blaze through social networking acting as though a whole network of personal relationships is just billboard space where they can blast their news. The Internet is a tool, but it isn't one giant ad space sequence for your promotional efforts.

Be neither reticent nor rule bound. Be neither cavalier nor brand stamping. You know how to meet people in real life, and how to introduce yourself, and how to find out what you have in common with people. Connecting with people online is really no different.

I have heard people talk about how the amount of time you spend connecting vs. sharing should break down into certain percentages. But it's my opinion that this is overthinking the whole process. More folks are afraid of saying what they have to offer in the first place then are so awkward that they can't have a conversation. The tricky part is how to balance having something to offer and being in the conversation at the same time.

Just remember that in social networking, balance is the key. Spend part of your time chatting with whomever you would like to chat with and spend the other half of your time sharing what you have to offer. Just show up as you would in ordinary life, connect authentically, then log off and get back to your muse.

Priority is a function of context.

—STEPHEN R. COVEY

If you had gold, how would you invest it? Your e-mail list is your gold. Always remember this and don't let anyone convince you otherwise.

Here are types of lists that writers may wish to track to better succeed in today's marketplace:

WARM LEADS

- Editors who buy your work
- Students who take your classes
- Audience members who attend your appearances
- Colleagues who support your career growth
- Your newsletter subscribers
- Readers who buy your books

PUBLICITY LISTS

- Local media
- Regional media
- Niche-specific media
- National media
- International media

GROUPS & ASSOCIATION OUTREACH

- Groups related to your niche
- Associations related to your niche
- Not-for-profits related to your topic/audience/niche
- Schools interested in your niche
- Online groups associated with your niche

PROSPECTIVE CLIENTS

- Corporations
- Universities/community colleges
- Like-minded enterprising others

Tools strategies, tactics, apps, and vehicles are all great. But, it starts with being willing to hunker down. Day in, day out, regardless of the weather. Show up. Dig in. Own the work. Because that's what pros do.

—JONATHAN FIELDS

One of the benefits of being a writer is how much you enjoy inclement weather. Writing when the sun is shining and the temps are just right for a trip to the beach can really be tough stuff for a writer on a deadline. But crummy weather—the colder and windier and lousier the better—can be wonderful.

I love bad weather. Even when my dogs truck half their weight in mud into the house, I don't mind because bad weather is a convenient excuse to slink down into the basement and click away at the keys.

Give me a frigid, icy, sleeting, hailing storm any day. I love it. These are the best days for cozying up to write.

In the winter, when the days are short and nights are long, relish how good it feels to stay in and just write. Writing in winter reminds me of how good it feels to write without any reservations or hesitations or fears. At some point in your career, after you've written enough, you'll be able to just let it rip, and it feels really good.

However, when you become a writer who can write no matter what the weather, you are a writer who has stopped apologizing for choosing writing in the first place. You are a writer who has made writing the norm in his life, to the point where you don't need to apologize for it or explain why you do it.

There is really no such thing as "writing weather" unless you set up a schedule to get more writing done while the sun doesn't shine.

But you don't want to do that. Write with the weather. Write in spite of the weather. Write however long you need to write. Set your life up to make room for and accommodate the writing you long to do. This is what makes you a writer who writes no matter what the weather.

Your personal capacity to handle more valuable projects will go up when you appreciate yourself more.

—BRIAN KOSLOW

One of the most important habits for any writer to develop is to learn to give up on what isn't working. Ironically, you will never know what won't work until you try. But you will learn fairly quickly when something isn't going well.

The way to determine whether something is simply a steep learning curve or is just not right for you is to close your eyes and try to imagine yourself doing the same thing in five years. In five years, will what is challenging or difficult be easier for you?

If it won't be easier, pay attention to the reasons. Maybe the issue is that you just don't like using your time in this way. If you don't like the way you are spending your time, what you are doing is probably not sustainable.

You are allowed to pick and choose. Nobody says you have to do everything. Even if all of your friends are successfully teaching writing, and you try it and just don't like it or it doesn't go well, don't feel like you have to keep trying. There are plenty of writers who don't teach. You can pull together other job options that work best for you and create a custom career.

Have some of your writer friends become consultants or ghostwriters or coaches? Does this mean you should try those things, too? Maybe. Or maybe not. It's up to you.

The key is to notice whether you feel on track in every pursuit. If your future feels uncertain, you may want to continue adjusting your professional-efforts dial until you feel like you can click to the right channels when you want them.

Often this is a matter of diversifying skills sets, but other times you may simply need to erase some of the old channels from the menu that no longer serve you so you will have room for new channels.

Today a writer is likely to have a lot more channels than writers had and maintained in the past. Over time and with practice, you will learn how to find your best channels and turn back and forth between them easily.

ORCHESTRATE, DON'T MANAGE

That tendency toward full immersion is something I've always con-sidered a strength—and for anyone in a community organizing/ engagement role, an absolute necessity, in my opinion—though the downside is it can often leave little room for other interests, even directly tangential ones.

—GUY LECHARLES GONZALEZ

Isn't it more poetic somehow to become the conductor of your writing career rather than merely the manager?

You know what managers are. They do the hiring and the firing. They nag. They make sure the paperwork gets done.

Why should you schlep through your career? Don't!

Orchestrators do not schlep. They design. They direct. They evoke.

Conduct your career like an orchestra that performs gorgeous music in many forms. Sounds a heck of a lot more fun than just getting all the paperwork done, right? Of course it does.

Now tap your baton on your podium, lift up your arms, and bring all that you do into harmony in your career.

The moment you become a manager instead of an orchestrator, your writing career is going to become something to dread.

But if you can remember to orchestrate not manage, you can do more in less time while making more money and enjoying yourself a heck of a lot more.

Consider the following tasks that might be delegated to other people so you can have more time to focus on the work that's more important for you to do:

- Housecleaning
- Child care
- Bookkeeping
- Tax preparation
- Technology services
- Yard work
- Landscaping

Try to keep and maintain any tasks that are pleasurable for you. In other words, don't hire someone else to plant the garden and walk the dogs if these chores help keep you mentally and physically fit. You know which tasks you want to do, enjoy, and are good at. Hire the rest of them out and watch, you'll earn more and enjoy your work more.

It takes a great deal of courage to stand up to your enemies, but even more to stand up to your friends.

—J.K. ROWLING

Do you have any false friendships? This is a confusing time for friendships both online and off. You never know when your ideals and your friend's ideals may come into conflict.

If you pay enough attention to your current loyalties, I bet you can perceive which people you know, if you know any, who are in it for what you can do for them. You don't have to go along with a relationship with a person who pretends to be a friend, who is actually just waiting for an opportunity to take whatever resources you have that look good to him.

You might not want to see it. And they probably don't want you to see it. But once you take a closer look, you may start to notice behaviors that are likely to turn into future disappointments.

What you have accomplished may look good to other people and they may develop a sense of entitlement about what you owe them, if you don't clarify where you end and where other people begin.

The other dynamic to be careful with is the "I'll help you, if you help me" exchange. Consistently opt for quality of character in individuals you recommend and quality of products and services you recommend, or pretty soon your word or recommendation won't be well regarded.

Learn that you don't need loyal friends if the cost of loyalty is too high. If this is a troublesome area for you, you may want to consider separating your friends, or at least your closest friends, from your work. Because sometimes mixing work and friendship muddies the waters.

If and when this happens, put yourself in the other person's shoes and try to learn from both your point of view and the other person's. Whatever you decide, don't let people take from you just because they have decided you should not mind.

Healthy people don't need the appearance of loyalty; they need genuine friendships with no strings attached. They don't need a string of favors, just mutual respect and mutual admiration.

Fair warning: When you choose to limit inputs and withdraw from social requests, not everyone will understand this behavior. Some people may get frustrated with you. Meanwhile, you'll be getting more done and doing more things that you like than all of them.

—CHRIS GUILLEBEAU

I'd love to be friends with absolutely everybody, but what I've found is that this isn't reasonable in practice. In real time, I can only maintain meaningful relationships with so many people and still have time for my immediate family, my pets, and my extended family.

Every year, through my work, I probably personally meet or interact with over one thousand new people. Triple that if I have a new book out. I realize that friend overload is a high-class problem but it's also a modern challenge. I know that I am not the only one who deals with trying to balance personal life with professional life and public life.

Everyone needs to find her appropriate balance in these situations. So when you start to feel the pinch in your professional life, ask yourself some questions that may help:

- Which people are your greatest priorities?
- Which people are important to you and your personal happiness?
- Which people are important to your writing business?
- Which people would you remain loyal to even if there were no professional benefit for you in the relationship?
- Which groups of professionals do you need to touch base with on a regular basis?

I think these are important questions in the technological age. Any writers who say that they don't need to consider these questions or that they are "just friends with everyone" may be on a collision course with their own limits. At some point the sheer volume of people may no longer scale. And certainly everyone has their own personal comfort level when it comes to amount and quality of social interactions.

Nobody is asking you to be a robot. We prefer the human being, anyway. Know as many people as you reasonably can. Meet as many people as you can. But keep your priorities in mind and never trade your integrity for exposure.

Interdependency follows independence.

—STEPHEN R. COVEY

I suggest that, even if you work for others, you work for yourself first by establishing yourself as an expert and then turning your expertise into multiple income streams. There has never been a more enterprising time to be a writer, and there are many ways of earning in addition to writing.

For me, social media is the last thing you do when you are setting yourself up in the world as a communications professional. It's not more important or most important; it's simply a natural extension of how you express yourself authentically in the many worlds writers move through, including the online world.

Social networking is important, but only if the work you are doing is important first. The best "paid" blogging or tweeting gigs you can get as a writer are going to result from selling your own services and products directly to your audience.

If you freelance, you owe it to yourself to mix up writing for others with writing directly for your readers so you don't only live deadline to deadline. I have more to say on selling direct in the final section of this book. In the meantime, you can gear up for selling direct as another thing you do in the gig economy by specializing, building your platform, and networking.

The two key words for social networking are *caring* and *sharing*. Caring while earning is tantamount to success in our new connected economy. It's okay to slip in what you offer while you are caring and sharing, as long as you don't overdo it. If you overdo it, folks will simply stop listening.

I keep the volume of my online networking manageable for me. I work my e-zine, my blog, and my networking into my daily routine, getting it done here and there, and using it as a break from concentrated work. This way, it doesn't take over my whole life—which it would, if I let it.

PLEASE DON'T: PART ONE

The Web has become a raging river filled with tweets, status up-dates, photos, and videos.

—STEVE RUBEL

Unless you are interested in how to lose friends and alienate people, *don't* try these methods to market yourself or your work online. Don't:

1. Use other people's personal or professional virtual spaces or contexts as billboards for your sales message (their blog comments, Facebook page, Twitter stream), even if you are only promoting your blog. Go for attraction, not promotion.

2. Hard sell. Use too much time pressure. Overpromise. Exaggerate benefits.

3. Friend/follow everyone or anyone. Be selective.

4. Have private conversations in public. TMI!

5. Take e-mail addresses from social media sites and use them to spam folks who made the mistake of friending or following you.

6. Dictate to people you just met on social media how to interact with you in an "or else" tone. No one wants to be threatened.

7. Needlessly or thoughtlessly criticize or rant against a person or product. The moment you start to rant, regardless of what you are ranting about, you make the topic *you*, not whatever you are ranting about.

8. Ask for an agent referral or some other major favor upon meeting someone for the first time over social media. Awkward.

9. Swear at someone and then unfollow or unfriend them because they didn't give you the answer you wanted. This happened to me once. It was unpleasant.

10. Make thinly veiled threats or place unrealistic conditions on a networking ac-quaintance. "If you truly want 2 connect with me I will add you to a column on tweetdeck, otherwise you will slip through the feed." Um, okay.

11. Presume that just because someone did something kind or nice for you once upon a time that they want to give you their time now. "Hi, you wrote an ar-ticle about me five years ago, would you be willing to do that again?"

12. Partake in games or other pastimes on social media, and then send invitations to folks who are clearly using the Internet for professional networking only, even if the person is your cousin, childhood friend, or an acquaintance you just met.

You always have a choice. It's just that some people make the wrong one.

—NICHOLAS SPARKS

Inevitably, at some point in your career you are going to encounter a situation in which someone assumes you are going to behave a certain way and that person lets you know what that should look like in her opinion. And if you don't see it coming, you might feel upset and react badly when she is disappointed in you.

So, slow down. Tread carefully. Don't be an automatic-yes person. If you are an automatic-yes person, you are setting people up for disappointment down the road when you eventually get up the guts to say no.

Remember that scene in *It's a Wonderful Life* where Mr. Potter invites George Bailey into his office and makes him a really sweet offer because he knows that George is the only person in town who poses a real threat to his power? There is that moment when George almost gets snookered because he is tempted by the shortcut Potter dangles in front of him like a carrot. In the nick of time, George remembers himself and refuses the offer.

Staying on the right side of integrity is not a choice that will always spare you pain. But make a pact with yourself and make it right now: Don't cave into the pressure of other people's agendas if they are not what you stand for. There are certain deals with the devil you probably can't live with in good conscience. So don't make them.

Ask what is for your highest good and act accordingly. It's always the right choice.

Black ice is a slippery situation that happens when somebody has decided how you should behave—or else (he will react unpleasantly). The pressure is either suggested or implied. (Ick.)

Black ice is almost blackmail. The situation is blackmail because someone has made a threat that you are going to "get it" if you don't act in the prescribed way.

Keep your wits about you at all times, especially if things are moving very quickly for you, or you feel rushed or pressured in any way. Slow down, pay attention carefully, get your bearings, and think. What would George Bailey do?

PLEASE DON'T: PART TWO

You can hustle and market and network all you want, but if your sports drink tastes like trash, or if you're putting out bad information, you're going to lose.

—GARY VAYNERCHUK

More ways to lose friends and alienate people. Don't:

13. Assume that people are playing by your social media rules. Your approach to social media and another person's approach to social media may be different.

14. Use any kind of misleading messages or bait and switches. Promising folks one thing and providing another is unforgiveable and should be a deadly sin.

15. Chronically spam. There is a special section in the fiery place (I hope) for people who do so.

16. Ignore everyone else as you pursue a stubborn and one-sided agenda.

17. Blast people's heads off with you-you-you.

18. Offend people needlessly or thoughtlessly. I unfriend and unfollow folks who use gratuitous profanity because I am not a teenage boy. And I don't wish to hang out with perpetually angry people online or off. Who would?

19. Be slick. Glib. Flip. Sarcastic. Haughty. Or high-and-mighty. Just be as you are in real life.

20. Friend and follow absolutely everybody. Better to friend someone specific, rather than everyone indiscriminately.

21. Go off on others either formally or informally. Doing so is never cool.

22. Kiss up to people who have more influence than you do in the hopes that some of it will rub off on you.

23. Auto DM. Especially an auto message that comes back to me when I follow you that says, "Sorry for the auto DM …"

24. E-mail or tweet that you wrote a blog post. That's nice. Grab our attention legitimately or don't share.

25. Go bananas on religion or politics. If you must say something, temper it so as not to offend needlessly. If you feel the urge to go on a religious or political rant, pause. Let the topic cool for twenty-four hours.

*Our ultimate freedom is the right and power to decide how any-
body or anything outside ourselves will affect us.*

—STEPHEN R. COVEY

Because I am in business for myself, I often receive a request for my attention or effort
that signals to me that maybe I need to create a policy about the issue for the sake of my
own sanity. And so I don't waste my time or other people's time needlessly.

Editors ask me for quick turnarounds. Students ask me for special treatment. Authors approach me for free advice or to review their platform progress. I used to try to
say yes to everyone. I don't know where I came up with that idea but it certainly wasn't
sustainable.

Now I decline, if that's what feels right in my gut. If a person's request is going to
put me out or diminish me unnecessarily, I give myself permission to decline an invitation without feeling guilty.

In the short run, it may be hard to see what harm can arise from always saying yes.
But I suggest you say no when you mean no. And when you find yourself feeling con-
flicted about how to respond over and over, it's time for a new policy.

What a policy does is it lets you off the hook more easily because when something
comes up, you know that you have already given the situation enough careful consideration to merit a policy in the first place.

Because I have policies, I understand that I can control how I respond to people,
but I can't control how they will feel or respond to what I say. In order to be a business
professional, I have to let go of the idea that I can control a person's response or please
them every time. If I tried to do either, my life would be unmanageable. So I say yes to
what I can manage, no to what sounds unmanageable, and let go of the conclusions I
imagine others may draw about me.

When it comes to policies that you make for running your business, whether they're
about the writing you do or the services you provide or the products you create, be sure
to revisit them as you go along to make sure the new direction you are going will be
sustainable and helpful.

265

OWN IT ANYWAY

As new formats, media, and devices come along, creators with well-conceived platforms will be better positioned to make the most of them.

—GUY LECHARLES GONZALEZ

To arrive at a point where you have built up a magnetic, thriving platform that attracts respect and fans on an ongoing basis is a huge accomplishment.

The good news about growing your own visibility is that it creates a growing sense of ownership in a creative person.

The rough news is that it takes hard work and many years to go from being not visible at all to being known and widely appreciated.

If someone else did your platform work for you, they would basically own you. So you have to do your platform building yourself, even as you partner with others. You have to be the force inside your writing career through which your work is constantly reborn.

How else would you know when to say yes and when to say no, unless you felt like you were the owner of your own value in the world?

The experiences writers gain in naming and claiming our platforms help us better position ourselves in the world of new media. Without the ownership that comes from the steady cultivation of craft, selling, specializing, self-promotion, and lifelong learning, writers cannot find themselves in a position to compete in the new playing field that the online marketplace has created.

However, writers who can see the potential available in this space, who can feel fear and do what they need to do anyway, will evolve and thrive.

Those who don't embrace self-promotion in all the realms now available are not going to be able to compete with a new generation of tech-savvy, well-connected online mavericks.

You have two choices. You can feel the fear and give up. Or you can feel the fear and build your platform anyway.

You can make mistakes, but you are not a failure until you blame others for those mistakes.

—JOHN WOODEN

You are one writer with two lives: a business life and a personal life. You determine what you want to share and what you don't want to share. These choices are your call.

I prefer to keep my personal life and my work life separate from each other, with a little bit of gray area in between. There was a time I didn't feel this way, but when I started social networking more, my work life grew to the point where it was swallowing up my personal life, and I wanted to be able to have both without either overwhelming the other. The solution: I decided to keep my online life focused on business and my offline life focused on my personal life.

Doing so allows me to use one identity on social networking sites, rather than creating different identities for public and private, which would make me feel schizophrenic. And since I'm not doing a lot of personal networking online, this keeps things simple and cuts down on how much time I spend online.

Think about which of your selves you want to appear in a Google search. Do you want a search to turn up windows into your personal life or your work? Once you decide, leave a trail of digital artifacts behind that will all add up to who you are and what you do whenever anyone goes searching for you.

Of all of the people you know, only some of them are going to use social networking. And then, even if they do, you might be focused on other topics or groups than they are, so you and your best friend in the whole wide world may both be networking online and rarely cross paths. And there is absolutely nothing wrong with this.

Social networking offers us the chance to pursue what interests us. If your time is spent otherwise, take a closer look and see what is holding you back from following the dance of your passions rather than your obligations.

FILTER YOUR ATTENTION

Our limitations and success will be based, most often, on our own expectations for ourselves. What the mind dwells upon, the body acts upon.

—DENIS WAITLEY

Are you eternally frustrated by the siren calls to hurry up and build your platform before you have even had a chance to find your legs as a writer?

Forget that nonsense! Find your writing legs first and work on your platform later, when the timing feels right to you.

There is only one logical time to start working on your platform and that is when you feel moved to do so. Even if you are the most reclusive writer in town, I believe that you know on an intuitive level when the time is right to start ramping up your platform.

The right timing usually coincides with the desire to take your work public. But don't forget to give yourself time to adjust to the learning curve. Just because we decide we are ready to learn about something, it still takes time to learn and apply all that there is to absorb and use.

When I built my platform far in advance of my first book deal, nobody told me to do it. I did it because it was a natural part of my creative momentum. What was bubbling up inside was ready to come out and be shared. I was seeking and building an audience intuitively.

If you do not heed your own internal promptings and instead turn outside yourself in search of the answers on timing, you are going to cut yourself off from your own natural instincts.

Would it help your writing to shut out the all of the yammer and calls to action that can be found everywhere and that only serve to throw you off your game?

Now that we have the Internet, we had better get used to the chronic calls to action. And we better get used to ignoring all but the quality messages we don't want to miss. Because the alternative is living in a constant state of overwhelm.

A writer is somebody for whom writing is more difficult than it is for other people.

—THOMAS MANN

At some point in your writing career, you will suddenly realize that you are doing more writing than you've ever done before. This is wonderful, but you have to maintain a delicate balance between writing, selling, specializing, and self-promotion without burning out. And all the while, you must keep learning.

If you don't keep these skills in balance, you may lose income or readers or gigs or risk not staying current in your field. What you are after is a customized work rhythm that works best for you. Here are all of the skills we have to weave together:

- Cultivating your best ideas
- Matching your ideas with appropriate markets
- Determining who your best audiences are
- Overcoming editor phobia
- Accumulating increasingly stronger clips and credits
- Expecting good things from good effort
- Getting more writing into every day
- Balancing your introverted and extroverted sides
- Finding a community of writers with similar goals to yours
- Learning from the careers of others
- Seeing your name in print regularly
- Becoming increasingly recognized as the expert that you are
- Repeating whatever you are doing that works
- Submitting to increasingly wider-reaching publications
- Getting faster and more efficient as you go along
- Recognizing what works for your career and turning those thrusts into habits
- Keeping a portfolio of your work and revising it quarterly
- Picking a time of year that is best for you and doing your planning then
- Continually increasing the size of your goals
- Finding supporters who help you stay accountable to your goals
- Pausing and appreciating your own efforts when something good happens
- Learning from any unfortunate things that happen
- Becoming the most creatively resilient person you know
- Inspiring yourself and others
- Reminding yourself of what you can't control
- Controlling your attitude, your effort, and how you assess your own progress
- Committing to your career and helping it prosper
- Developing a body of writing for a growing tribe of readers

STOP COMPARING

Remember that you are all people and that all people are you.

—JOY HARJO

Can you study what other professional writers do, ask questions, and learn from their example, without comparing yourself? Not many writers can. Comparing causes fears and self-doubt to arise, which can create more of a stumbling block than a helpful example you might follow.

That said, you must attempt to see what you notice without comparing yourself to others. It's always self-defeating (even if you secretly think you are better) to compare ourselves to others. I suggest learning how to be in another person's glow without doing anything.

When you are clear about how you wish to express your energy, it will be great, I'm sure. In the meantime, admire what's worth admiring about others' self-expression without bringing yourself into the equation whatsoever.

Here are tips for how to admire and not compare:

- Stay detached. You are a visitor in another person's world. You are not there to take over, stir up a controversy, become instant best friends, or ruffle feathers.
- Connect loosely through social networks with authors, experts, and publishers who share the same focus as you.
- Connect with other groups, associations, and events that focus on your topic.
- Connect with other groups, associations, and events that focus on your audience.
- Admire what others are doing, taking note of any writing, topics, or debates you'd like to respond to in your own blog or writing. You might start with a quote or excerpt from a written work and then respond to it.

Above all, never stalk. Realize that idealizing people or putting them on a pedestal is a form of stalking. Anytime you hold someone in such high regard that you put her on a pedestal, you set yourself up to eventually knock that person back down to earth.

Remember that people are just people. Learn what you can from each, and then get back to your own creative process. Make sure you never tie your creative cart to anyone else's expression, projection, or career.

If you choose to self-publish because you can't handle the rejection of the query process, you're setting yourself up for worse pain later on.

—ANNE R. ALLEN

Once a writer gets to the point of having multiple pieces in print, there is truly something to celebrate. Most of us are not ready to go from being completely unknown to being famous for our writing. But most of us are ready, and even impatient, to get on with the journey from wannabe to published writer.

Writers who are getting published are challenged and tested and confronted and stretched in ways that a writer who sits back and proclaims himself a writer without doing much about it isn't.

A publishing writer is a growing writer, although, naturally many publishing writers get stuck in ruts. Their ruts don't usually last long, however, because their own restless desire to move on to the next level of accomplishment starts nagging at them and they get back to growing.

Writers who write for publication grow steadily and see results for their efforts. They begin to understand how their words can touch readers and the kinds of responses their writing can engender.

I have read an ample number of pronouncements that claim we are all writers, and I even believe that we have entered the age where everyone *is* a writer. But every writer is not necessarily a published writer, and there is, in my experience, absolutely no denying the waxing creative power of a writer who is not only writing but also getting regularly published.

The quest for publication is a kind of journey that most writers approach backwards. They think they are going to write a masterpiece before they have even tried for an op-ed. They think "best-seller list" before they have received an acceptance for publication of any kind. This kind of pipe dreaming is an invention of the ego, not the heart. It certainly doesn't come from the hands, either.

Of all the developmental phases that I see writers go through in their journeys from unpublished to published, probably one of the most inspiring is the moment that a writer validates his own identity.

Once you have a strong inner sense of being a writer in your own right, you've crossed an invisible line. You've become one of us.

Fame lost its appeal for me when I went into a public restroom and an autograph seeker handed me a pen and paper under the stall door.

—MARLO THOMAS

Have you had any close encounters of the celebrity kind? They might be fun to write about. You never know where these ideas will take you.

Try it and see.

First list every major celebrity you have ever crossed paths with. (Obviously "major" is a relative term. Go with whatever it means to you.)

Here I go:

- Brian Dennehy
- Lily Tomlin
- Ted Turner
- Jane Fonda
- Diane Sawyer
- Tony Danza
- Jodi Picoult
- Julia Cameron
- Marianne Williamson

I have shared some of the stories of brushes with celebs already. But it sure would be fun to write them again or to collect them together in one piece of writing.

One of the most memorable books I ever read was Jean Houston's *A Mythic Life*. In this book the human potential movement leader shares her encounters with well-known great minds of her younger years and considers how those encounters shaped her future thinking and career. It's a fascinating read.

Another fun idea is to write about the people you worship. If you devote a lot of energy toward openly or secretly adoring someone, you likely have plenty to say. Crack your adoration open by writing about fan devotion you either have or have had. These stories are bound to be juicy.

TAKE BACK YOUR ATTENTION

The mind is fickle like a fast galloping horse and the only way to control him is by involving him in good actions beneficial for the welfare of all. The person who does so shall achieve success and peace.

—THE RIG VEDA

There is a trend online and it goes like this: Folks start using social networking, they start having fun with it, they get into it, and then they look at the clock and gasp.

Their days are flying by in a blur of "conversational" banter—meanwhile their productivity has come to a screeching halt.

This has definitely happened to me. Perhaps it needs to happen to all of us. Maybe it's part of the online initiation process that we all lose and then reclaim control of our attention.

When it happened to me, I realized that what I needed to do was redesign the entire way I invested and distributed my creative energy. I had to take social media into account without letting it hijack my entire daily routine.

So I grabbed the wild horse of my attention and led it back into the ring. I threw a saddle on it, employed a crop, put on some English riding gear, and started retraining my attention to get back in line.

That was over a year ago. This past year, I accomplished more than I ever have, and I'm in position to accomplish even more next year. That's the payoff for being able to control and direct your attention in the ways that are constructive and empowering for you.

Today, when I hop on and offline a few times a day, you know what I see? I see lots of really nice people drowning in the social media undertow.

Next comes the announcement that they are using software that will tame their attention, keeping them from getting online during certain hours of the day so they can get their work done.

While they are at it, maybe they could put a timer lock on their refrigerator or have the Stairmaster come over, tackle them, and drag them to the gym?

The only way to tame your attention is to train it. And the only way to train it is to know what you are doing and why you would even spend one second of your valuable life on social networking. If you don't have a clear sense of purpose and mission that feels authentic and empowering, consider taking a break.

I don't think any novelist should be concerned with literature.

—JACQUELINE SUSANN

When you've been working long and hard and you need a mental break, movies can offer a comforting refuge. As with books, writers have never had a greater variety of films featuring writers and writing.

Films about writing and writers are based on fact, fiction, or both. Either way, if you are a writer, watching movies will probably help you tap into the field of sympathetic resonance that exists among writers.

For example, when I watch *Isn't She Great*, I vicariously share Jacqueline Susann's disdain for too much emphasis on literary tradition and convention. I feel her pain when she discovers her son has autism. I cheer her on as she tries to do the impossible: turn a trashy novel into a bestseller by driving all over the country to meet with booksellers.

In *Julie and Julia*, I share two writers' experiences. One the one hand, I can relate to Julia Child, devoted to her magnum opus cookbook project for eight years while juggling delicate writing partnerships and international travel. On the other hand, I can relate to a young, self-absorbed blogger trying to prove that she can do something right in her life. Despite the contrasts, there is much to appreciate in the delicate balance of both points of view.

When I watch *Driving in Cars With Boys*, There's a lot to chew on: the role women are supposed to play in society, whether or not it's acceptable to choose writing *and* motherhood, and the gut-wrenching emotional and creative cost of marrying the wrong guy.

Why not select your favorites? My husband, Jason Katz, helped me put together a comprehensive list of "Movies About Writers and the Writing Life." You can download the complete, updated list at my website christinakatz.com/free and tap into our collective writer zeitgeist.

Every secret of a writer's soul, every experience of his life, every quality of his mind is written large in his works.

—VIRGINIA WOOLF

Imagine you are standing in an open field.

The sun is shining, there is a cool breeze, your fists are on your hips, and your legs make an upside down *V*.

A camera pointing up at you would grab a snapshot in which you look like a superhero. You feel competent and ready for whatever is ahead.

Now I'm going to hand you a shovel. Maybe the shovel handle has a nice rubber coating so you can grip it better. Or maybe it's made of wood. Imagine it however you like.

Grab your shovel and start digging. The ground is not hard. The dirt is loose and light underneath a layer of field flora. You dig easily, tossing the dirt back over your shoulder like it's nothing.

You're making progress. The hole is getting wide and deep, about a foot by a foot. The next time you jam the shovel it hits something with the sound of metal crunching metal.

What is this? You've found something. You are intrigued.

You start to dig around it. A metal box becomes visible, about the size and shape of a shoebox. The box is old and blackened by being buried for a long time.

You dig around the box carefully, get down on your knees, and pull it out.

There is something in the box that you are ready to consider. You may not have been ready three or five years ago. But you are ready today. You have a strong sense that you can handle whatever the box contains.

The latch on the box is shut, but not locked. You take the back of your thumbnail and flick the latch open.

You take a deep breath, steel yourself, and open the box. And there it is. Something you always knew you were going to write about some day, when the time was right.

Maybe the time is finally right. You decide.

WINTER:

COACH YOURSELF

If art is the bridge between what you see in your mind and what the world sees, then skill is how you build that bridge.

—TWYLA THARP

The happiest and most successful writers have always understood that they work in a service industry that revolves around readers, not writers. So any opportunity for redirection always starts with a reflection on whom you serve and how you can serve them better, regardless of genre or path to publication. Writing careers are cyclical. Once you have been writing, selling, focusing, and self-promoting consistently, you will be more familiar with your strengths and how to best steer them within a constantly evolving professional landscape. Once you can align your wants with reader needs, you will no longer need a coach other than yourself and your best instincts. There are plenty of people out there who can offer you terrific advice, but at the end of the day, and at every major crossroads, there is only one person you can ultimately rely on to choose the best course for your career, and that's you.

*Traditional publishing and indie publishing aren't all that different,
and I don't think people realize that.*

—AMANDA HOCKING

In the recent past, we had a name for writers who created and sold their work directly to their audience: self-published (or indie) writers. We also had a name for writers who worked with publishers: traditionally published writers.

Now it's time to free ourselves from this black-and-white thinking and live in the land of gray. Every writer is capable of, and should exercise, both types of publishing.

The two practices compliment each other a lot more than you might expect. In my experience, the happiest writers are those who do both without choosing one camp or the other exclusively, and who do both without attributing unnecessary angelic or demonic qualities to either.

Embrace the idea of a detached approach to how you are going to publish your writing. Instead of joining one camp or another, embrace the idea that you will do whatever is best to match your aspirations to their appropriate audiences.

How you publish no longer matters. It only matters that you publish. This permission to go either way, as you deem appropriate, does not exonerate you from all of the other responsibilities that come with publishing. You are expected to be professional and poised no matter which way you go.

If you are going to write, you may as well become a professional in all of your writing-related dealings regardless of how you go about broadcasting what you have to say.

In fact, since we don't know what's going to happen next, let's take the concept further and say that it's your birthright to check the box that says "all of the above," whatever that is going to mean in publishing in the future.

So let's assume, for the sake of this book, and with a nod to the times we are living in, that in the long run you will both traditionally publish, i.e., have your work published by others, and self-publish, i.e., publish some of your own work yourself.

I don't want to be a passenger in my own life.

—DIANE ACKERMAN

When most writers come to me for classes and coaching, they don't know what they have to offer, so they don't know what they have to author.

And most writers I work with who go on to succeed in becoming regularly published, or even to publish books, find their strongest topics through writing and then go on to champion and expand those ideas further and further.

Therefore, one of the most important aspects of your writing rhythms is your annual inventory. You annual inventory helps you plan what you hope to accomplish next via an inventory of what you accomplished this year. Take a look at all five parts of your writing career: craft, sales, specializing, professional development, and self-promotion.

Publications:

Self-published projects:

Pieces under consideration:

Started, not completed:

Online platform-building progress:

Social networking strides:

Paid gigs:

Volunteer gigs:

Shared/gave away:

Gather all of these up and take a good look because what you have accomplished today is the foundation of what you will accomplish tomorrow.

BECOME A THOUGHT LEADER

An original writer is not one who imitates nobody, but one whom nobody can imitate.

—FRANCOIS-RENÉ DE CHATEAUBRIAND

According to e-media professor and publishing industry expert Jane Friedman, there are four predominant ways successful authors carry out their online platforms.

NICHE CRAFT

This is similar to what I do. I concentrate the lion's share of my efforts on writing for writers, specifically mom writers launching writing careers. By focusing on one area and working within that area, I test and grow ideas that become stronger in the process of sharing. Niche craft takes patience. Niches grow slowly over time. Trust and consistency are important for the thought leaders who grow them.

COMMUNITY BUILDER

Author Cory Doctorow is a good example of a community builder. He has built community through his work on BoingBoing.com and his own blog, Craphound.com. His fans interact with his work, test-driving it, sharing it, mashing it up, and transforming it. Cory has created an environment that encourages fans to splash around in his body of work.

MEDIA MAVEN

Gary Vaynerchuk grew himself a huge platform using Wine Library TV. How did he do it? By combining two contradictory things: wine and randomness— two things that did not previously go together in the carefully curated wine culture in which he grew up. But you don't have to be from Jersey to do something with this much panache. Anyone can do exactly what Gary has done, so long as you do it in the way only you would do it. Start something and grow it over time.

THE CONNECTOR

Jane is the epitome of the connector. The connector is a person of influence who lowers the rope and lets others in by sharing what she notices, as she notices it, and inviting and sharing the participation of others. She participates in two blogs: her own, Jane-Friedman.com and Writer Unboxed. Whether she is attending conferences or giving a webinar, she is accessible via every communication tool. As a result, she has grown her network of influence astronomically in the past few years. The secret handshake of the connector? Be accessible and available, and share what you learn and know as you go. (It helps if you have a wide and deep knowledge of a few specific topics.)

As for my next book, I am going to hold myself from writing it till I have it impending in me: grown heavy in my mind like a ripe pear; pendant, gravid, asking to be cut or it will fall.

—VIRGINIA WOOLF

So you've had a really amazing idea. That's great!

There's only one problem. Out of the millions of writers out there right now, about 100,000 of them are also having an amazing idea right about the same time as you. And some of those writers' ideas are going to sound remarkably similar to yours no matter what you do.

But maybe you know the difference between an idea that has legs and an idea that flops over. Or maybe you are not sure if your idea has legs. Bounce one off of this list to get a better idea of just how long its legs are:

> **LITTLE LEGS:** An immediate local audience would be interested in the idea.

> **MEDIUM-SIZED LEGS:** A regional audience would be interested in the idea.

> **PRETTY LONG LEGS:** Most of the people in the United States would be interested in the idea.

> **DADDY LONG LEGS:** All English-speaking people will be interested in the idea.

> **WICKED LONG LEGS:** Many of the people in the world would be interested in the idea.

> **LEGS THAT JUST WON'T QUIT:** Everyone in the world would have reason to be interested in the idea.

Once you get in the habit of skipping over ideas that are not ready yet, you may notice that later some of those ideas come back stronger and more ready to roar. Keep in mind that some of your ideas need to simmer, even if you don't act on them today.

In the meantime, don't waste an iota of energy regretting ideas that are gestating. Focus on the ideas that have enough right now. Because time spent on an idea that is ready is time better spent than time spent on an idea that is not yet ready.

A man will turn over half a library to make one book.

—SAMUEL JOHNSON

When all of the following converge for you, maybe it's time for a book:

- You have mastered short and long pieces.
- You know who you are speaking to.
- You know what they find compelling.
- You are the person they are going to listen to.
- You have cultivated expertise for several years.
- You are well connected in the community that is your audience.
- You are a sensor of what is needed in the community.
- Once you get the universal yes, you strike out in that direction.
- When you articulate your clear-cut mission it will attract interest.

When you hold that intention over time, you are in your power and you can steer your own ship.

Publishers have done really great things for a really long time. They aren't some big bad evil entity trying to kill literature or writers. They are companies, trying to make money in a bad economy with a lot of top-heavy business practices.

—AMANDA HOCKING

Let's tip the balance in the direction of the traditional publishing industry here. Does this sound like a good match for you?

1. Letting the publisher carry half the project load
2. Letting the publisher worry about distribution
3. Gaining legitimacy from the publisher's brand
4. Benefitting from the publisher's experience in audience targeting
5. Partnering with others
6. Gaining amazing project-management skills and all the connections you'll need to create the kind of product you envision
7. Being taken more seriously; inheriting cache; acquiring clout
8. Using publisher resources to back your idea so you don't have to go into debt doing it
9. Getting into brick-and-mortar stores with ease
10. Working with set deadlines
11. Avoiding the stigma of self-publishing
12. Receiving an advance
13. Doing the necessary work to get the deal

Nobody notices normal. If you want to get noticed, get remembered and get business, you've got to stick yourself out there.

—SCOTT GINSBERG

Memorable means you are unforgettable. *Memorable* means you make an indelible impression on others. *Memorable* means there is something remarkable about you. *Memorable* means that you operate from excellence.

When we apply the concept of memorable to writers, what does it look like?

It looks like a writer who cares, not only about herself but about delivering value to others regardless of what kind of value we're talking about.

It looks like a writer who is nimble, one who can juggle multiple tasks, like writing the next book and the demands of his personal life, with a rigorous appearance or promotion schedule.

It looks like a writer who took the time to write a great book. In a *Writer's Digest* article that I wrote about self-promotion for fiction writers, every single writer I polled said that quality writing was still the most important thing.

It looks like something about you that others want to share. Something makes you a standout. It can be anything, but it has to be something that gets others talking about you.

What do you think makes writers memorable? What makes a writer memorable to you? Think of a writer you admire. Then jot down ten reasons why that writer is so memorable for you. What is that special ingredient? Then ask what it's going to be for you.

How many writers would you pay—I mean more than once—to see them take off their clothes, paint themselves gold, and parade around on the stage with a giant egg?

—MARGARET ATWOOD

In my experience, here's what people are willing to pay writers for:

EXPERIENCE

This is a person who knows what she is talking about from a depth of personal know-how. The deeper the person's experience, the more you should expect to pay for their time. A person with less experience but a lot of enthusiasm should do more for less, but still charge something.

SATISFYING INTERACTION

Nobody wants to go it alone, so many people may be willing to pay for a satisfying interaction with either you or a group of folks led or facilitated by you. People today desire companions along the way. They crave community, and there are as many different kinds and different qualities of communities as one can imagine. And yet, communities are fickle, so they are tricky to contain and sustain. I would say that communities are probably the trickiest contexts to charge for because you have to strike just the right balance. What does that mean to your audience? You'll probably have to experiment to find out.

PERSONAL PROGRESS

In my role as a teacher, I have consistently offered my students deadlines, challenges, lessons, and a gentle kick in the pants to remind them to keep going and growing. It took me some time to find the confidence and authority in myself to offer this kind of service with just the right tone, while being neither too pushy nor too authoritative. In the long run, my advice usually ends up being fairly grounded and practical, therefore it works for people who are comfortable combining inspired and creative with grounded and practical.

TRANSFORMATION

You can create contexts for the transformation of your audience members' minds. You can create contexts that transform your audience members' emotions. You can create contexts for the transformation of your audience members' bodies. And you can create contexts for the transformation of your audience members' souls.

The questions remains: What do you have to offer, and how do you want to offer it?

By some strange, unknown, inward urgency they are not really alive unless they are creating.

—PEARL S. BUCK

When you keep the focus on service, the possibilities of what you can do with a writing career are unlimited. There is a kind of purity about a person who not only knows what she is doing but also knows why she is doing it. People with pure intentions magnetize good things to them. And every business success story is a combination of a great idea, consistent effort, growing the reach, and attracting success.

Let's review the steps:

1. Plan to do more than merely write (if you've already been writing, consider what else you can offer).
2. Get to know the audience you wish to serve very well.
3. Address your audience's needs and meet them.
4. Understand how your audience will benefit from what you offer.
5. Price your services competitively.
6. Time your offers appropriately.
7. Package what you offer to appeal to your audience.
8. Write your way to increasingly longer salable forms.
9. Spoke services off of your most successful topic(s).

By steadily expanding what you do with your topic while at the same time expanding your audience, you increase your impact. The measure of your platform is the amount of influence you have on others. I want to make sure it's clear that your influence will not increase because you obsessively focus on how others respond to you, but when you focus on how well you are doing at the services your provide.

Keep your focus in the center of your fountain flowing upwards and outwards and you will fare far better than if you give in to the temptation to view your career, your writing, and yourself from the outside. There is only one power point in any creative career, and that place is firmly rooted in the center.

People feel no obligation to buy books. It isn't their fault.
—SHERWOOD ANDERSON

In the last section, we covered the many reasons readers might follow you on the Internet, but when it comes to books, according to Kevin Smokler, the CEO of Booktour.com, there are only five reasons people buy books. I've added a couple more .

THE READER IS DRAWN TO THE SUBJECT MATTER

This means the reader needs the book or wants the book or feels a connection to the book based on the subject matter. If you want to renovate your own home, you purchase a book that breaks it down into manageable steps. If you are a huge baseball fan, you might pick up either a baseball biography or a fictional tale with a baseball story.

THE BOOK WAS RECOMMENDED TO THE READER VIA WORD OF MOUTH

Whole cultures have been built around reading and readers in the past ten years, and because they are online, they are international. So now you can garner book recommendations, not only from your friends, but also from a wider context of referrals.

THE READER HEARD ABOUT THE BOOK THROUGH MAJOR MEDIA

Major media is still a major player in influencing the books we buy. Think about it: You may not purchase a book just because a friend recommends it, but if you also see a cover section story on the book in your daily newspaper, you might decide to buy.

THE READER IS ALREADY A FAN OF THE BOOK

If you follow and enjoy a particular author, you are quite likely to buy the next book and the next and the next. It's possible for readers to lose faith in a favorite author, but assuming he does not let you down, you will continue to buy what he writes.

THE BOOK IS SHORT

In a digital age where life is increasingly hectic and free time is at a premium, you might read something by an author you never heard of—even if you are not drawn to the subject matter and the book wasn't recommended to you—if the book is short.

YOU TRUST THE AUTHOR/IMPRINT

If you like writing books, and you trust Writer's Digest, you are more likely to purchase a book by Writer's Digest than another type of writing book because you expect a certain level of quality and comprehension.

DIRT CHEAP

Another reason people buy in these tight economic times is price. The risk of buying a book for a buck or two is a lot less than buying a book for ten or twenty bucks. Admit it. You have always loved a bargain and you always will.

What makes *you* pay hard, cold cash for a book?

PUBLISH YOURSELF

Publishing is the mode of transmission from brain to brain.

—MARGARET ATWOOD

Let's flip the publishing coin to the self-publishing side and see when and how it might make sense:

1. The project would not work as a traditionally published project for whatever reason.
2. Time pressure. You want or need to turn the project around quickly.
3. You want to keep most of the profits yourself.
4. You are taking an artful or limited edition approach to the book.
5. You want to test-market a topic before tackling a longer, more labor-intensive project (perhaps take a micro-publishing approach).
6. You are just getting started as a writer and you don't really have the platform for a traditionally published book, but you think you have an idea that would sell itself.
7. You are already an established name and you want to publish your backlist or your unpublished work.
8. You plan to work with a niche market only, so no point going after a mass market.
9. You are extremely patient, have strong administrative skills, and are good at project management.
10. The resources to create quality products and partner with professionals are now widely available.
11. Publishing some of your own work will increase your feeling of ownership.
12. You like marketing and self-promotion, and you are good at both.
13. Your book is location specific, and you live and work at the location you want to write about.

No author dislikes to be edited as much as he dislikes not to be published.

—RUSSELL LYNES

What we are experiencing right now is a rapid evolution in publishing where only the fittest will survive. And this applies to writers as much as it does to agents and publishers and bookstores and every other business related to publishing. And if you are going to prosper in this economic landscape, you are going to probably want to get your game face on and give up any fantasies you might be harboring about being chosen by Oprah's Book Club or becoming discovered, because these are not goals that lend themselves to small actionable steps.

This is not the publishing landscape of bygone days. These are modern times. Exciting times. Rapidly shifting times. Precarious times. And, believe it or not, for some writers who work at a focused, consistent rate, prosperous times.

And, sure, if you want to speak squarely about what is going on in publishing right now, advances are down. Bookstores are in jeopardy while online stores are doing well. E-books are on the rise, and there is a very long way up to go. Niches rule, both for nonfiction writers and nonfiction publishers. Publishers, editors, and agents are hard pressed to make time for their authors, while increasing amounts of responsibility fall on the authors who are traditionally published. Community building, sharing information online for free, and distance learning are hot.

Regardless of everything going on, I still believe that the traditional book deal is the best thing that can happen to a writer not only for the potential money, because there is still *some* money to be earned, but also for the increase in visibility and credibility in the a writer's career. I believe that writers still need agents. And I know many publishers wish that agents would simply go away so they could renegotiate the rights they want to get from their authors' works to stay viable. I believe that there has never been a better time to be a writer, perhaps since the invention of the printing press.

So, if you work well within a structured context with parameters and deadlines set by others, persevere. Publishing opportunities are narrowing, but they will not likely disappear any time soon.

The only constant in your life is you. The best audience for what you write is you—the child you were, the adult you are.

—JANE YOLEN

Have you ever watched the Winter Olympics when the skaters are doing their routines and they are working up to the perfect spin?

The perfect spin is, of course, the moment when the audience is the most stirred because the movement is so poetic and inspiring.

Have you ever noticed that the perfect pirouette isn't something the skater puts out there on demand? A skater doesn't go from standing on the ice to ta-da! Look at my perfect pirouette.

You have to skate your way into the perfect spin. You don't get the big applause until you have practiced for hours and hours and hours.

In other words, your whole writing career isn't going to be a perfect pirouette. And expecting this of yourself or your writing is going to inhibit your growth and put a damper on your mood.

Just like you are not a perfect person every minute of your life, every single thing you do in your writing career isn't going to be a perfect pirouette.

What you will likely experience instead are a lot of long hours of practice, a lot of learning new techniques and putting them into practice, a lot of building up the stamina and the strength to do something amazing every once in a while. And then, finally, applause!

You're going to have your peak experiences in your writing, and the reader is going to feel them. But a writer who brings perfectionism into the process and expects of herself perfect spin after perfect spin ad infinitum is going to be a writer who ends up feeling badly most of the time. Because perfect spins 24/7 are simply an unrealistic expectation.

I see this type of imposter syndrome with my writing students. They have the perfect pirouette syndrome, which means they are constantly holding out for the feedback that tells them they have finally performed the perfect pirouette. When it doesn't happen, they discount everything they have done up to that point. They disregard the less than perfect path they are on, which is actually the thing that will eventually lead them to a very solid spin.

Don't be confused. Continuous perfection does not exist on this plane, nor is it an attainable goal. No matter how many of your books are published, and even if each of those books *is* your perfect pirouette, even if millions of that perfect book are published, it doesn't mean you spend every minute of every day perfect. Perfect is not humanly possible.

Work hard for peak moments. Cherish them when they come, more because they are fleeting than for any other reason. And then, the rest of the time, go back to being your imperfect old self. That's the you we like best anyway.

DECLARE OWNERSHIP

Can you explain something or teach a skill in a clear, organized, and entertaining fashion? If you can, then you can succeed as a how-to writer.

—ROBERT W. BLY

When you first started writing, you might have written only for yourself. Maybe your writing was limited to journaling. Then, after a while, you probably got antsy to make a little money. So maybe you started writing short pieces that paid a bit of money. Then maybe after you wrote a couple of dozen of those, you felt restless again and expanded into longer pieces that took longer to write but paid better. In order to do this, you may have learned how to query for assignments.

But after a time of juggling a variety of types of writing and submissions, you started to feel restless again. Maybe you have an idea at the back of your mind that you think might be a good idea for a book. If so, this is probably a good time to start thinking about writing an e-book first, before you attempt a book.

What's nice about e-books is that they give you ownership. And at a certain point in your writing career, you are going to start craving ownership and you are going to find that fulfilling your desire for ownership makes you feel a lot more cheerful about serving others.

There is no reason you shouldn't heed the call of an e-book when it comes around. For one thing, it's never been easier to create e-books. But e-books aren't the only way to cultivate ownership. There are plenty of worthwhile ways to do it. You could create a paid newsletter, teach, speak, consult, or train.

If you've been writing for a while, you are more likely to make good choices of an e-book topic because you are a seasoned writer. Unseasoned writers often make rookie publishing mistakes. Of course, mistakes can help you learn faster, so you may as well make some.

Once you think you are ready for ownership, you'll want to be pretty sure that your idea is going to fly before you invest your time and money. Outline your ideas in detail and test run them by a large sample of folks who are like your target readers before you commit a lot of time and energy to the publishing process. You'll know when your idea is a winner.

One hates an author that's all author.

—LORD BYRON

When you are approached for a donation of time, money, or energy, it helps to have a plan. The problem with not planning how much you will give each year is that you won't know what you can and want to give in order to gauge what's reasonable.

I am regularly asked to give more than I possibly can. On the other hand, I don't want to be selfish or greedy, so I strive to find a balance and I give in as many ways as possible. Here are several ways you can give that are all good practice:

TIME

Giving away some of your time is good for others and it's good for you, too. When you consciously give some of your time away, you appreciate the time you keep. Often the time we willingly give can lead to good ideas for getting paid in the future.

MONEY

No matter how much you make from your writing, start giving a small percentage to good causes. You can start with five or ten dollars at a time. Keep your eyes and ears open for opportunities to do so. Or make your purchases through retailers that are also good causes or who give back to good causes. When you give money, you feel the good will that comes with sharing a portion of your money with those in need.

CONTENT

What causes or organizations would you like to support with your writing? This might take the form of a book, an e-book, a special report, an article, a checklist, or whatever you wish to give. Maybe you will write marketing copy for a nonprofit or contribute an article to your most valued nonprofit writing organization. As long as you limit what you give for free, you can feel good about contributing.

A RESPONSE

If someone contacts you just to ask a question, you don't have to take the time to answer. And maybe you won't have the time to answer. But once in a while it's good practice to try to answer a question that someone asks. Think of it as your small part in the saying, "Ask and you shall receive."

GOODS

How often have you purged your home and then turned the leftover stuff to a local family or charity? If you are like most Americans, you do this several times a year. Giving is great preparation for receiving because in clearing out the old, you make way for the new. Donate books to reading charities and libraries.

If you were to make an annual giving plan that included time, money, content, a response (or a few), and goods, what would your giving plan look like?

The trouble with the profit system has always been that it was highly unprofitable to most people.

—E.B. WHITE

Every kid in kid-dom knows how many days off from school she has coming. So one reason a snow day is such a big cause for celebration is because it's a bonus.

Snow or no snow, everybody gets excited when they receive something they hadn't expected. And writers are no exception. This is exactly how it feels to receive a bonus check you hadn't expected.

When bonus checks come, it means you wrote a piece and you had a clause in your contract that says if your piece is repurposed you will receive another payment.

This has happened to me more in recent years. I've been in a better position to receive these extra checks after a dozen years of writing for publication. The longer you write, the better the chance some of your old pieces will get repurposed.

Once I even eventually collected as many bonus checks as I had been paid for the original piece—that was really thrilling. I essentially doubled the money I'd made on one feature because the publisher repurposed it so often.

The thing about snow days is they have to be paid back. Bonus checks never have to be paid back. They are 100 percent profit. Plus, you get another clip or credit for your work.

Bonus checks trump kill fees any day. A kill fee is what you get instead of your contracted rate if a piece is cancelled (aka killed) instead of going to print. I don't know too many writers who receive a lot of kill fees.

Before you sign a contract, take a closer look. Make sure your content cannot be leveraged by your publisher without compensating you. You should receive a percentage or flat amount per each use.

Also make sure there is a clause that says you will receive a percent of the original amount promised (a kill fee) if your hard work is not used.

HELP OTHERS BENEFIT

Authors sustain many other life forms: Many others are employed because of authors.

—MARGARET ATWOOD

I am taking my car into the shop for an oil change today. What are the benefits of my car getting an oil change? On a purely practical level, my car will run better and perform better longer than it would if I did not regularly get the oil changed.

On a financial level, I will save money by keeping this car, which I don't have to make a car payment on, running longer by paying a little today. From a mental perspective, getting the oil changed will put my mind at ease, because I drive an older car and might otherwise worry if I didn't have an expert check under the hood once in a while.

On an emotional level, I will feel better about taking my car in for service than I would if I procrastinated and my car suddenly died on me.

By taking my car in for an oil change, I clearly benefit on many levels, and this makes me feel good about spending the money to do so. In fact, I had to call three times to get my appointment and I would have called ten, if necessary. That's how loyal I am to my mechanic.

And you know what? I would do all of this without any incentives from my mechanic, and yet, he also sent me a fifteen-dollars-off coupon for a holiday promotion. So my mechanic can pretty much do no wrong as far as I am concerned at this moment.

This is the kind of relationship we all want to have with the folks who pay us for products and services. That's why if you don't know ahead of time what the benefits are going to be for the folks you serve, you are going to have trouble convincing them to belly up and pay you.

What you must do is analyze your product or service's benefits. What are the immediate benefits? What are the long-term benefits? What are the purely practical benefits? What are the emotional benefits? What are the mental health benefits? What are the financial benefits? Are there any other benefits? List them all before you get to work on marketing copy.

Last time I checked, most people like to save boatloads of money. So be like my mechanic if you possibly can. And if you can't, be sure to offer a product or service with multiple benefits on many levels. If you do, you will prosper in both the short run and the long haul.

Writing is like prostitution. First you do it for love, and then for a few close friends, and then for money.

—MOLIERE

Let's explore multiple ways writers can profit in addition to writing and while continuing to get writing projects done. There are plenty of ways you can create fresh, ongoing income streams that don't and won't compromise your literary integrity.

And yet, many writers dislike talking about money. Why?

Chalk it up to humility, low self-esteem and, occasionally, self-righteousness. Regardless, we still have to dirty our hands talking about money if we are going to find ways to stay afloat as writers. If you are going to be in business for yourself, you are going to need to think about, talk about, and discuss money. And treating your cash flow like a shameful secret, or if you don't have cash flow, like something you don't need, is not going to help anyone become more flush.

As a collective, writers could stand to cultivate a more prosperous attitude. So let's roll up our sleeves and talk frankly about money. I've learned a lot over the past decade by pricing things and then seeing how it goes. And once you start pricing your offerings, the feedback process begins, which is really crucial, because the response you receive to your price offerings tells you everything you need to move forward.

Here's what you'll learn when you begin pricing your own stuff:

- You'll learn what people think your value is.
- You'll learn how much people trust you to deliver quality.
- You'll learn how much is too much and how much is not enough.
- You'll learn how to adjust your prices as you go according to what your audience will pay.
- You'll learn how your success or lack of success selling products and services is impacted by what's going on economically with the rest of the country.

Avoid confusing controversies. Let's say you are pricing your first e-book. I just did this and it is pretty darn confusing with all the hullabaloo about e-book pricing right now. So I suggest that you ignore all the nonsense going around about low-balling your e-offerings. This is your business and you can and should price according to what feels right for you and your audience. Your audience will let you know how you are doing. And your audience is necessarily like any other audience, so ask for their opinion.

To avoid criticism say nothing, do nothing, be nothing.

—ARISTOTLE

If someone were going to criticize your product or service offer, what would they say? For example, I'm working with a student right now who is offering a class that some might consider controversial. The truth is, it's an incredibly powerful topic. Yet, knowing in advance that some people will take offense or call her motives into question is helpful to her from a marketing point of view. It's also helpful from a professional point of view so she won't be blindsided when and if she is verbally attacked, which is something that is likely to happen thanks to the anonymity the Internet offers to provokers.

Here are the kinds of questions you can ask yourself about your product or service to make sure you are ready to address folks' resistance to what you wish to offer:

- Will anyone be offended by my product or service? If so, why? Which aspect or aspects will they find offensive?

- Will anyone be turned off by my product or service, even if only mildly? Which aspect or aspects will turn them off?

- Does my product or service bring up questions or issues that I have not thought to address in advance? If so, what are the questions or issues and how can I address them?

- Is there any way someone might feel disappointed or let down by my product or service? Have I made provisions for this such as offering a makeup class, a refund, or a guarantee?

- Is there something about the timing, cost, or features of my offer that might cause someone to hesitate before purchasing? Have I considered how to respond to these concerns in advance, or have I looked for ways to alleviate the concerns altogether?

- When and if someone does decide to take a swipe at me, for whatever reason, will I be ready? Will I bounce right back or will I perceive the attack as personal and something I may never recover from? (I want to warn you now that if you plan to do anything in the public eye, you will likely be attacked or harshly questioned at some point. Be prepared for this day so you won't think it's more personal than it really is.)

To monetize your personal brand into a business using social market-ing networks, two pillars need to be in place: product and content.

—GARY VAYNERCHUK

Basically my advice to you about pricing is the same as my advice to writers about every-thing. Be mindful of your value according to you and others. Be responsive to your audi-ence and communicate clearly and thoughtfully what you have to offer them. Trust your audience and your instincts to guide you through the process of developing products and services that others want, need, and will pay for. And then price appropriately.

DECIDE WHAT YOU THINK YOUR PRODUCT OR SERVICE IS WORTH AND THEN LOWER THAT AMOUNT JUST A SMIDGE. You'll end up with a good "beta version" price this way. A beta version simply means that you are still improving the product or service. And since this is true of most products and services launched today by small businesses or creatives, your most loyal customers will appreciate a price reduction for being first-time buyers. They will also be more willing to provide you with constructive feedback you can use to improve your product or service, which is key.

DON'T PRICE SO LOW THAT YOU GET A PAIN IN YOUR STOMACH. Your hard work is worth something. You have a lot to offer and what you have to offer has value. You deserve to be paid a fair amount for your time and energy for the products and services that result from your time and energy. Got it? Good. And when you price yourself too low or give yourself away too cheaply, you will feel low and cheap, not to mention a little nauseous. So don't. Or if you do, make note of how that feels and try to do better next time.

STAY OFF YOUR HIGH HORSE ABOUT PRICING. Your experience in another field or area of expertise may lead you to believe that your value should be a lot higher than your audience believes it is. So keep things real. Professional experience does not always cross over just be-cause you'd like it to. You can expect your audience to tell you when you've overpriced your-self by not purchasing your products or services. People who are overly focused on how no one values them enough may be suffering from self-consciousness, and self-consciousness interferes with good communication. When you care about your audience, you are focused on them, not on you. You price appropriately and make sales that create happy customers. Aiming for win-win-win is not just about you. It's a three-way proposition.

UNDERPROMISE AND OVERDELIVER. Start what you offer at a modest price and increase it over time. Let's say you are pricing a six-week e-class, like one of mine. Soon, I will price my e-classes at $299. I had priced them at $275. Prior to that, they were $250. And prior to that, they were even less. The primary touchstone I use in pricing my classes is to listen to my students. When it was priced too low, they suggested I raise the price. If your audience says they would pay more, it's time to raise your price.

STRUT YOUR SOCIAL SIDE: PART ONE

The illiterate of the twenty-first century will not be those who cannot read and write, but those who cannot learn, unlearn, and relearn.
—ALVIN TOFFLER

I want to give you some tips for how to use social media once you have a strong sense of identity, purpose, and a mission or call to action.

Be you. You're enough. Your presence is welcomed at the table. There is no exclusive club. Join in. Speak up. Chime in.

See yourself as profitable and productive rather than starving and desperate. Focus your energy. Spend some time on self-reflection. Then move forward in a thoughtful, constructive manner.

Become magnetic. Connect with whomever is right there in front of you wherever you are, either in person or online. Forget "the masses." Instead of spraying your energy outwards willy-nilly, pull people in. Rather than splattering others with your agenda, engage in dynamic interactions that are mentally stimulating and inspiring for everyone involved. If you do interesting things, you will be interesting to others.

View social media channels as communication tools for building your platform. If your platform is just another to-do list or litany of musts and shoulds, that feeling of "have to" will leak through. There is an art to platform building just like there is an art to writing, selling, specializing, and continuing to evolve as a creative businessperson. See your platform as a lifelong creation that grows and evolves alongside your art. You have to keep it fresh for readers and for you.

Share your process. Once you know your identity, purpose, and mission, share the process of where your journey meets the world. This is interesting to folks who are interested in your message. They will stay tuned to find out what is going to happen next.

Embrace the business of your art. No one is going to come along and launch your career, manage it, and send you checks to live on. I've said it before but it's worth saying again: If you are writer and you don't see yourself as a businessperson as well, you are never going to thrive creatively. Discover the right balance for you between business and art and groove it!

Helped are those who create anything at all, for they shall relive the thrill of their own conception and realize a partnership in the creation of the Universe that keeps them responsible and cheerful.

—ALICE WALKER

Consider how building a readership with simple online strategies like this one can lead to opportunities for your future writing. Bruce Holland Rogers is an example of an enterprising writer who set up a site where readers could pay him ten dollars a year to receive thirty-six short stories on a regular basis.

Charging twenty-eight cents a story may not seem to you like a model for blockbuster success, however, when you crunch the numbers, you begin to see how a humble direct-subscription model like this one can truly work. If Holland Rogers builds up to a thousand subscribers, twenty-eight cents per story starts to work pretty well. Even just seven hundred subscribers adds up to seven thousand dollars a year.

You might think that's not much. But are you making seven thousand dollars a year directly from readers for your writing? I bet for those who are that it's a pretty satisfying feeling.

That's more than the size of a lot of book advances these days. What Holland Rogers has done is create an income stream that supports his writing career while also helping him cultivate a readership.

At the other end of the spectrum is building up a readership through generously sharing your content for the promise of future earnings or readers. There are many examples of people who do this out there, but two that jump to mind are Gary Vaynerchuk and Ali Edwards.

Gary Vaynerchuk created Wine Library TV online. It's a show focused on the everyman approach to drinking and appreciating wine.

Ali Edwards, a designer by training, started scrapbooking as a hobby and has grown her passion for words and images into a full-time career as a scrapbooking blogger.

Both Vaynerchuk and Edwards have used a combination of traditional and nontraditional publishing to create readerships for their work. Through a combination of what I call "gigging"—writing, teaching, speaking, selling blog ads, and direct selling—both Vaynerchuk and Edwards have established handcrafted careers that are fueled by words.

Neither strategy is "right." What's right is deciding what to do to earn from your work because it's a good fit with your skills and your readerships needs. And when you figure out that balance, you are going to feel rich no matter how much you make.

Customers want you to tell them the truth. Sure, they want quality and service and value and entertainment, but above all they want to know that the person they're dealing with is being honest.

—GARY VAYNERCHUK

Here are more tips for how to use social media after you have a strong sense of identity, purpose, and mission:

ESCHEW PRESSURE

If you are a person who commonly bends to peer pressure or who worries overly about what others will think, consider social media your new fresh hell. Learn how to acknowledge mistakes, say you are sorry, and move on without taking even one minute to beat yourself up, obsess, or freak out. Make mistakes daily, if possible, or you won't grow.

USE GOOD JUDGMENT

You don't need to be a brand. You can't be genuine friends with everyone. Nor can you be available 24/7. Not only should you rock the community boat just for the sake of rocking it; if you are being truly authentic, it's inevitable that you will rock the boat at some point.

AVOID THE ECHO-CHAMBER

The echo-chamber effect plagues blogging communities and collaborators. The echo-chamber effect happens when everyone who writes on a topic seems to feel the exact same way about everything instead of folks having variations of opinions. It's more healthy for a group to feel yes, no, maybe about an idea than for everyone to be automatically nodding and feeling and saying the exact same thing all the time.

HAVE BOUNDARIES

Never let anyone else's rule book dictate what and how much you should share. You should share what you are comfortable sharing, period. Trust your internal compass with regards to where to set your filters for personal and business privacy. Your gut knows when to say when. Guard your privacy as though it were gold, because it is.

BE CREATIVE!

You are a writer, so take your creative impulses and apply them to other pursuits. What would happen if you were as creative in selling, specializing, professional development, and platform building as you are in your writing? Magic! That's what.

If writers desire to spread a message, have an impact on a reader-ship, and be heard, there are many ways to do that aside from publishing a book.

—JANE FRIEDMAN

Once upon a time, in the dark ages known as the twentieth century, the end-all and be-all of being a real writer was writing a book.

Today things have changed, and they have changed dramatically. Today we have the luxury and the headache of thinking beyond the book. I say luxury, because aiming for a book was a measurable goal and therefore a doable one. I have worked with many students who have accomplished this goal. The steps from completely unknown and unpublished are rigorous but known and easy enough to map out.

However, now that the publishing world has cracked wide open, the opportunities for writers are unlimited. And this is where the overwhelm, and therefore the head-aches, begin.

If writers can write anything, what's the most logical path from where you are to-day to where you'd like to be? How long will it take? What can you expect along the way? How can you speed the process up or slow the process down?

Say what you like about the old ways of doing things in publishing, there was something reassuring about knowing that you could climb the ranks if you set your sights on it and proceeded wisely. Today there are still ranks, but there are other op-tions, as well.

What happens when the people with great ideas start organizing for themselves, start leading online tribes, start creating microproducts and seminars and interactions that people are actually willing to pay for?

What happens is that they become leaders and people follow them. I think what we are going to see in the future is not merely that there are no rules in publishing, but that there is no such thing as publishing, per se. What we are going to see is that everyone is a publisher or a potential publisher, whether or not they are trained and professional. And just as everyone will be a potential publisher, everyone will also be a potential author.

I think what we will see is that the future ends up being not about bending the rules or breaking the rules, but abandoning the concept of rules altogether. The tricky part in all of this will be figuring out in a world where there are no rules what to say yes to.

SYNCHRONIZE YOUR EFFORTS: PART ONE

Don't cast sidelong glances, and compare yourself to others among your peers! (Writing is not a race. No one really "wins." The satisfaction is in the effort, and rarely in the consequent rewards, if there are any.)

—JOYCE CAROL OATES

Timing has always been important. And when we are talking about *timing*, we are actually talking about two things: What's *timely* right now, and how well you *time* your offerings. You need to become a master of both of these strategies.

Go with your most timely ideas. Planning products, services, and events can be complicated. So let's keep this simple. Think of keywords for your topic.

Let's say your topic is "writing." Your specific topic is "memoir writing." And when we take your audience into account, we get "memoir writing for seniors."

Great! This is a hot topic. Seniors are motivated to get their memories down on paper as they enter their golden years, in order to leave a legacy. Next consider what's happening right now with this topic. Or at least what's happened recently to do with this topic.

Frank McCourt didn't become a writer until he was well into his sixties— this information could provide a crucial promotional concept for your offering. (McCourt has since passed away, but you might trace the arc of his publishing success and present this information to seniors in your audience to motivate and inspire them.)

Or perhaps you are not coaching seniors to write for publication. Perhaps, instead, you simply want to help seniors get their recollections down on the page so they can self-publish a book for family members and friends. Also a great idea! How can you tie this offering into trends that make the idea more appealing to your audience?

If providing writing assistance to seniors is your offering, you are off and running today, right? Because you have positive proof that the concept behind your offering is a legitimate niche that you can fill. So go ahead and fill it.

Giving yourself away is about bringing your humanity to the moment.

—SCOTT GINSBERG

For writers, social networking represents excellent opportunities. We can poll our networks, create hubs of students, and participate in a virtual round table discussion that never could have happened in the past.

There are benefits for our networks, as well. They can connect with people whose work they admire and discover what they are actually like in real life. For example, if you are my friend on Facebook right now, you know my husband is directing a musical, my daughter is playing her first leading role, and that I am very busy writing this book on top of my regular teaching and writing load.

But what I'm not is constantly accessible because if I were constantly available I would not be able to run my writing career. Instead, I use social networking as a way to be in touch with those I want to connect with without taking on any pressure in the relationship to perform tasks or accommodate behavior I did not explicitly intend or invite.

I do not follow the advice of marketing gurus, who might advise me to milk every ounce of tolerance out of my network of friends and followers. Instead my behavior is professional and consistent, even while occasionally sharing some of my personal life and some of my offerings.

I use the Internet gently as a tool to connect with others where we can hang out, take a break, blow off steam, vent, and find refreshment. And that's why I don't get sick of it, because I don't abuse it or worship it. I see social networking as a tool that we are very fortunate to have.

Social networking is a place to chat, to share, to decompress—and the folks who want to turn this lovely water-cooler break into a constant marketing machine are going to wear out its good graces.

Who forces time is pushed back by time; who yields to time finds time on his side.

—THE TALMUD

Don't just offer anything, anytime. You must consider the importance of your timing. Offer something specific and plan it for the very best possible time for your audience, as well as you. If you serve your audience needs, they will participate. And then they will thank you. And then your offering is win-win-win for everyone involved.

To continue with our example from chapter 299, what kind of timing would work well when offering presentations or workshops to seniors who want to write? Think about the audience's specific needs and concerns, because the strength of your timing is going to play a big part in your success (or lack of it).

Let's say you live in Arizona. And you know that one of the most boring times of the year for members of retirement homes is summer because of the brutal heat. So you might decide to offer an eight-week writing workshop during the summer because you know that is a time when seniors are looking for something to do indoors, to take their minds off of the limitations of the weather.

Who is your primary audience? Is your audience impacted by the time of the year? Specifically, which times are good for what you are offering and which times are not good? Schedule accordingly.

If any of this sounds like the kinds of things query writers and book proposal writers take into account, that's because it is a very similar way of thinking. If you are a writer with strong sales skills for selling your work, you are going to have an easier time conceiving of offerings that will fly based on good timing, just as you make the most of timing in selling your writing ideas.

You want all of your offerings to be fresh and connected to what's happening right now. Paying attention to the buzz related to your topic and audience will help you think like a marketer of multiple product and service possibilities, not merely a writer. Being selective and sensitive about the timing of your offerings helps you create mutual appreciation between you and your audience.

LET IT GO

A high-quality life of abundance has much more to do with what you remove from your life than what you add to it.

—CHERYL RICHARDSON

If you are going to enjoy the process of becoming an author, you are going to need to let go of the following:

- The need to be liked
- The need for approval
- The need to be put on a pedestal
- The need to become famous
- The need to please your mother, your editor, your ex-boyfriend, or anyone else who didn't approve of you in the past
- That book in the drawer you think should have published
- The friend who drains your energy, time, or bank account
- The need to be right all the time
- The need to make every single decision
- The need to control everything
- The need to be creative every second of every day
- The idea that you will never have normal human emotions
- The need to write a bestseller on your first try
- The need to network with every published writer in the known universe
- The need to do everything the exact same way you've always done it

Each of us has an inner compass. This is an instinct that points us toward health. It warns us when we are on dangerous ground, and it tells us when something is safe and good for us.

—JULIA CAMERON

May the best agent, not the one who plays the "exclusive" card most, win.

After attending Willamette Writers for many years and watching one agent in particular use flattery and the coveted "exclusive read" request with naïve writers, I've soured on the tactic.

Sure, it's great … for her. If she can cordon off the writers she perceives as the most likely to succeed in the publishing pool and get them to wait for her go ahead before they share with other agents—after the conference—instead of encouraging aspiring authors to mingle with all the agents at a conference, she increases her odds of landing promising clients quite a bit.

However, the strategy that is beneficial for the agent is not necessarily beneficial for the writer. Indeed, if an aspiring author focuses all his energy on only one agent at a conference, where he has paid for exposure to the many agents in attendance, then the practice would seem to conflict with the spirit of what writing conferences offer.

Certainly exposure to agents is one of the primary reasons writers attend writing conferences. Therefore, as an attendee, recognize that if you get a request for an exclusive, the agent making you that offer is jockeying for first dibs.

In what special cases should you give one agent first dibs?

Well, certainly, if the person making the request is one of the most well-respected agents on the planet, you might want to do so. But be clear that when an agent asks for an exclusive read, it's a acquisition tactic, not a necessity. There are plenty of agents out there who do not ask for an exclusive read on a project they are excited about. They just get back to the writer faster than they do in response to projects they are less excited about.

Furthermore, a reputable agent relies on the strength of her own track record to convince a writer to choose her over another agent, not jockeying tactics. Remember, writers: Agents are in competition with each other for authors, just as you are in competition with other writers for agents.

Over the years, I've seen quite a few writers disappointed because they took one person's recommendation for a particular agent without doing more due diligence. You can learn about any cautions about agents at the website Preditors & Editors (http://pred-ed.com).

If you get an offer from an agent to represent you, try to track down *past* and *current* clients of the agent. Contact the author politely with a simple question such as, "Would you mind sharing whether you would work with this agent again?" This will get you the information you need to make the most informed decision possible.

Eighty percent of success is showing up.

—WOODY ALLEN

Writers can learn a ton from actor, director, screenwriter, comedian, musician, and playwright Woody Allen. Regardless of what you think of him personally, I hope, as a writer, you will follow his creative example and give the world what you see through your eyes in the long run of your creative career. Here are a few career highlights:

Allen has cultivated a huge body of work. Some of his films are terrible, but some of them are brilliant.

He knows how to get financial backing, and he gets it for his films.

He is a flawed person and everyone knows it. This does not seem to trip him up creatively in the least. In fact, he has drawn a wealth of creative work from a well of common neuroses.

Better than anyone, Allen combines mood, conflict, and humor—the combination is memorable.

He did not have a particularly happy childhood. This did not stop him from becoming a creative success.

Allen is a lifelong learner, reportedly drawing inspiration for his work from a wide field of interests including literature, sexuality, philosophy, psychology, Jewish identity, and the hsitory of film. His films show a depth of understanding and respect for the filmmakers who came before him.

He does the 1920's time period exceptionally well (check out *Bullets Over Broadway* and *Midnight in Paris*).

Allen has always understood the idea of gigs. Some of his early gigs included writing jokes, writing comedy scripts for television, performing stand-up comedy, television acting, writing plays, writing short stories, writing cartoon captions, and collecting his written works for publication.

He considers his best films those that came closest to his original vision (*Purple Rose of Cairo, Stardust Memories*, and *Match Point*).

Over the years, Allen came to understand the importance of ownership over the production process of his films. Even though this has meant his actors earn less and the films do not gross as well, he retains complete control.

Allen's work is often better received overseas than it is in the United States. He has said that he "survives" thanks to the European market.

Allen has not let the public scrutiny of his romantic life interfere with his personal lifestyle or creative choices.

Allen has cultivated his own unique take on life and repeatedly turned it into art. About his most recent film, *Midnight in Paris*, he has said, "I just wanted it to be the way I saw Paris—Paris through my eyes."

There no longer has to be a difference between who you are and what you do.

—GARY VAYNERCHUK

What people really need is to be seen.

People want to be seen and appreciated for who they are while they are still around, not merely praised and missed once they are dead and gone.

Being seen and having people acknowledge who you are is one of the most basic human needs, though sadly, for some people, the need may go forever unfulfilled.

There are things we can do to help others in our midst see us more clearly so they can recognize us in the crowd.

We can express ourselves every day in as many clearly articulated ways as possible. If we are waiting for others to recognize us or acknowledge us but we are not expressing anything, we may end up waiting to be seen for a long time. Showing others who we are and expressing what we have to say is our job.

Another thing you can do is like and accept yourself for who you are before you start expressing yourself widely.

Neither of these things (communicating clearly and liking yourself) is the kind of thing you do once and then you are done. These are the kinds of things you do daily, steadily, regularly. And you will make mistakes along the way, probably daily, so plan on doing extra accepting and liking right after you make a mistake. As for the whopper mistakes, they will happen, too. If you've been kind to yourself regularly, you'll be able to handle them. If you haven't, you won't.

If you can't do these things—express yourself, accept yourself, and like yourself— you may as well forget about becoming visible. If you see yourself only through other people's eyes, the experience will be downright painful.

If you want to be seen, not just by one other person in the world but by many other people, practice these basics first. And when you feel like you've got them down, start putting yourself out there for more people to see.

If you do, they will recognize you. I guarantee it.

With so many new opportunities for writers to tell stories and reach and engage with (and sell to) their readers directly, why would you ever want to limit yourself to just writing and publishing a book?

—GUY LECHARLES GONZALEZ

Dabbling in self-publishing can be extremely empowering for writers. For one thing, working on your own book-length projects can be good preparation when ramping up for a traditional book deal. Self-publishing is a great way to test a market and see how contagious your ideas are. And self-publishing can be a confidence booster that helps you keep growing your body of expertise and building your platform.

Here are a few ideas (many of them drawn from *101 Niche Marketing Topics* by Gordon Burgett) of the types of things that might make a good first self-publishing effort:

- A booklet
- A comprehensive checklist
- A guidebook or minireference guide
- A list of insider secrets
- How to do something or tips for how to do something
- How to do something better
- How to be the best at what you do
- A collection of interviews with celebrities in your field
- A collection of the best case studies or examples
- How to do something difficult, complicated, and expensive yourself
- A directory of resources for your field
- An anthology of curated works
- How to develop specific expertise quickly
- How to get more of any of the big four: sex, money, time, and happiness
- How to be the most successful _____
- A way to help people improve their timing
- A calendar, almanac, or recipe book
- How to parlay something small and pleasant and make it bigger
- How to take something large and unwanted and make it smaller
- How to get more out of something you already have
- A gift book, photo book, or humor book
- The ten biggest problems related to something specific and how to solve them
- The most concise information on the topic
- The latest news about how to do something
- Predictions about the future
- A collection of ephemera and nostalgia related to something specific

307

HUG YOUR INNER RENEGADE

Successful writing is permeated with an adversarial spirit demonstrated in suspicion, opposition, confrontation, and refusal.

—SOL STEIN

What we have right now is a lot of what I would call "The Renegade Mentality." The renegades decided that people who work for publishing companies aren't really people at all, they are uncaring drones put on earth to make them feel less-than. Of course, this is not true. In my experience, people who work for publishing companies are typically passionate about books, incredibly smart, well-read, and well-meaning people who are doing the best they can.

But the renegades decided to disdain not only people in traditional publishing but also everyone and anyone involved in the process, while they headed off to the self-publishing camp to band together and talk about how awful and mean all those people were in traditional publishing who were keeping them out of the club.

The ironic part is, once the renegades got to the self-publishing camp and availed themselves of the more experienced professionals there, they discovered that the self-publishing camp people and the publishing camp people were teaching and valuing the exact same things!

And what is at the root of success in both camps? Focusing so much on hard work and perseverance that you don't have any energy left over for knocking other people down. But you feel a little foolish now for choosing a camp now, don't you? Don't feel badly. Anyone can fall for this old rabble-rouser ruse.

Today, let's do ourselves a favor and be flexible and open to both camps. There are bright, interesting, innovative folks in both camps, and neither group has cornered the market on either sainthood or evil as of yet.

If and when you have the opportunity, I hope you will publish every which way you can with every which kind of format. I have, and I will continue to do so because I learn so much from everything I try. But I've learned the most from my cumulative experience. We all will in the end because there are many paths up the self-expression mountain. I hope you will use them all.

If you can just assemble these 30,000, 50,000, 100,000 people who love literary fiction, then you've earned the right to be the ringleader, the leader of that tribe—and you'll never, ever again have trouble selling literary fiction. What's missing is you don't know who those 100,000 people are, and you don't have permission to talk to them.

—SETH GODIN

We've already discussed how to identify your best audiences for the purposes of pitching your writing. Now let's expand that concept and imagine those same audiences as tribes.

Consider the broadest possible audience. The result is our tribe. My four words were *mother, wife, writer,* and *teacher.* So my tribes would be: all the mothers in the world, all the wives in the world, all the writers in the world, and all the teachers in the world.

First, broaden your four best audiences into tribes (find your best audience in chapter twenty). Finally, you want to turn your tribe into readers. Selling your work directly to readers is an income source for your writing. Here's how to find the readers in your tribes: 1. publishers or publications 2. online content providers (websites, blogs, databases) 3. your audience or readers or fans 4. businesses or corporations (all sizes) 5. organizations and associations (all sizes) 6. anyone with something to say who needs help saying it (individuals).

Take each of your tribes and clarify where you might find its members. I'll use "mothers" as an example. Work on all four of your tribes below and see what ideas pop into your head.

MARKET	EXAMPLE	FOR	FOR	FOR	FOR:
PUBLISHERS/ PUBLICATIONS	Publishers/ publications <u>for mothers</u>				
ONLINE CONTENT PROVIDERS	Online content providers <u>for mothers</u>				
YOUR AUDIENCE/ READERS/FANS	My audience, readers, and fans <u>who are mothers</u>				
BUSINESSES/ CORPORATIONS	Businesses or corporations <u>that target mothers</u>				
ORGANIZATIONS/ ASSOCIATIONS	Organizations or associations <u>for mothers</u>				
INDIVIDUALS YOU CAN ASSIST	Any mothers <u>who need help ___ fill in what you offer</u>				

Writing is an act of faith, not a trick of grammar.

—E.B. WHITE

In 2010, Cory Doctorow launched a self-published book experiment called *With a Little Help.*

Doctorow took some of his previously published stories and self-published them together with one brand-new commissioned story, which he wrote for $10,000.

In one commission, he says he made more than he probably would have made on an advance for a short-story collection from a traditional publishing house. While Doctorow admits that wearing all the hats was a grueling and often frustrating process, he has set a great example of what an author with a following can accomplish with a little help from his friends.

I hope his example will serve as both inspirational and cautionary tale for writers who are considering playing all the parts in their careers. Here are the versions of the books he then offered and their various price points:

> Commissioned storybook
> Price: $10,000
> Copies available: 1
>
> Super-limited handbound hardcovers
> Price: $275
> Copies available: 250
>
> Paperback on-demand
> Price: $18
> Copies available: unlimited
> Bonus: Four cover choices available, updated monthly with the balance sheet from the project
>
> Audiobook as MP3 download
> Price: $10
> Copies available: unlimited
> Bonus: Celebrity readers
>
> Ogg CD
> Price: $5.50
> Copies available: unlimited
> Bonus: Celebrity readers
>
> Free electronic editions/free audio downloads
> Price: Free
> Copies available: unlimited
> Bonus: Creative Commons Share-alike license so fans can copy the material and create their own editions but not sell or profit from them.

Sit down, and put down everything that comes into your head and then you're a writer. But an author is one who can judge his own stuff's worth, without pity, and destroy most of it.

—COLETTE

Flesh out your self-produced project a bit before you run with it, and it will all go so much better.

THE BROAD STROKES

Why are you doing the project?
What's the intended outcome?
Who will be served?
How is the project a win-win-win?

THE DETAILS

Name of this project/event:
What it is:
When it is:
Where it is (with a link to location directions):
Format of the project/event (how will it work?):
What prompted this project/event was (why should anyone come/participate?):

AUDIENCE

Primary audience for this project/event (who is it for?):
Secondary audiences for the project/event (name three other audiences who also might be interested):

    1.
    2.
    3.

NEEDS

Audience needs that are addressed by this project/event:
This audience needs:
This project/event will address these needs by:

BENEFITS

By the time the project/event is over, the audience/participants will benefit because (what will they have gained from the project/event?):

If you know all of the above about your project, and you perceive all green lights, you are likely ready to move forward.

KEEP IT COOL

Just about every successful author going forward (except for the lucky exceptions like Dan Brown) will own her own media channel.

—SETH GODIN

Publishing is undergoing a massive transformation. We are in the death throes of mere brick and mortar bookstore publishing and inching ever closer to a customer-demand-driven marketplace. Print-only publishing is basically over, except in cases where it makes the most economic sense or the product is collection worthy.

And everything is changing all at once. My own reading habits are changing, too, sometimes quickly and sometimes slowly. With a spectrum of reading choices, I am developing a spectrum of habits. And I don't think I'm that unusual. Readers are not going to be any one way in the future. We are going to be every which way.

We are going to exist on that same sort of continuum that Cory Doctorow served in his *With a Little Help* project. As it turned out, at least as of the writing of this book, serving the readers who wanted the first-class service ended up being the most profitable branch of the effort. Readers want a spectrum of choices from first-class treatment all the way to quick and cheap.

Are libraries and bookstores over? I don't think so. I think instead we must embrace a multiplicity of possibilities. Consider the possibilities for customization. Focus on pleasing readers as many ways as possible. And forget about being offended by anybody as things change. Resist making innovators evil. In fact, cheer the innovators on and support them because they are providing important pioneering for us all.

In my mind, the publishing industry has a natural evolution just like everything else. Of course, it's going to be survival of the fittest. Of course, businesses that find new customers and serve those customers according to their tastes can and will take customers away from legacy businesses.

Keep in mind that the transition is going to be bumpy. Embrace a steep learning curve. If we can remember that we are all in this together, we will be able to understand when the customers follow the business that offers the best customer service and serves the widest variety of needs. You can't do this if you are ranting, righteous, angry, or pointing the finger at the publishing industry. The change will be calmer and less painful if we all keep our cool amidst a whole-system change of the publishing industry. Take a deep breath, and carry on.

312 BEWARE OF PIGGYBACKERS

Imitation is the highest form of pissing me off. Quit stealing my content and violating my copyright.

—JEN T. VERBUMESSOR

There is probably no better example of the nature of piggybacking than the story depicted in the film *Exit Through the Gift Shop*. In the film, a piggybacker decides to shadow street artists, saying that he is planning to create a documentary about the phenomenon of street art. He gains access into what is typically an elite club of street artists because his cousin is a street artist, therefore a member of the club.

A piggybacker takes from someone else what is not being offered. In the case of *Exit Through the Gift Shop*, the piggybacker took the famous artist's techniques and copied the processes he had honed from many years of effort. The famous artist might have been more protective of his process if he had realized how the relationship was going to play out.

A piggybacker does not recognize or value other people's investment in craft or hard work. A piggybacker sees the world as being full of fruit that is ripe for the taking. He doesn't care if he is taking someone else's fruit. He will tell you that there is plenty of fruit to go around, while grabbing the fruits of other people's hard work.

The essential problem with a piggybacker is that she wants the results that someone else has worked for. The piggybacker may adopt or co-opt the guise of the person he is imitating, either as a show of loyalty or perhaps because she is not ready to express her own identity. You have to embark on your own creative journey in order to be able to do this.

Piggybacking is like plagiarism because if you borrow from just one source that's stealing, but if you borrow from many sources that is research. If you are a student and you study the publicly shared documentation of artists who have gone before you, you are not a piggybacker. You are a student apprenticing yourself to those who have gone before you.

Apprenticeship is good so long as the person with less experience is committed to finding his own way and style of self-expression and not relying overly on imitation of a mentor or teacher to advance his career.

The best way to protect yourself against piggybackers is to be aware that they exist and that you will likely attract them once you become visibly successful. If you have resources you would prefer to not share with the whole world, keep them in the back of the house. If you have resources you would like to share with the world, keep them in the front of the house.

Anything you make public should be considered public property available to anyone who wants to leverage it. If you don't want piggybackers to leverage what you value, you have to protect it.

If you are concerned about being a piggybacker yourself, make sure you don't rely overly on one person or a few people while you are ramping up for creative success. Avoid stepping on other people's toes and don't closely imitate others unless it's for the benefit of an exercise—not something to sell or leverage for your own advancement. Draw research and inspiration from many sources, and credit those sources appropriately.

Just as many entrepreneurs no longer need venture capitalists to launch their companies, authors no longer need publishers to publish.

—MARK COKER

What's changed about the way I teach writing over the years is that I no longer assume that traditionally published writers won't self-publish at some point in their careers. In fact, I assume that pretty much all traditionally published writers will self-publish, sooner or later. And I think we should plan on it sooner, rather than later. Why? Here are five good reasons.

1. You can spoke off some of your best ideas that don't work in traditional publishing into self-published materials because you control the process. I did this with my e-book, *Author Mama*, which I had originally drafted as part of a blog tour to promote my first book, *Writer Mama*. I sell copies of *Author Mama* at $5.99 each to a small, appreciative market.

2. You can self-publish one idea in a myriad of ways and expand on your profits from the rest of your existing work. Not only was *Author Mama* too short for a traditional book deal, no publisher would have ever gone for a book on such a narrow topic. *Author Mama* arose from reflections on the book-writing process that I wanted to share with my students and readers.

3. The stigma on self-publishing is rapidly diminishing. Soon it will likely be considered foolish to avoid self-publishing. Personally I have been surprised how hard of a time I had getting myself to add self-publishing to my repertoire, even though I'd done it before with my students' work. Surprisingly, I found it harder to publish myself. I think a lot of writers feel this way.

4. Writers need to produce themselves, and self-publishing is good practice for learning how to administrate the creative process. Some writers will never go for this because they don't feel confident enough about their administrative abilities. But you will likely encounter many other writers with strong administrative skills who will embrace the trend and succeed.

5. The technology for publishing your own work has become more accessible and less expensive in recent years. If it's easy and cheap, why not try it? What do you have to lose?

314
MELD MULTIPLE INCOME STREAMS

The more you build your platform in your niche, the more money you will make.

—ROBERT W. BLY

Whether you write fiction, memoir, children's books, or nonfiction, it's a good idea to expect your income to come from other places besides your long-term writing projects for the first ten years of your career.

Multiple income streams are where making a living comes from for most independent writers, authors included. In case you don't believe me, check out this quote from Cory Doctorow, which appeared when he launched his column in *Publishers Weekly*:

> I've been a full-time writer since I quit my day job as European director of the Electronic Frontier Foundation (a charity that works for online civil liberties) in January 2006. Since then, I've made my living through a combination of royalties and licenses (foreign translations, film options, etc.); earnings from Boing Boing, the popular blog I co-edit and co-own; speaking fees; column writing; and the occasional grant, teaching gig, or residency. Mine is the semirandom hodgepodge of income sources that characterizes most of the freelancers I know, as skills, circumstances, and capacity dictate.

When you work for yourself and maintain your own business, you don't receive paychecks on a particular date each month. You receive checks and e-payments willy-nilly on no particular pay date. Therefore, the only way to stay in the black is to pull in enough income streams to add up to a full-time income.

Even though I'm not a novelist, I have a similar setup as Cory Doctorow to keep the money flowing in from a variety of long- and short-form writing gigs and a variety of media outlets.

I write long in the form of nonfiction books. I get published in national, regional, and online publications on topics of professional writing and parenting. I write a monthly column for the Willamette Writers newsletter. My blog earns a modest amount of referral income.

I have developed about a dozen curricula over the past ten years. I currently teach about a hundred writers a year. I train writers in monthly conference calls and offer them ongoing support for five months, twice a year.

I give talks, readings, workshops, keynotes, and appear on writing-related panels. I do a little one-on-one coaching by phone, mostly with former students. I publish e-books, which are helpful to my existing readership.

Basically, I take the skills I have and put them to work in a variety of ways to serve my best audiences. And that's what I recommend you do, as well.

I decided I had to stop wasting time and money on things that weren't working and focus on things that were. What wasn't working for me was my small publisher, which couldn't get my books into bookstores. What was working for a lot of people was the growth of e-book sales. I set aside the novel I was writing and got busy saving my career.

—L.J. SELLERS

What writers have today are more choices. We may as well flex these opportunities wisely without expecting any one choice to create an overnight sensation. I encourage you to have reasonable expectations with your self-published book projects as well as your traditionally published book projects. Here are five more.

1. Self-publishing is a lot faster than traditional publishing. This is likely to become a handicap for the publishing industry. The fleetest executors of popular ideas will likely win. But I believe that there is still a place for traditional publishing, and this will be the case for many years to come.

2. Distribution becomes less and less of an issue with the shift toward digital reading via e-readers and personal computers. Of course, not everyone has a computer or an e-reader, so we need to keep this in perspective over the next couple of decades as e-reading evolves and becomes more status quo.

3. Reaching new readers with a broader variety of published materials can expand your readership by attracting new readers to your already published books, whether self-published or traditionally published.

4. A midlist author can use self-publishing to expand the size of her platform and gain credibility that can be leveraged into more traditional book deals. With self-publishing, you can create a decent income stream from a committed group of readers, whereas you can't create much of an income stream with traditional publishing anymore unless you have readers in the high thousands.

5. Fans like materials that are expressly for them, and self-publishing offers easy-to-use tools to accomplish this. What writer doesn't want to please his fans? The Internet helps with easy crowdsourcing (outsourcing tasks to the community at large) opportunities, for example using existing social media outlets, while the sheer variety of self-publishing possibilities (PDF, e-reader, podcasting, apps) offers many possible ways to please fans.

A mental fitness boom is brewing.

—FAITH POPCORN

At the beginning of 2010, there was a lot of panic about whether writers would be able to continue to make a decent living writing. But most of the professional writers I know are still earning, even if they had to dig deeper into a niche or diversify their services to keep doing so.

Freelancers are always challenged to adapt their strategies to the changing marketplace. But new marketplaces seem to be opening up even as old writing opportunities become scarce. There does not seem to be any shortage in business writing, for example. In fact, companies are communicating more than ever.

E-books create a new revenue opportunity for writers without diminishing the value of that writer's other products. In fact, it may soon become a known fact that the more you have in print, the more you sell overall, especially if everything you offer exists simultaneously in multiple formats.

Writers are also adding on new services like teaching, coaching, and training. Combining the old ways of earning a living as a writer with the newer ways of earning a living like e-books, apps, podcasting, and selling special editions as a writer is the most prosperous way to run a writing business.

Many people in this country (and around the world, no doubt) are eager to express themselves in written form, and this also presents opportunities for writers. The need for ghostwriters, personal biographers, teachers, and all kinds of people who facilitate and midwife the process of self-expression has escalated with the explosion of available self-publishing tools and a large number of people who need assistance in order to express themselves at a professional level.

The full-suite-of-services approach means that you, as a writer, have identified a niche market and are committed to serving all of their needs in the long haul. For example, my publisher does this for me, offering writers publishing advice, craft advice, creativity advice, tips, prompts, conferences, classes, webinars, books, digital downloads, e-books, online communities, blogs, magazines, competitions, annuals—you name it, they've got it.

Similarly, I think it's helpful for writers to think of the products and services we provide in terms of a whole range of offerings that meet as many of the needs of the people we serve as possible.

So whether the people you serve are editors, businesses, event planners, or someone else, think about how you can provide a full range of offerings that will meet the needs of your audience as completely as possible.

We live on the leash of our senses.

—DIANE ACKERMAN

The packaging process for your offering is extremely important and should not be rushed. The way you pull together your offering and expertise will determine whether you succeed or not. To manufacturers, *packaging* often refers to plastic, cardboard, and sticky or twisty things to hold the offering together. But for writers, *packaging* refers to presenting what you offer in words and images so others can partake of your class, e-book, audio download, or whatever it is you have to sell.

Here's how to package your offering so you can take it to the marketplace:

ASK KEY QUESTIONS AND THEN ANSWER THEM

Your offering has arisen to address specific needs, and now it's your job to let the audience know what kind of thinking went into creating your offering. Think of an advertisement that uses this kind of teaser method like the "Got Milk?" campaign. It's a simple question and yet it begs to be answered. You should kick off your offering with either one or several questions and answer them in the description of your offering.

OFFER SOLUTIONS TO CHALLENGES

You took the time to make sure your offering was needed and wanted, so this is no time to forget to mention how solution-oriented your offering was designed. List all the problems presented before your offering came along, then list all the solutions your offering provides. Incorporate some of these ideas into the marketing copy for your offering.

DESCRIBE THE KEY BENEFITS

You also took the time to make sure that your offering would supply some kind of transformation for your audience. By describing the benefits of your offering, you are providing your audience with a glimpse of how they can expect to become changed by it.

PRICE AND TIME ACCORDINGLY

Your offering is competitively priced and matched to the affordability of your audience, so be sure to highlight this aspect. You also have gone out of your way to time your offering appropriately for your audience. Mention these points in your marketing copy.

Appealing workplaces are to be avoided. One wants a room with no view, so imagination can meet memory in the dark.

—ANNIE DILLARD

Your productivity in your first year writing and your productivity in your tenth year writing may not end up looking anything alike because your habits will evolve the more time you spend cultivating your career.

So when my beginning students ask me for systems to help them become more productive, I am hesitant to make sweeping suggestions. In over twelve years of professional writing, I've never found one system that works for me. I will use whatever system or nonsystem gets the job done.

Your organizational thinking should serve your daily goals. A key to productivity might be keeping your eye on exactly what you hope to accomplish this year, one day at a time.

What are you planning to accomplish? Is it writing and placing ten articles? Is it drafting a novel? Is it crafting six personal essays and submitting them to magazines? What are you going to do with your writing skills? How are you going to turn them into action?

Once you determine your goals, you are halfway through planning. Now all you have to do is pace out each goal as realistically as possible. Can you write one article a week, or is one article a month more realistic? It may turn out to be one every two and a half months, but you'll figure that out later. In the meantime, strive for your best guess of what you can accomplish.

Once you've set the pace, it's time to get to work. In order to meet one of your goals, what steps will you need to take? Can you turn those steps into a checklist for yourself? Go ahead and draft your best effort in a detailed checklist. Then use it, and as you use it, revise it to make that list better and better at serving your specific purposes.

Guess what's going to happen if you envision these goals in advance and then turn them into simple action steps? You are going to start meeting your goals.

Be sure to modify this concept to suit your needs. Creative minds often resist straightforward approaches. In my experience, the straightforward approach not only works, the structure provides a helpful pressure to reel in a freewheeling mind that, left to its own devices, might not otherwise reach any goals.

PACKAGE YOUR OFFERINGS: PART TWO

People are always looking for the single magic bullet that will totally change everything. There is no single magic bullet.

—TEMPLE GRANDIN

A lot of forethought goes into creating an offering for your audience. You don't typically wake up one day and decide to offer something out of the blue, launch it that day, and succeed. Although today might be the first time you conceive of an offering that will take you far in your career. Often a successful offering emerges out of momentum you already have. Here are more ways to package your offerings for the marketplace:

TIE YOUR EXPERTISE TO THE SOLUTIONS

Your short bio plays a critical role in illustrating how you are the very best person to present an offering. In fact, the more your name is tied to the kind of expertise behind your offering, the better. Keep your bio short and to the point of the offering, rather than long and rambling and trying to include your entire CV.

CREATE WAYS TO ACCEPT PAYMENTS

By far the easiest way anyone can accept payments for offerings today is via Paypal. In exchange for accepting payments and transferring them to you, Paypal takes a small cut of your fees. Try to serve the widest possible audience by combining payment methods. Set up a post office box to accept payments by check, if you like. Be sure to comprehensively explain how you accept payments.

BE AVAILABLE TO ANSWER QUESTIONS

Undoubtedly folks will have questions about your offerings. They will want a clear and easy way to contact you to discuss their questions in a timely manner. E-mail provides the perfect communication tool for this kind of exchange. For the sake of your privacy, I suggest that you don't publicize your home address and phone number. If you check your e-mail regularly, you should be able to keep up with the needs of your audience just fine. You do not have to be available 24/7 simply because you are offering something, but you do want to be consistently responsive in a reasonable amount of time.

SHARE PAST SUCCESS STORIES

Once you have provided your offering consistently over time, start to solicit and accrue feedback from your audience. The most important use of this information is to constantly strive to improve your offering based on what you learn from clients and customers. A secondary benefit is that you can gather and share their testimonials, which provide proof of the appropriateness and helpfulness of your offering.

Just because it's not in a crafts fair doesn't mean it didn't demand craft.

—SETH GODIN

Fiction writers are like snowballs: They get bigger as they roll down the fiction-writing hill. As they create stories, fiction writers accumulate worlds of knowledge, inspiration, stories, research, writing tips, and more.

If you are a fiction writer, here's a taste of what else you might have to offer. You might, in fact, be an expert on:

- Fiction writing
- The location or place of your story
- A topic you had to penetrate to write the story
- A particular time period
- A truth or phenomenon
- A universal human theme such as redemption or compassion
- A particular age or phase in people's lives
- The creative process or an aspect of the creative process

321

UPDATE YOUR PLATFORM: PART ONE

Most important, try to view every opportunity you pursue as part of a long-term, big-picture endeavor. Build relationships. Be willing to market yourself. Stay open to possibilities you may not have thought of before. Act professionally at all times.

—I.J. SCHECTER

Every three months or so, my blog is badly in need of an update. If it's been six months since the last update, so much has happened that much of what is posted becomes embarrassing.

This happens to everyone, so don't let it throw you. Instead regard outdated info as a signal that it's time to comb through your old site and get all your info current again. Here's a list of the kinds of things you may need to update at your home base:

NAME IT AND RECLAIM IT. What do you do? Who do you serve? Has any of this changed? Is all of this reflected in your blog/website title? Judy M. Miller's blog says, "Parenting Your Adopted Child: Tweens, Teens & Beyond." Jenny Kales's blog says, "The Nut-Free Mom: Raising a Nut-Free Kid in a Nutty World." Malia Jacobson's website says, "Writer, Editor & Sleep Journalist: Better Information. Better Living." Now, your turn.

DELETE OUT-OF-DATE INFO. Approach your blog/website as a visitor and see what you find. Last time I updated, some of the information on my classes page was no longer relevant since I am not offering those classes at this time. Down that copy came. You can always save anything you think you might use in the future in an archive document on your computer.

CONSOLIDATE INFO AS NEEDED. You need to consolidate the information you already have to make room for what's current and coming next. Just as your house would become hopelessly cluttered if you never decluttered it, your blog/website info will often need to be trimmed, rewritten, and rearranged. For example, the old information about my books was on two separate pages, so I consolidated all the relevant info onto one page when my e-book was about to come out.

CLARIFY ANY FUZZY IDEAS. When I approached my page as a visitor, I noticed that my page headers were too esoteric. I had gone with an idea that seemed clever to me at the time—so clever that they were likely impeding navigation of the site. Now my page headers just say what they are. Take a look at yours. Is your cleverness impeding clickability?

REPROOF ALL COPY. As time had marched on, I had partially updated some pages, which led to typos, of course. And some info, like expired contact info, was just outdated. Always check your fine print!

Rather than trying to cover a wide variety of subjects, I started to concentrate on a handful of topics that interested me and were a part of my life—health, fitness, nutrition, and relationships—and began developing a specialty in those areas.

—KELLY JAMES-ENGER

Chances are very good that you are going to invest your creative energy in things other than just books throughout the course of your career. Keep tabs on this content because it's likely to come in handy the next time you write a book or an e-book. Let's count seventeen ways to capture and share your content:

1. Video
2. Video scripts
3. Audio
4. Audio transcripts
5. Courses
6. Teleseminars
7. Card packs
8. Gifts
9. Speeches
10. Presentations
11. Webinars
12. Newsletters
13. Proposals
14. Blog posts
15. Grant-writing proposals
16. Kits
17. Panels

The trust you learn in your own voice can be directed then into a business letter, a novel, a Ph.D. dissertation, a play, a memoir. But it is something you must come back to again and again.

—NATALIE GOLDBERG

Most platforms have a home base—a blog or website or combo blog/website that needs a certain amount of updating in order to stay current. Schedule a half day or two every three months and you will maintain a better online presence. Here are more ways to update your home base:

SAY WHAT YOU ARE GOING TO DO. Nothing makes a blog/website look neglected like really old appearance announcements. Now I have one place for upcoming appearances and another place where I thank the organizations that have hosted me.

AMPLIFY YOUR CREDIBILITY. If you have a variety of credits, cast a wide net when listing them. It took a bit of time to gather all of my credits together, but I feel better now knowing that they are all there, updated, at least until next time.

HIT THE HIGHLIGHTS. On my credits page, I made an effort to compile works that search engines would not necessarily list in the order I think makes sense. In the past, I had linked to a lot more online sources, but links require constant updating so I decided to let search engines take care of that.

SHARE WHAT OTHERS SAY ABOUT YOU. Remember to request testimonials from folks as a regular part of what you do. I realized that I had been collecting feedback from students but not audience members or coaching clients. So I've started to make these requests part of my routine.

DON'T FORGET YOUR MISSION. I have a page called "Trust," which is the way to let folks know what I'm all about. I want them to see both that I have a mission and that I'm a real person. I'm a real person who works with real people, not a faceless brand. I want my blog to reflect this.

COMPLY WITH FEDERAL RULES. I also state in my "Trust" page that I run a blog as part of my business and list my affiliations to comply with the Federal Trade Commission's guidance that calls for full disclosure of business relationships between bloggers and advertisers or sponsors.

TWEAK YOUR BIO. My bio evolves as my writing career evolves. If I kept it the same year after year, it would get pretty stale. Therefore, I come up with something fresh and new to say about what I do every year.

Every author does not write for every reader.

—SAMUEL JOHNSON

When you reach out to the world with your words, you will want to do so in both print and digital forms. Think of digital and print as the yin and yang of publishing. If you can keep them in balance, you will likely fare better than if you go just one way or the other.

I think the best way to consider how to create, share, and market content forms in the future is to keep these three E's in mind and then combine them with balance between print and digital formats.

- Extend your reach.
- Enable your audience.
- Empower yourself by empowering others.

You may decide to use other media as well (audio, video, multimedia), and this is not a bad idea, but since this is a writing book, I'll keep the focus on writing.

Should you go with digital first or print first, or do them simultaneously? I think you will fare best if you consider your audience and what it needs. Go with the combination and timing that works best for them.

Writing is hard work and bad for the health.

—E.B. WHITE

Here are the typical health pitfalls for writers, or heck, for anybody, but especially creative types who have some not-so-healthy lifestyle habits.

NOT ENOUGH HYDRATION: A lot of writers drink caffeinated and alcoholic beverages. If you are among the ranks who overdo both or either, you may need to drink more water.

NOT ENOUGH FRESH AIR AND SUNSHINE: Get outside every day. Walk briskly even if only for a short time. Consider a pet, such as a dog, that will require a daily walk. Find a walking buddy in your neighborhood. Take up a hobby like gardening.

NOT ENOUGH HEALTHY FOOD: If you are not eating plenty of fruits and vegetables on a daily basis, you probably should take a daily multivitamin.

NOT ENOUGH EXERCISE: Raise your hand if you have exercised at least three times in the past week. Due to the necessary amount of sitting we do, writers have got to move it or face steady weight gain.

NOT ENOUGH FUN: Answer quickly: When is the last time you laughed your head off? You don't know? You can't remember? Watch funny movies, read humorous books, call your silliest friend.

NOT ENOUGH EXPOSURE TO OTHERS: Studies have shown that people who have the most meaningful relationships live longest. So why not spend the time you have on the planet with people whose company you really enjoy?

NOT ENOUGH INTIMACY: Who loves you, writer? You need to know. And you need to love and appreciate them back. Giving and receiving love is just as important as loving your work.

NOT ENOUGH DOWN TIME: Sleep much? How about enough? Are you allowed to do nothing, or are you constantly on the go, go, go? Don't forget to catch some Z's.

INADEQUATE HEALTH MAINTENANCE. Certain health appointments must be maintained for optimal health: physical checkups, teeth cleanings, eye screenings, blood and sugar analysis, and any annual screenings your age makes pertinent.

CONCERN ABOUT MENTAL HEALTH. Be a good friend to yourself first, and make a life-long commitment to peace of mind. Seek professional support or assistance if you can't find it on your own.

By three methods we may learn wisdom: first, by reflection, which is noblest; second, by imitation, which is easiest; and third by experience, which is the most bitter.

—CONFUCIUS

There is one thing I have consistently noticed about successful writers. They put the lion's share of their energy into their own efforts and don't get hung up on the efforts of others.

This may sound counterintuitive when there is so much propaganda out there about championing the efforts of others, but I've already written frankly about having standards and choosing partners wisely.

Another aspect of influence is knowing when to use it and when to keep your mouth shut. I give a lot of advice because students and readers constantly come to me for my opinions. However, one thing that I have had to learn the hard way is when to offer input and when to keep it to myself.

I don't want to participate in every conversation nor can I work with every person. I know which conversations make sense for me to join and which people I want to work with intuitively. I don't have a particular profile I'm looking for. I am open to working with anyone, so long as the person clicks as a good person for me to work with.

This may seem needlessly discriminatory. Why can't I just work harder to be everything to everyone?

Over the years, I've learned that it's better to offer my opinion less frequently, to very specific people, and to make sure that my input is of the highest qualtiy when I do offer it. The rest of the time, I mind my own business.

I trust that if someone really wants to work with me, she will seek me out and find me. And after I have worked with someone once, she decides whether she wants to work with me again, and I decide if I want to continue working with her.

This advice goes decidedly against the most common views today, which say that it's best to work with and for everyone. I think that advice is fine for some people who are comfortable with it. But I'm going to stick with what works best and feels best to me, and that's working with people I want to work with and working on projects I want to work on. In the process of focusing specifically, I learn lessons that I can share more widely.

Feeling gratitude and not expressing it is like wrapping a present and not giving it.

—WILLIAM A. WARD

I'm not much of a thank you-note writer, mainly because I have bad handwriting. But one thing I really enjoy is giving professional gifts. I think the people on the receiving end enjoy receiving them as much as I enjoy gathering, preparing, and sending them.

Over the years, I have given gifts to my favorite editors, my students, my teachers, my contributors, and my co-workers. The gifts are typically modest: books, candy, gift cards, and fun, colorful items.

For me, the process of gift giving is pure pleasure. I would like to start a professional gift-exchange movement because I've noticed that a lot of folks don't give professional gifts, especially since the recession.

I pride myself on being prosperous enough to give gifts. And it's a virtuous cycle because giving modest gifts makes me feel more prosperous.

I would like to see a comeback in gift giving among publishing professionals. Nobody says the gifts have to be expensive—we can support our own industry by giving books and book-related items.

Give professional gifts if for no other reason than the opportunity to thank those who have helped and supported you. And never forget that books make great gifts!

Here are a few more ideas:

- Blank notebooks with colorful markers
- Gift cards tucked into a to-go cup or mug
- Colorful or classy business card holders
- Thoughtful magazine subscriptions
- Magazine holders: canvas, cardboard, metal, or plastic
- Marginalia kit: bookmarks, highlighters with sticky notes, and book plates
- Bookstore gift cards: online, indie, or a cash card to use anywhere

The skill of writing is to create a context in which other people can think.

—EDWIN SCHLOSSBERG

I have been hosting the Northwest Author Series for going on five years now, and I've learned a thing or two along the way. Here's how to have a win-win-win event or series:

1. Name your program, claim the purpose, have a mission, create a tagline—have fun with it.
2. Choose a magnetic event coordinator with an extended network who can synergize your events.
3. Give your event a year to find its legs in a trial run, and let it evolve into what it wants to be.
4. Consider spoking out sponsorship so you can include as many pertinent sponsors as possible while creating continuous excitement and synergy.
5. Photos forward, give your event a face or design identity and add visual elements to communications when possible.
6. Get ongoing feedback, collect testimonials, publicize them, and blow your own horn.
7. Develop a publicity practice of approaching traditional and new media, and keep expanding.
8. Make your event multisensory—add food, exercises, discussion, anything to engage audiences.
9. Host giveaways, drawings, raffles, anything that adds interest without cost
10. Be ready for the spotlight, have a short and long media blurb, and prepare an online media kit with photographs that provides all the info journalists might need.
11. Spread the word exponentially by using an e-mail newsletter program, multiply your impact by asking cosponsors to publicize, too.
12. Balance digital materials with "real" promo pieces like posters, postcards, and bookmarks.
13. Don't skimp on quality; invite "the best" or "the best known" folks available like award winners, up-and-comers, and famous out-of-towners.

HONOR WHAT SERVES ALL

You can't sue your way to attention, and we shouldn't legislate writing back to a world of scarcity.

—SETH GODIN

With so many opinions coming at us all the time, it's easy to forget what we think and absorb the mind of the status quo. This has happened to me in the past, but thinking other people's thoughts always proves unhelpful in the long run. I want to think my own thoughts. I want you to think your own thoughts.

If you think you might be absorbing the group mind like an over-saturated sponge, try to wring what you think from what you have accidentally absorbed. Here are a few examples of how to transform beliefs that won't serve you in the long run into those that will:

- I will become friends with everyone. (Change to: I will be as friendly as possible.)
- I will help everyone. (Change to: I will be as accessible as is practical.)
- I will give all the time. (Change to: I will offer assistance when asked and ask for help myself in return.)
- I will say yes to everything. (Change to: I will create personal policies that help me gauge when I need to say no.)
- I will always have fun. (Change to: I will have ups and downs in my career but I will always strive to align and realign with my passion.)
- I will be organized and on top of everything all the time. (Change to: I will regularly make time to get on top of my affairs and manage my time and schedule.)
- I will never get ahead of myself. (Change to: I will try to get ahead of myself so I can hurry to catch up and therefore grow.)
- I will always be in control. (Change to: I may not be in control but I will simply show up and do my best.)
- I will never complain or need to complain. (Change to: I will ask for permission to grouse before launching into it. I will limit the time I spend grousing and then move on.)
- Once people learn how great I am, all will go well. (Change to: I will cultivate personal power on easy days and bumpy days.)

BE ACCOUNTABLE TO QUOTAS

Sleep on your writing; take a walk over it; scrutinize it of a morning; review it of an afternoon; digest it after a meal; let it sleep in your drawer a twelvemonth; never venture a whisper about it to your friend, if he be an author especially.

—A. BRONSON ALCOTT

One way or another, writers constantly churn out a steady stream of content. I am constantly updating the best of my content. And I am constantly inspired to write more because my deadlines keep the writing pistons pumping.

If you have daily, weekly, and monthly accountability in your writing career, you will end up accumulating more completed projects than if you don't have accountability.

All of these productive habits add up to an accumulation of content. When you write salable content steadily from within your area of expertise, your career is going to grow steadily.

I meet certain annual goals, monthly goals, and weekly goals without being a perfectionist about any of them.

I know in a general sense what I need to get done this year. I also know what I want to accomplish this week and this month.

Ask yourself what you hope to accomplish within the next year. How many of each of these can you reasonably write?

Books _____

E-books _____

Articles _____

Columns _____

Blog posts _____

Newsletters _____

Guest blogs _____

Freebies _____

New projects _____

Collections of old projects _____

SYNERGIZE SUCCESSES

I don't want to get to the end of my life and find that I lived just the length of it. I want to have lived the width of it as well.

—DIANE ACKERMAN

Synergy happens when writers connect with readers. A lot of writers think that synergy is happening between themselves and their writing. But that's not what I mean by the word.

When I'm talking about synergy, I mean that which occurs when writer reaches out to readers and interact with them. This may happen before readers have even looked at their writing, while they are reading their writing, or after they are done reading their writing.

Whenever the opportunity to connect with readers arises, synergy between authors and readers becomes possible. And it's almost always this interaction where lasting good impressions (or the opposite) are made.

So go ahead and have a powerful experience with your work when you write. But don't forget that equally important synergy is going to happen between you and your readers before, during, and after the writing process.

Synergy comes from the interplay between writers and readers, when the writer has the opportunity to receive input and sense how to better serve readers. Here are a few ways to actively create synergy:

- Conduct research on the people you serve.
- Poll your audience.
- Ask for feedback and testimonials.
- Improve what you do as you go along.
- See what you do as a process not a product.
- Partner with credible others.
- Create/join teams of professionals assisting each other.

The polls you take and the opinions you solicit may not always be constructive. You may need time to perceive the value in some feedback and integrate changes into your work habits. Improving your craft, sales skills, focus, and promotional skills will likely all be impacted by feedback you receive as you grow your writing career. A certain amount of your success will be determined by how well you can roll with and grow from the synergy between yourself and those you serve.

The Beatles did not invent teenagers. They merely decided to lead them.

—SETH GODIN

Devices are not the only game changers, you know. People are the ultimate game changers. The most worthwhile forms of social artistry are those that change everything: the game changers.

Seth Godin says that the only way to change the world is to be a heretic, and by being ready to stand up and be counted instead of following the rules. He says if you are not upsetting anyone, you are not changing the status quo.

Right now, if you are reading this book, you are already a leader. Because you would not have read this far if you weren't. Perhaps you are a latent leader: a leader who has yet to actualize your leadership skills.

Godin also says, if you tell a story, connect a tribe that already wants to be connected, and lead a movement, you can create change. He says that you don't need charisma to be a leader; you develop charisma by leading.

But leadership skills are not learned; they are cultivated by leading, just as writing is not learned through merely reading about writing or talking about writing.

You can't buy leadership. It can't be downloaded into your brain. You can only learn leadership through leading.

If you've been following along in this book, you have identified your best audiences and you have served them through your writing and other platform-building strategies. Your tribe is out there, and you are getting to know them intimately.

When will you be ready to lead?

If you don't want to lead, maybe you should consider selecting a different topic or audience and see if that feeling changes.

If you are reluctant to lead, baby steps apply here just as they do with writing momentum. Maybe you are not ready to lead today, but you will be ready tomorrow. Don't be too hasty with this leadership stuff. If writing takes chutzpah, leading takes more than just chops, it takes confidence. When you have your confidence up, and you are used to drawing strength from it on a regular basis, you'll feel ready to step up.

Lead a little or co-lead and see how it goes. See if there is a subgroup in your audience or a combination of groups who are just waiting for you to take the reins. Meet them where you both and are lead them your way. Then see what happens.

Experience is the best teacher of all. And for that, there are no guarantees that one will become an artist. Only the journey matters.

—HARRY CALLAHAN

Once upon a time, when I was in graduate school, I had the opportunity to interview several prominent Chicago architects. I loved the feeling of being an interviewer. Once I became aware of this fact, it became an important nugget of personal information that was very valuable to my writing career at the time.

As writers, we're always collecting an inventory of satisfying moments to bring to bear on our career in the future.

At the end of the day, the most successful people are those who are most satisfied with what they do every day. When we embrace the idea that we are the creators of our own destinies, we embody this idea.

You can never please others enough to "make it." You can, however, please yourself enough to experience joy.

Joy comes from breaking out of the prisons we have chosen to live inside in the past and striding forward to embrace the writing career we were born to have. You can cultivate a career based on satisfaction by making more time to be grateful for what you have already done. Start by blessing today and then bless your journey so far. And then watch: Tomorrow will be a little easier.

I consider myself very fortunate not because I am rich or famous, but because I love what I do. I take pride in my work. I see the positive results of the past years of my efforts working with others. I feel like all my efforts have been worthwhile and satisfying.

The funny thing about satisfaction is you usually can't plan it in advance or force it to happen. It almost always comes from the process of looking back or reflecting, and when you look back, you recall what you experienced as satisfying. Embrace it all. Let it be enough.

If I have lost confidence in myself, I have the universe against me.

—RALPH WALDO EMERSON

Evil is as evil does. Do good, not evil.

- Focus on cultivating your own skills and body of work. Don't focus on what others are doing.
- Don't be codependent. Don't make self-destructive deals with other codependents. Have boundaries and use them.
- Give credit where credit is due. Don't borrow from others without giving them a nod.
- Don't become addicted to anything, not even the creative process. Love what you do, but don't forget about life.
- Grow your confidence by doing, not watching. If you are scared to act, get yourself around encouraging, expressive people. They will encourage you to express yourself, too.
- Don't try to take or gain from what rightfully belongs to others. If it's not being offered to you, don't take it.
- Recognize your biases and turn them into strengths.
- Don't make choices that effect others based on anger or frustration. Cool off and redirect your energy. Let time pass if it helps.

Create your own definition of success. Then live it.

No author: no book. Think about it.

—MARGARET ATWOOD

In the course of the past year and a half in which I have spent developing and writing this book, I have accomplished a lot of messy yet satisfying good.

I have spent more time greasy, unshowered, and in a variety of sweat clothes than I care to admit. At one point my *Writer Mama* baseball cap had to be replaced because it was so discolored and disgusting I was too embarrassed to wear it in public.

Okay, truth. My husband was too embarrassed for me to continue wearing it in public. Either way, I got a bright, white new hat to cover up my greasy, unwashed hair.

So here's the part you probably don't expect me to say: I would do it all over again in a heartbeat.

Maybe I would not do it all over again tomorrow. But check back in a year or two and I bet you I will have undertaken another impossibly large deadline. There is no easy, perfect, film-friendly way to write a book.

The truth about writing long works is that they require immersion and personal sacrifice. As long as we look at this state as temporary—something to get through until we get to the other side—we writers will be fine. At the point at which we become comfortable fat, broke, and suffering, we have flipped into subservient victim mode. And we'd better get out of it, quick.

Subservient victim mode can be addictive if you are not careful—even if you are mostly serving deadlines that you agreed to. Perhaps it's not a good idea to work on long project after long project after long project. Perhaps a better idea is to jump from project to project of varying lengths or to switch things up in the course of a day so you are not merely working on one giant project all day long.

There is something to said, however, for the long, immersive process of writing a book. And there is something to be said for the glorious moment at the end of an extended writing paddle when you reach the shore of your deadline and throw yourself upon it for a long and much-deserved rest.

Take a step back, look at the bigger picture, and ask yourself: What have I done to bring potential book buyers to the table?

—RACHELLE GARDNER

The reason to balance your marketing efforts is because you will want to call on all of your resources when you have major news. When you announce a book, for example, you will want to share the news locally, regionally, nationally, and internationally. You will want to share the news with everyone you know online.

In the meantime, continue to build up those contacts.

Remember when I said you are not a brand (chapter 171)? Well, what I meant by that is someday you are going to want to make changes to or expand your creative trajectory. And before you make those changes, you are going to want to consolidate your resources in preparation to expand in new directions.

Here are several steps I suggest you take in preparation for a new direction:

- Read all the latest info about your specialty or niche.
- Update yourself on all of the latest technological tools.
- Listen to what your established audience says they want and need from you.
- Watch what thought leaders in your niche are doing.
- Check out what thought leaders outside your niche are doing.
- Try out any tools you need to be familiar with before you relaunch
- Take a break if you are about to embark on a period of heavy effort, you probably deserve it!

Customers don't want to constrict themselves into a predetermined mold; they want to create their own personal media landscape. Let them. Turn down your control freak knob and leave it up to them to close the loop. After all, people buy what they have a role in creating.

—SCOTT GINSBERG

When books are written with the intention to create a win-win-win effect on the reader, that's what happens.

Multi-published nonfiction author Kathy Sierra lectures on the topic of creating passionate users at writing and publishing conferences. Sierra says passion has to be "baked into a book"—the information in the book has to be useful, useable, and user-friendly. The author has to turn a book into an experience, or a series of experiences.

If the reader feels like an author is focused on helping her, according to Sierra, the reader will gladly become a fan, tell friends, share what she's learned, and engage others in sharing the experience of the book.

Sierra says that authors with passion are not afraid to show off, continuously improve, spend time, spend money, evangelize, elevate the meaning of their work, and connect with readers.

The key to writing a really great book, says Sierra, is to take out all the stuff that makes the author look good and jam-pack the book with all the stuff that helps the reader look good.

She explains that readers pick up a book to feel better. So if an author writes a book about how great he is, this makes the reader feel bad, and the reader won't like the book. Then the reader won't like the author.

When it comes to writing books, Sierra is absolutely right. If your book doesn't rock your anticipated readers' world, readers probably won't want your book.

Sierra says, "Reader awesomeness produces a change in the reader." Notice she said reader awesomeness not author awesomeness.

So, rock the reader's world with your passion or weep, folks. Nothing less will do.

338

TAKE IN CRITICISM

I read those fifty to one hundred negative reviews on Amazon on Crush It! I took them in the chest and I was like, Ugh, what can I do better? I didn't get mad. I respect the negative reviews. I said next time I come out, I'm going to come out stronger.

—GARY VAYNERCHUK

A lot of writers want to make it seem like only special people can become writers. But that's a lot of bunk. Anyone who works steadily and consistently can become a successful writer.

The thing is, you have to have a zeal for communicating. You have to relish getting through to people better than you did yesterday. If this describes you, you can be a very happy, healthy writer. You can create writing-career success.

So I have an idea. How about you go ahead and put yourself out there, and you invite input on your work.

Now here's the trick about being able to receive, digest, and process criticism. It's all in the timing and how well you know yourself.

If you know that you will take negative criticism personally for a period of time after you put some of your best efforts out there, here's what you should do: Receive the criticism, gather it up, but don't try to take it all in immediately.

Put it in a folder, and face it when you are ready to face it. This will be, preferably, when you feel prepared to digest and respond to the criticism with a certain amount of detachment and objectivity that you won't have when you are still raw from just putting yourself out there.

Once you have taken in and absorbed what's helpful, see if you can turn the feedback into tips or suggestions for yourself to draw on next time.

Create a list using two columns. In the first column, write the gist of the criticism, and in the second column, give yourself some advice based on what feels right in your gut.

How can you improve? How can you better serve? How can you take in other people's opinions of your work and help them help you?

PLAN ON FUTURE SUCCESS

I would feel more optimistic about a bright future for man if he spent less time proving that he can outwit Nature and more time tasting her sweetness and respecting her seniority.

—E.B. WHITE

The publishing industry is struggling to reinvent itself and is redefining the way writers will fit in with their economic wants and needs.

In the meantime, you are likely creating your own definitions of success based on what feeds and satisfies you and what you need and want as you go from gig to gig, trying to juggle all your responsibilities and make it all work.

I have a prediction: Everyone involved in publishing, meaning writers, agents, production people, and publishing companies, will succeed or not succeed based on how well they can create mutually beneficial partnerships. If we can muddle through all of the change and get to a place where all partners benefit, publishing will experience a new renaissance, a bright, prosperous period, where reader needs are met and writer needs are met and publisher needs are met.

I suspect during these lean economic times that all of the roles in the process that are not absolutely necessary will disappear. This isn't and won't be personal, but some people may need to find a new line of work. I am probably not sophisticated enough to know which of the publishing roles are needed and which are not, and likely there will be some trial and error in the process.

Once we see what is workable in the new economy and what isn't workable in the new economy, we will learn how we can best partner with each other in ways that are win-win-win. Until then, we'll have to keep muddling our way through, doing the best we can. And just accept that we have an increasing number of free agents out there who know an awful lot about the legacy system of traditional publishing.

The folks who will still be standing will be those who are willing to evolve, cooperate, and share the wealth.

I want your map of superpowers.

—KATHY SIERRA

In *Get Known Before the Book Deal*, I came up with an exercise in which writers imagined their own action figure doll, and it turned out to be a popular part of the book.

The idea was to imagine that you became so successful that Accoutrements, the company that makes the action figure dolls of people like Shakespeare, Seth Godin, and Librarian Nancy Pearl, would create an action figure in your likeness.

- What would your doll look like?
- What kind of accessories would it have?
- Would it have any specific kind of action? (Nancy Pearl's doll has a shushing action.)

These were the kinds of questions I asked. Now let's take that idea a bit further.

Let's come up with a transformer doll that is not in our likeness but in the likeness of our reader. Since we are hoping to create a transformation in the reader, this doll will have two appearances: before she reads our book and after she read our book.

- Describe your target reader.
- Describe some of the accessories that characterize her life.
- Describe the frustration your reader has that your book will change.

Your reader doll will go from mere mortal to empowered superhero thanks to reading your book. Next describe your target reader after she reads your book.

- How does the doll look different?
- Does the doll need or want new accessories now?
- Describe the super powers that have been activated in the reader as a result of reading your book.

Once you have fully described your empowered reader, tell us what was in the book that enabled the reader to become superpowered.

Now write the book. Include all the secrets. Don't leave out any important ingredients. Help your reader become the fully actualized person she was meant to be.

341

EXECUTE UNIQUELY

Your challenge is to figure out which unique attribute of your personality, life experience, and expertise you can leverage in a remarkable way. That means: Values before vocation, individuality before industry, and personality before profession.

—SCOTT GINSBERG

Lately I have been thinking about the timing of creative projects. It used to be that it was always better to be early, even better if you could be first. But a whole new competitor culture has sprung up online around "anything you can write, I can write better."

It's impossible to stop this phenomenon to a certain extent because once you write something, anyone who can benefit from what you have shared can write something bigger and better on the topic because they have the benefit of what you already wrote.

This person can also expand the context of what you wrote, swallow up what you covered, and then widen, broaden, and deepen the topic to ultimately cover more ground.

What I'm trying to say is, don't worry if you are not the first person to think of an idea. Just execute the idea in a way that is uniquely yours. You can include your competition in your research, if you like. Just be sure to cite his words and ideas properly and secure permission as needed.

Your focus should be squarely on one objective and one objective alone: serving the reader and writing the best book on the topic for the times. But be careful that you proceed respectfully. Just because you can take another person's ideas and make them generic without attribution (because you are a skillful enough writer to pull it off) doesn't mean you should.

Having appropriate intentions as a writer always means giving credit where credit is due. You probably have a ton of great ideas that are all yours. But when you pull from someone else's body of work, you should give credit where credit is due.

But, before you start curating your way to fame and fortune, there's one more secret to great digital curation. You can't just re-post something. You've got to add value and relevance beyond the original content.

—JONATHAN FIELDS

When you write, you first become rich just in the process. Writing feels great—most of the time.

The second way you feel rich when you write is with the accumulation of finished pieces. As I said in chapter ninety-six, they start to line up like stones and then you start laying another row on top of them, and the next thing you know, you have the equivalent of a wall or a chimney or a house.

The third way you feel rich when you write is when you can exchange your words for money. I don't know who invented this concept, but I would like to kiss them. I have made the most money I've ever made because it is possible to exchange words for money.

The fourth way you feel rich when you write is when you receive a response from readers. I don't know a single writer who dislikes hearing from readers. But I know many who felt moved, inspired, compelled by their responses.

The fifth way you feel rich when you write is knowing that you are leaving a legacy. What if you were to die sooner than you'd like? Wouldn't you feel better knowing that you'd put many of your most important ideas down on paper as you possibly could? Wouldn't you feel proud if some of those most important ideas had been published?

The sixth way you feel rich when you write is by achieving ownership of your own destiny.

Therefore, if you are not writing down and cultivating your best ideas, you are throwing away not just money but wealth every single day.

Not every person feels called to write. But if you do, why wouldn't you answer the call? You just might become the richest person in town.

Self-publishing and traditional publishing really aren't that different. One is easier to get into but harder to maintain. But neither come with guarantees. Some books will sell, some won't.

—AMANDA HOCKING

You decided to self-publish. Somebody told you that self-publishing was better, easier, and less labor-intensive than traditional publishing. And now you are looking for someone to help you move the stacks of books in your garage.

Unlikely. No one can is going to be able to help you move those books unless yours is well written, well conceived, and most importantly, is well-received by readers.

It's true that there have been some hugely impressive self-published to bestseller success stories over the years. According to Dan Poynter, *A Time To Kill* by John Grisham, *The One-Minute Manager* by Ken Blanchard and Spencer Johnson, and *What Color Is Your Parachute?* by Richard Nelson Bolles were originally self-published before achieving outrageous traditional publishing success.

But we need to cut through the hooey here, and get to the reality of self-publishing success.

If your book is well written but not selling, you may need to increase your marketing and self-promotion efforts.

If you book is not being well-received by readers—meaning they are referring the book like crazy to all of their friends after they read it—the problem might be that you wrote a book that won't sell.

If this is the case, you may need to start over. If you self-published and the book is not moving despite your best marketing and self-promotion efforts, your best bet might be to simply move on to new projects.

I'm not saying that this is what happens to every person who self-publishes because it isn't. There are always going to be the standouts like *The Shack* by William P. Young, but, of course, these kinds of self-publishing successes are not the norm.

The solution is to keep things real. What is the truth about the book you wrote? Was it a good practice book? Did you learn a lot about the process of book writing? Do you feel ready to move on to the next project?

Self-publishing can be an educational experience. And then, as always, it's time to keep moving forward. Count your self-publishing as equal in value to your traditional publishing experiences, regardless of the outcomes.

I don't have to have faith, I have experience.

—JOSEPH CAMPBELL

Failure can be turned into success in this business. I've seen it happen before and I'm sure I'll see it happen again. Because when a person is willing to learn and grow from mistakes, she can really do well in the long run.

At the end of the day, success means different things to different people. I strive to maintain a balanced approach to the writing life because professional writing has not traditionally lent itself to balance.

If I love the work that I do and the people I do it with, I'm going to feel like a success at the end of the day, whether my life is perfectly balanced or not.

My work could quickly lead to a pretty serious imbalance in my personal life if I let it. That's because writers often operate on steep deadlines that require long hours of sitting at the computer.

Writers are prone to extreme behaviors. Long story short, writers are creative types. And creative types—although, used loosely, the phrase could apply to anyone—are sensitive souls who need to strive for balance.

But don't take my word for it; take Bill Peschel's word for it. He wrote *Writers Gone Wild: The Feuds, Frolics, and Follie's of Literature's Great Adventurers, Drunkards, Lovers, Iconclasts, and Misanthropes*, which, if nothing else, will make you feel better about any imbalances you may have in your life.

If we don't take care, imbalance is always there, right around the corner, waiting for us to fall into its folly.

You can be a success from the very first day you launch a writing career until the very last breath you take, if your focus is on having a good day today and not on what you have yet to accomplish.

One-day-at-a-time is a method that people who are not balanced use to get back to balance. Therefore it's not a bad approach for sensitive creative souls who are striving for balance in a career that easily tips the scales.

Be successful today, just today, and you will be all that much more successful tomorrow.

> *The reality of book publishing is that there are too few resources to support every book. This means that some books will get publicity campaigns and budgets while others will go without.*
>
> —JACQUELINE DEVAL

By the time this book comes out, I will have published five books. This will be the third traditionally published book, and I also published one e-book and one anthology, a collection of my former students' writing.

I will have referred or assisted about a dozen writers in procuring a book deal, writing a book proposal, or getting an agent. Between my own experience in writing and publishing and the experience of my students and close friends, there are some essential things I've learned that I think will remain fairly consistent going forward.

1. The most important time to promote a book is the six months before it comes out, the day it is released, and the next six months after it comes out.

2. If you want librarians to purchase your book, you'd better get it reviewed in *Booklist, Library Journal,* and *School Library Journal.*

3. If you want people to review your book, don't just wait for them to review it. You have to ask them point-blank, "Will you review my book?"

4. If you want awesome book blurbs for your book, you'd better start lining them up six months in advance otherwise, you'll be stuck taking whatever you can get.

5. If you are writing your first book, do all of these things: Get a better-known author to write a foreword for your book, get really great blurbs, plan an epic blog tour, and hire a cutting-edge book publicist.

6. During a book launch: Take extra vitamins, get plenty of sleep, and schedule downtime ahead of time, or you won't take any at all because you will be so concerned about book sales.

7. If this is your first book, pull together a team of advisors composed of folks with more professional experience than you. Call on all of them, but don't just ask the same person for advice over and over as you make your way toward launch. Spread your questions around or ask each question to a few different people so as not to wear out your welcome.

Several of your "friends" aren't that. They're more like "friendlies."
—CHRIS BROGAN

You have become an author, congratulations!

You've launched your book into the world and, oh my goodness, the response is overwhelming. I repeat: OVERWHELMING.

Propositions are coming at you, seemingly from every direction.

Not that you are complaining about your success. You are thrilled beyond words with your success, it's just that you can't even seem to go to the bathroom without somebody stopping you midstride to ask for a favor that holds the promise of something called "exposure" for you and your book.

Listen for this word.

You might hear it like this, "I'm sure this would be *great exposure* for you and your book." Did you catch it? You have to listen for it because you are going to be hearing it a lot.

Offers are going to start flying at you from e-mail, phone, snail mail, Twitter, Facebook, LinkedIn, and any other way or place where you are visible.

The requests will vary but are likely to include:

- Requests for coffee with complete strangers
- Offers for you to drive long distances to reach crowds of unknown proportions (for no speaking fee, of course)
- Requests for guest blogs ... with original content only, please
- Requests for you to do teleconferences so that the person coordinating the effort can package the teleconference and sell it (hopefully to some of your e-mail list)
- Ditto providing your content to for-profit membership organizations that would like to use your expertise to attract more paying members to their group (paying them, I mean, not you)
- Requests for phone interviews, podcast interviews, e-mail interviews, Skype interviews, and Twitter interviews
- Requests to volunteer your time for a myriad of good causes or to give your books or earnings to support good causes
- Offers from unknown production companies to share their peoples' offers with your permission-based e-mail list (something called "database leveraging," which quite possibly could alienate everyone on your list for good)
- This list does not include the requests you will get for a mysterious thing called "help" — as in "Here is my terrible situation ... (I can't get published, I can't take classes, I can't pay my bills, I can't, I can't, I can't ...). You seem to have things figured out. Can you possibly HELP?"
- Or you'll get requests from people who read your book and applied what you suggested ... and now, they were just wondering if you could you take just a few minutes to take a quick look at what they've done and discuss their progress?

347
ORGANIZE YOUR PAPERS

Putting words together in a way which is unique, to me is some-thing I still think is one of the most thrilling things that one can do in one's life.

—SEYMOUR SIMON

Is it arrogant to think you have papers that might interest someone else some day?

I don't think so, especially when the organizing and updating of your papers can lead to so many great ideas for your current writing.

Besides, now that we have publishing tools basically at our fingertips, why shouldn't you self-publish your best work as you go, instead of leaving it behind and risking that no one will ever see it?

Here are some preliminary categories that may help you get started:

PERSONAL CORRESPONDENCE
- Letters
- E-mails
- Telegrams
- Cards

PUBLICITY
- Flyers
- Posters
- Ads
- Articles
- Coupons
- Postcards
- Business cards

YOUR WRITING
- Student work
- Published work
- Articles
- Stories
- Poems
- Opinions
- Contributions
- Books
- Contributions to books by others
- E-books
- Curriculum (classes, workshops, etc.)
- Training materials
- Speeches

It doesn't matter if you're an aspiring writer, traditionally published or going the DIY route, marketing is every writer's responsibility, and it takes the same level of commitment, dedication and self-discipline as sitting down and actually writing does.

—GUY LECHARLES GONZALEZ

Initially, when you are publishing books, you will heroically think you can do everything for everyone. And you'll think you should try to. You will try to say yes to everyone. You might even pat yourself on the back for getting so many requests for your time.

But the next thing you know, you won't have any time. No time to go to the bathroom or shower or speak to your child or your spouse or your friends. You'll miss out on paying opportunities to write, teach, and speak for vetted audiences who would likely become long-term fans. And all because you are trying to keep up with a deluge of requests that are big on promise and low on value.

You will become poorer and poorer because you will be so busy spending money to promote your work only to be overwhelmed by the demands of the very people you are paying to market yourself to. Given all of this back-and-forth, you can lose sight of the big picture.

Until one day you will start to wonder, "How the heck did this happen?"

It happened because you never dared to say one little word.

So repeat after me. It's just one little word. And the word is *No*.

Once you figure out how to say it graciously, you'll be able to create the results *you* want.

And you deserve it after all of your hard work.

We've talked about saying no before, at other busy times, earlier in your career. But once you are a published author, you might fall into the trap of thinking that *no* is a word you can no longer afford.

You can afford it. In fact, you need it during book promotion more than you ever needed it.

So it's a good thing you've already practiced.

349

BALANCE INSIDE AND OUTSIDE

Writing a book is a horrible, exhausting struggle, like a long bout of some painful illness. One would never undertake such a thing if one were not driven on by some demon whom one can neither resist nor understand.

—GEORGE ORWELL

Another thing we've learned over the years is that writing careers don't make you happy.

You either were already happy when you embarked on the writing path or you were not.

And doubtless, whether you have earned external writing-career success or not, you will end up exactly as happy as you were when you started.

So hopefully you have not looked to something outside yourself, like the idea of a writing career, to bring you the happiness you seek, if happiness has been elusive.

Happiness doesn't come from external things. And it also won't come from a marriage, a child, a big house, a nice car, or any of the other usual trappings of the American Dream.

If you want to be happy, practice listening to and trusting your idea of happiness. Your concept of a satisfying career won't like look like anyone else's in the long run.

Happy means you accept yourself, you trust your natural instincts, and you embrace what you really want. None of your choices are for show.

Don't think, what does a successful writer look like? Think, what does my future look like when I'm a successful writer?

And build, happily, toward that ideal.

Creating is heaven. Or close enough.

—ERIC MAISEL

Now that Oprah's twenty-five-year-old TV show is over and even Oprah is leaving a major television network and going her own way, I think it's time to break apart two very old and entrenched aspects of a writing career: creativity and fame.

Ever since Oprah launched her book club in 1996 and started selecting one new book each month, recommending seventy books over fifteen years. a writer's imagination has been dominated by the hope of securing Oprah's favor.

You know how the rest of the fantasy goes. Lights, action, camera, Oprah! The writer is then delivered from obscurity, the book becomes a huge international bestseller, and the rest is best-selling history.

Because this is the experience most writers have, especially with their first books. Right?

Of course it isn't.

And now there is a new pressure that goes like this: We have social networking so now we no longer even need Oprah.

Well, not so fast. Haven't you heard that Oprah is planning to launch a TV show on her new network for books and authors?

Let's not throw the biggest book endorser in the history of publishing out with the bathwater.

In the meantime, the fantasy of enormous overnight success has been replaced by something much more sane, human, and rational. It's been replaced by author ownership.

Every writer in the world is now a publisher, just as Oprah has launched her own TV network. What this means is that creative power can now be tapped and exercised by authors in a fashion appropriate and proportionate to the experience of the creator.

Now that there is no reason to be waiting for the stamp of approval from Oprah, you may as well just be where you're at and do what you can with it. It's enough. Maybe even Oprah will notice that it's enough.

35 PREPARE DESPITE EXPERIENCE

Nobody said writing was easy.
Selling your writing is even harder.
Do your homework. Don't waste your own time.

—JANE YOLEN

Let's say you've been writing articles and getting them published and you've even established a writing specialty for yourself that is leading to better and better paying gigs. This is great.

And by now you are getting bored.

Why? Because you are a writer, and you are always going to need to keep growing or you will die a thousand creative deaths.

So what would I suggest? I might suggest that you take an essay-writing class or a fiction-writing class or a poetry-writing class. I'm not going to suggest that you tackle a book-length work right out of the gate because that's counterproductive unless you've written so many books already that the process of writing a book has become habitual.

At some point in your writing career, if you haven't already, you're going to want to scratch that itch to try new genres. And when you first started on the writing-for-publication journey, I wanted you to be prepared. None of that advice has changed.

If you are on the cusp of trying your pen at new-to-you formats or genres, you will want to be adequately prepared. What's the easiest way to do this? Probably to take a short, inexpensive class in the genre or form you want to master. You'll make so much better use of your time if you do.

If it were freezing cold outside, no matter how intense your cabin fever, you would not just throw on your coat and run out the door. You'd make sure you cover all your needs. You'd put on your coat, your hat, your scarf, and your gloves. You would not want to be outside suffering; you'd want to enjoy being outside.

The same is true when you attempt a new form or genre. Why merely survive the experience? Cover all of your bases so you can enjoy your writing time.

GO ABOVE, BEYOND, AND BACK

Deliver me from writers who say the way they live doesn't matter. I'm not sure a bad person can write a good book. If art doesn't make us better, then what on earth is it for?

—ALICE WALKER

You can always just get by. But you won't feel good about it.

What you will feel good about is going above and beyond every time you do your work.

This applies to what you are writing. Make it the best it can be. Don't settle for good enough.

This applies to what you are planning for the future. Don't plan something acceptable when you could plan something outstanding.

This applies to speaking. Say something that will bonk everyone on the head and wake them up a little.

This applies to teaching. Aim to teach the skills and knowledge that people need the most. Then go for it. Cram as much learning in as time allows.

This applies to consulting. Always coach people to tackle the necessary things—both the things that most people can handle and the things that you know most won't want to tackle. They are paying you to anticipate and provide solutions for challenges.

Figure out what it takes to pump you up to do your best. Does listening to inspiring music help? Does going for a run help? Do whatever you have to do to get to your most outstanding work.

BE WISE AND OPEN

The road to enlightenment is long and difficult, and you should try not to forget snacks and magazines.

—ANNE LAMOTT

If you know everything already, maybe it's time to start over.

Part of being wise is also being open. Part of being open is becoming a channel for the work that wants to come through.

I was helping my husband mount a production of *Les Miserables* with kids ages eight to eighteen. We were almost at the end of the run. There were only three more performances left. Yet there was still room for improvement in the show—if not in the actors' performances, then in a timing issue or a technical effort.

The kids just kept getting better until they were performing one of the major musical undertakings of all time as though it were as easy as hanging out with their buddies at the pool. I get inspired by their commitment every time I watch the DVD.

If only we could see our writing career as three-dimensionally on stage as we see a play or musical in a theater, we would realize that there is always room for more improvement. There are always more ways to awe and impress our audience. There are always aspects to tweak to deliver a more quality experience.

Use all the space on the stage. Sing out. Hit the back wall of the theater your voice. Leave your best performance on the stage. Make sure the space where you were just standing continues vibrating long after you have made your exit.

Don't be afraid to weep, when weeping is called for. Laugh, uproariously, when appropriate. Collapse with exhaustion. Dance with exultation.

You can do all of these things on the page as well as on the stage. Never settle for just good enough. Most people don't push themselves hard enough. They settle. Settling is human nature. Don't let yourself off the hook until you've milked every writing opportunity for everything it's worth.

A lot of times settling is connected to the groups and colleagues we associate with. We stay where we are in order to fit in. We don't want to rock the boat. We don't want anyone to say, "Who do you think you are?"

Don't give up until you feel satisfied that you have done all you can do. At that point, it's okay to move on. Especially since there is always going to be a next time.

Becoming a writer is about becoming conscious. When you're conscious and writing from a place of insight and simplicity and real caring about the truth, you have the ability to throw the lights on for your reader. He or she will recognize his or her life and truth in what you say, in the pictures you have painted, and this decreases the terrible sense of isolation that we have all had too much of.

—ANNE LAMOTT

Don't worry about creating drama so you will have things to write about. You don't need to do that. Life comes with challenges intact. You will never run out of bumps and bruises, because this is earth and earth is school and class is always in session.

Life will literally hand you things to write about over and over again, and all you have to do is stay strong, keep putting one foot in front of the other, and remember that you might write about it some day. Probably you can't just drop everything to write about it today.

But, then again, you never know, you just might write about it today if you can make the time. If you need to get it down on paper, get it down.

If you really want to have something to write about, challenge yourself to tell the truth, the absolute truth, and the whole truth for one whole year. And by this challenge, I mean tell the truth in your life *and* on the page.

No fudging now. You know what I mean. We can call it fudging to be kind to ourselves because we all do it. Or we can just call it what it is: lying.

What would happen if you stopped fibbing to yourself for a whole year about anything? No loopholes. Just the straight dope.

You could do it if you take to questioning every single thing you say and do with, "Is this true?" or "Is this the absolute truth?"

What would this practice do for your writing? What would this practice do for your life?

It would set you free first. And then it would set your writing free.

The point of the book is to be spread, to act as a manifesto, to get in sync with others, to give and to get and to hand around.

—SETH GODIN

I did not pursue writing; it beckoned me. It has always beckoned me. I answer the call from within. It still calls me all the time. And it never calls collect.

I practice writing in the real world, so I try not to use the fact that I am a writer as an excuse for eccentric behavior. I use short-term goals and deadlines to help me get the writing done. I also like working with others on writing projects sometimes.

I like working with my students most of all. I enjoy helping them succeed. I get a kick out watching them get published.

I suspect I am not alone in needing others. I'm a writer and a member of the human race just like everyone else. I would be a terrible writer if I had to do it all myself. I think our egos sometimes want us to think we are terribly important, when really we are only as important as everyone else.

Living from creativity is not the typical path in this country. I think it's okay to acknowledge that the writing path can take you to some pretty interesting places, and some of them are places that most people would never care to go and are probably not even remotely interested in anyway.

So, yes, writing makes us unique. It pulls us all into the same tribe: a tribe of writers.

Many in the tribe are eccentric. And that's okay. As in all tribes there is room for all kinds of people. You can be in the tribe and still be you.

And being a part of the writer tribe doesn't take you out of the other, bigger tribe that we were all born into: the human race. It feels good, when the giant, lumbering projects are done that may have felt like they would never be done, to rejoin the human race and just be nobody. Not an eccentric, not a person who is known, not even a person who does good work, but just, you know, you, whoever you are.

Step off the path once in a while and hang out with the folks who are not part of our exclusive group. The tribe is great but it can get a bit inscestuous if you never leave it.

So leave the tribe. Abandon it all together if and when you must. Membership is voluntary and the doors are always open. Come and go as you please.

The primary thing is to not get hung up or messed up by any group mind, not even by our exclusive little club of writers.

Preserve your individuality by stepping back once in a while and blending in with the crowd. Don't get addicted to striving. The tribe will still be there when you get back from wherever you need to go.

I arise in the morning torn between a desire to improve the world and a desire to enjoy the world. This makes it hard to plan the day.

—E.B. WHITE

I am not the kind of person who goes around encouraging writers to abandon their ideals for overnight success; I am the kind who teaches people to cultivate their own creative power and grow it over time, because this is the only kind of success that is lasting. It's also the only kind of success that is worth having at all.

Let the creativity that you experience every day be half of the reward, writers. That's where so much of the personal satisfaction comes from anyway.

Realize how many people walk around in this world cut off from their source of joy. While people who write every day get to splash around in the waters of creativity every single day.

Then afterwards, we channel some of our leftover creative energy into platform development because platform development is just as creative and joyful as writing. And, sure, when you have a book coming out, feel free to work extra hard. Put your whole self into it. Why wouldn't you? Be creative. Be visionary. Make as big of a splash as you can. Launch that baby into the world with as much fanfare as possible.

But remember that platform development means connecting how you serve to an incrementally larger audience over time, all the time. And anyone who doesn't talk about the joy and creativity that comes part and parcel with this effort simply doesn't know about it.

Start to see that authorship equals ownership. And ownership equals creative power. And creative power is where the joy is. It's where the joy has always been.

You can have joy after as little as a few minutes of experiencing your own creative power. Tap into that joy and share some of it with the world.

When we leave this world, we will ask ourselves one question: What's different? What's different because I was here? And the answer to that question will be the difference that we made.

—STEVE CHANDLER

At the end of your life, when you look back over your writing career, what will you feel most proud about leaving behind?

Will you have inspired people to become better people, to do more good in the world, express themselves, to reach out to others who are suffering … or something else?

What are you after with all of this?

There are no shortcuts. No easy answers to this question. It takes years of writing your way to the answer.

Certainly, you don't get to answer and then sit back and rest on your laurels. You still have more writing to do. Right?

Instead, think about why your life's work will have been meaningful to you. Who else will have found your work meaningful? Will you have managed to achieve what you wanted to achieve while maintaining happy relationships with family and friends?

If you can answer these questions now, you are going to be much further ahead in leaving behind the legacy you want to leave behind and not the one you leave behind by accident.

Even if you can barely glimpse what you hope to ultimately accomplish, you can begin building it today, stone by stone.

Never allow a person to tell you no who doesn't have the power to say yes.

—ELEANOR ROOSEVELT

You might expect that a veteran writer would get tired or worn out, but no, the opposite happens. A veteran writer eventually feels powerful just from her sheer ability to take a creative concept and express it over and over and over.

The true power of a writer isn't what you wrote last year, what you are going to write next year, or even what you just wrote. The true power of a writer is the ability to chart your own course, to learn from what you've already done, to open your mind to new opportunities, and to leverage your creative value in the current marketplace.

As I've said, writing isn't the only part of this process that is creative. The whole career path of a writer is the creative process. It's an adventure and journey. A learning process and a path of self-discovery.

Your writing career is totally in your hands. You are never limited by the choices you made in the past. It's never too late to start again or head in a new direction. A writing career is a blank slate for you to write your plan upon.

One reason I never tire of working with writers is because the possibilities for first, second, and third acts are endless. Even just one writer can produce herself in multiple acts as time goes on. And as the publishing industry changes, the opportunities to re-create ourselves over and over again become more exciting because we are not talking about merely creating books any longer, we are talking about creating whole worlds not only for readers but for folks who crave more than the experience of reading.

Once we get to this point in our careers, things start to get exciting. I imagine it's rather like the moment when Walt Disney realized he could build an entire theme park based around the characters he'd developed many years before.

Imagine the feeling that one thing that you created could lead to so much more than what your limited vision could conceive at the time.

What would happen if you took some of your best ideas and made them bigger?

What kind of experience do you long to offer your audience with your work?

If you imagine your creation as a multidimensional experience, what would it be like?

It's a good feeling to wake up every day and create your career. I wish you the very best of luck in creating something big that's perfectly suited to you.

STOP RESCUING

Caution is the eldest child of wisdom.

—VICTOR HUGO

I'm very fortunate that I often get to work with writers who embody the three *H*'s: They are humble, hard-working, and healthy. They tend to be lovely people with joyful personal lives, good boundaries, positive intentions, and energy.

However, there are writers who struggle, who actively hurt themselves and others with substance abuse, emotional imbalance, or compulsive behaviors. So just remember, you are allowed to choose to work with, learn from, partner with, and surround yourself with healthy, happy people, both writers and otherwise. There are plenty to go around. Don't ever feel like you are stuck with unhealthy people and there is nothing you can do about it. Choose again; there are plenty of healthy people to go around.

Numerous writers (and people) live in prisons of their own making. They might be in pain, and you might want to help them, but my advice is simply to get out of their way and stay out of it. I used to try to tolerate these kinds of people. In my twenties, I was attracted to these types of people. I thought alleviating other people's pain was my job. I was a rescuer.

Somewhere along the line I'd gotten the idea that the best kinds of people are kind, patient, self-sacrificing, and generous to a fault. This is a dangerous idea, completely devoid of self-preservation, which I learned the hard way.

As I've gotten older I've noticed that the healthiest people don't seek out self-destructive playmates. I finally get it. Not every person in the world is healthy. If I start to recognize that a person has a penchant for negativity, drama, or self-destruction, I gently lean away. It's too slight a gesture to be distinguishable but at least I know I'm out. I silently wish the person the best and stop engaging if I am participating in anything I might regret.

I am not a therapist. I'm a writer. Today I choose to be a healthy person and to associate with healthy, happy people, whether they are writers or not. This kind of clarity has been a boon for my career.

If you surround yourself with needy, impossible, difficult, self-destructive, self-absorbed, and addicted people, chaos will surely follow. And even one or two difficult people in your life might be too many. So choose your friends wisely. Steer clear of anyone on a collision course with serenity because it will likely cost you some of yours, as well.

The maker of a sentence launches out into the infinite and builds a road into Chaos and old Night, and is followed by those who hear him with something of wild, creative delight.

—RALPH WALDO EMERSON

When you are completely full it's hard to take in anything new. But if you can let yourself forget everything you know, if you can be willing to become a beginner again, you can open up to something new.

Sometimes when we have a lot of expertise in one area we have trouble getting out of our own way. I know I've tripped over the things I already know to the point where I can't say anything fresh about them.

In fact, this happened to me recently with an article I was writing on a topic that I write about frequently. The solution was to forget what I've already said a hundred times and expose myself to new ways the idea could be presented. Then I researched and played around with a whole new way of presenting these new ideas.

The other solution was partnering with my editor because my editor could see in my draft that I was getting in my own way. She gave me some input to help me cast myself beyond my own thinking, and that encouragement was really helpful.

Every writer, no matter how long she's been writing, needs to know how to become a beginner again, and how to do it frequently in order to have fresh input coming in.

If you can't embrace a beginner's mind, you will repeat yourself and everything you've already said over and over again. Like a song stuck on repeat play.

And this becomes very tedious for both the reader and the writer. What is written becomes compromised from overuse. It can become a cliché or worse: static.

Emptiness is the habit of letting your mind be a blank slate. It happens when you let your curiosity lead you to new unchartered places where what you create becomes a process of surprise and delight. You are most fully creative and alive when you let go and let what wants to happen, happen.

You can't get there from full. But you can get there from empty. Even if empty feels awfully hollow and echo-y.

You'll fill up again. Don't worry. But first, you need to make yourself blank.

361

ELEVATE YOUR PEARLS

And the point is to live everything. Live the questions now. Perhaps then, someday far in the future, you will gradually, without even noticing it, live your way into the answer.

—RAINER MARIA RILKE

By the time you become more seasoned in your writing career, you understand what prosperity means to you as a writer. You know intuitively that your success today and tomorrow is contingent upon your sustainable enthusiasm; your ability to write well; your ease in offering your work, services, and products; the scope and impact of your visibility; and your willingness to keep learning no matter how much you already know.

When you take all of this inner awareness and combine it with carefully selected partners, you actualize the potential of the creative writer.

You become a writer who has cultivated a readership by writing on a wealth of topics and penetrating the mysteries of many specialties. Rather than embodying that joke about the generalist who knows a little about a lot, you become a person who knows a lot about a lot. And if the areas of your expertise have had personal meaning to you, this is a very satisfying feeling.

If you've learned one thing and learned it well, it's to never to cast your hard-wrought pearls before the demands of snorting, hoof-pounding swine.

If asked to give everything for nothing, graciously decline.

You have bigger dreams to crusade than the demands of those who would like to monetize your insights and hard work.

You know when to say yes, when to say no thanks, and when to say sorry, not right now.

You've got pearls, all right. And you are not going to give them away.

It's easy to say "no!" when there's a deeper "yes!" burning inside.

—STEPHEN R. COVEY

Let's face it, there is only one word that folks want to hear when they ask you for something, and that word is *Yes*. We've already talked about *No*, and the importance of knowing when you have to use it and learning how to say it gracefully.

But every once in a while you are going to run into a phenomenon I have encountered where everybody seems to want you at the same time. This is a good thing because it means you are successful. But this doesn't make an onslaught of requests any easier to juggle.

However, if everybody wants you and you say, "Yes," guess what is going out the window? Your creative productivity. Here are three things that I need to stay focused and on track:

INSULATION

When you are under the pressure of a deadline, either your own or one imposed from outside, you need a certain amount of insulation. You need to be able to say, "Not now, I'm on a deadline." You can either say this out loud, in public, to select appropriate folks, or just to yourself. You are under no obligation to broadcast your availability. But you will feel better, calmer, and more focused if you insulate yourself to the degree you need to get your work done calmly. Simply adjust your availability dial according to what you need and what works for you; don't worry about how others set their dial. Other people's availability or lack of availability is not your concern. Keep a close eye on your own dial appropriate to your needs for each deadline and you will get your work done on time.

PROTECTION

Making sure you feel safe so you can get your writing done is not defensive. So when I talk about protection, I don't mean *defensive*, I mean guard and shield yourself and your work as you see fit. As with insulation, most writers need a certain amount of safeguarding to feel they can get their work done. Similarly, when I talk about protection, I don't mean paranoia. For example, it doesn't serve a writer to focus on how others might wish to steal or copy his work. In the Internet age, there is nothing you can do to stop people from taking whatever of your work is available, and you would not want to waste your time trying to stop the few who would. However, it makes sense to protect your ideas until they are developed to such a degree that you feel they are complete and ready to be shared. Protect your ideas until they are ready for prime time, and then let them fly.

PRESERVATION

The reason preservation of your work is important is that nobody cares about preserving your work as much as you do. And no one can leverage your work as well as you can, either. Certainly no one is going to volunteer for this job. So your long-term game plan for protecting your work is to have a preservation plan, which means collecting and protecting your body of work over time. Take stock and care of your work as you go along. Back it up and keep it safe for the future as you go.

No one can give you your subject matter, your creative content; if they could, it would be their creation and not yours.

—TWYLA THARP

The more you learn and know about writing and publishing and producing yourself and staying tuned into your audience and serving them through the best of what you have to offer, the more informed your responses become.

Earlier I talked about how important it is for writers to respond to what they notice. But at this point, what I'm talking about is how you need to respond more fully to what you notice as your career progresses. Sometimes, sure, the more you know, the more difficult it becomes to respond in the moment to what you notice.

Sometimes this can be a good yet confusing feeling. Especially when we have become such social animals that we are picking up stimulation from not just what we read, but from the groups we are a part of and from industry reports and discussions or events about our industry. It's not hard to get to the point of information overload that can lead to feeling stuck.

Remember that expression about knowing too much? It gets tricky sometimes knowing what to do with all the knowledge and information you have accumulated and communicated over the years.

Touchstone words can make all the difference. For example, at a particular point in my writing career, I was confused about what direction to move in next. If I stayed as is, with all the possibilities and what was currently going on in the zeitgeist, the choices felt overwhelming. But then I remembered that I had already been on a trajectory of writing for publication and teaching for over a decade, and when I took that trajectory into account, I remembered its value and what I have to offer.

I remembered what my priorities are and as soon as I remembered my place in the grander scheme of things, I knew that I had a lot of ideas I wanted to share and that they were enough to create a whole book. That's this book.

If you have been on a career trajectory for a while, don't be surprised if you go through periods of confusion. Take pause and conduct an inventory of what you value, what you've already accomplished, whom you serve, and what you love to do most. By following your instincts, you'll discover the best direction to take next.

I'm sure you have many books in you, as well as writing in many other forms.

It is impossible to discourage the real writers—they don't give a damn what you say, they're going to write.

—SINCLAIR LEWIS

Maybe it's time to break out. Take your most unique topic, the one you feel you have the best grip on, the one that is really you, and see what happens when you brainstorm different writing forms from one idea.

You've been doing this writing gig stuff for a while. And it can get a little tedious, even if you are consistently successful, if you don't shake things up every once in a while.

So maybe it's time to break out of your box.

Start by asking yourself: "What would I create if I let myself create *anything* I wanted?"

Spend five minutes jotting down nothing except what truly sounds the most fun.

Your ability to break out of your own box will inspire you, and you will inspire others.

CHILDREN'S NONFICTION ARTICLES OR BOOKS:	TIPS, LISTS, HOW-TOS, & FEATURES:	CHILDREN'S FICTION BOOKS:
INTERVIEWS & PROFILES:	YOUR UNIQUE TOPIC:	ADULT FICTION:
MAGAZINE FILLERS/ SHORTS:	ADULT NONFICTION BOOKS:	ESSAY OR MEMOIR:

365

JUST KEEP GROWING

Everyone is given an acre of attitudes at birth. It's yours to tend and garden and weed and live with. You can plant bitterness or good humor. Feel free to fertilize and tend the feelings and approaches that you want to spend time with. Unless you hurt someone, this acre is all yours.

—SETH GODIN

Remember that letter I suggested you write in chapter thirty-nine and put away or send to yourself at the beginning of this process? If a year has gone by, this would be a good time to get that out and take another look at it (otherwise, you'll have to wait—no cheating!).

What did you create that you intended to create?

What more would you still like to create?

How satisfied are you with your progress?

When it's time, write another letter and send it to yourself for next year.

What you are looking for is progress, not some perfect image. Perfect images are never as perfect as we thought they were going to be.

Create what you can reasonably create in one year given your best efforts and let it be enough.

Each year you will learn valuable information about yourself and your career that will pay dividends as you apply what you learn to your future.

Remember what I said at the beginning of this section: if you committed enough and paying attention enough; if you are tapping into to your highest good and what is being asked of you by the people who appreciate you most; and if you listen and respond to the work that wants you to do it, you are already the best coach you can possibly acquire or hire.

Like Dorothy with her ruby slippers, you've had the ability to guide your choices to the most comforting possible outcome all along.

So click your heels or meditate or go for a walk or punch some pillows or do whatever you need to do to tune into your inner wisdom. And then listen to what it says.

Yet as fast as the results seem to have happened, I can assure you that the whole process took a hell of a long time.

—GARY VAYNERCHUK

Now it's time to talk about doing nothing.

Even though I have advised you all the way through this book to do something and keep doing something rather than nothing if results are what you are after.

But let's give ourselves a little breather for a moment.

Take pause. Hang out. Do nothing.

Can you feel it? That feeling of fullness and emptiness at the same time? You deserve to experience this feeling before you move forward.

Enjoy that peak moment when you are done adding up all that you've accomplished but you are not yet ready to spring forward again.

Let yourself have feel a sense of completeness. Not that you are going to throw a party about it or anything. It's more like a feeling you relish privately.

For many writers the feeling of closure is elusive. The feeling comes from a job or jobs well done, from relationships full of respect and genuine warmth, from valuing yourself and your contributions. From knowing that the feeling doesn't come around that often.

If you have residual feelings of unworthiness or low self-esteem, it's hard to sit still and feel complete. If you are insecure, you may always be dancing as fast as you can, trying to please others and get the approval that you think will make you feel happy.

The way to dig deeper and find a feeling of completeness is through service that isn't selfless. When you find your self-infused service, you have found your calling.

Self-infused service means you are dedicating your energy consciously, not simply running around trying to address a sense of not being enough. When you finish the book you felt called to write, complete an article that will have a positive impact, or wrap up the piece of work that you think might just change lives, it's time for a break.

And before you launch into what you are going to tackle next, take some time to be in the moment of completeness that you have earned.

And every time you finish something or complete a project or your responsibilities are done, take a moment or a day or a week or a month to honor that accompanying feeling of closure.

Closure feels like curling up next to a roaring fire on a frigid day with a mug of something hot and a really good book. It feels like this feels. It feels like, "Ahhh..."

I wish you many of these blissful moments of repose in between whatever it is you love to create for the world.

ABOUT THE AUTHOR

 Christina Katz is the author of *Get Known Before the Book Deal: Use Your Personal Strengths to Grow an Author Platform* and *Writer Mama: How to Raise a Writing Career Alongside Your Kids.* She holds an M.F.A. in creative writing from Columbia College Chicago and a B.A. in English from Dartmouth College. A "gentle taskmaster" over the past decade to hundreds of writers, Christina's students go from unpublished to published, build professional writing career skills, increase their creative confidence, and prosper over time. Christina hosts the popular Northwest Author Series in Wilsonville, Oregon, where she lives with her husband, daughter, and far too many pets. Learn more at ChristinaKatz.com.

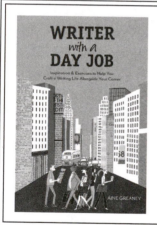